New Directions in Scandinavian Studies

Christine Ingebritsen and Andy Nestingen, *Series Editors*

New Directions in Scandinavian Studies

This series offers interdisciplinary approaches to the study of the Nordic region of Scandinavia and the Baltic States and their cultural connections in North America. By redefining the boundaries of Scandinavian studies to include the Baltic States and Scandinavian America, the series presents books that focus on the study of the culture, history, literature, and politics of the North.

Small States in International Relations, edited by Christine Ingebritsen, Iver B. Neumann, Sieglinde Gstohl, and Jessica Beyer

Danish Cookbooks: Domesticity and National Identity, 1616–1901, by Carol Gold

Crime and Fantasy in Scandinavia: Fiction, Film, and Social Change, by Andrew Nestingen

Selected Plays of Marcus Thrane, translated and introduced by Terje I. Leiren

Munch's Ibsen: A Painter's Visions of a Playwright, by Joan Templeton

Knut Hamsun: The Dark Side of Literary Brilliance, by Monika Žagar

Nordic Exposures: Scandinavian Identities in Classical Hollywood Cinema, by Arne Lunde

Icons of Danish Modernity: Georg Brandes and Asta Nielsen, by Julie K. Allen

Danish Folktales, Legends, and Other Stories, edited and translated by Timothy R. Tangherlini

The Power of Song: Nonviolent National Culture in the Baltic Singing Revolution, by Guntis Šmidchens

Church Resistance to Nazism in Norway, 1940–1945, by Arne Hassing

Christian Krohg's Naturalism, by Øystein Sjåstad

Fascism and Modernist Literature in Norway, by Dean Krouk

Sacred to the Touch: Nordic and Baltic Religious Wood Carving, by Thomas A. DuBois

Sámi Media and Indigenous Agency in the Arctic North, by Coppélie Cocq and Thomas A. DuBois

Sámi Media and Indigenous Agency in the Arctic North

COPPÉLIE COCQ AND
THOMAS A. DUBOIS

UNIVERSITY OF WASHINGTON PRESS
Seattle

Sámi Media and Indigenous Agency in the Arctic North
was made possible in part by support from the Department
of Scandinavian Studies at the University of Washington.

Printed and bound in the United States of America

Design by Katrina Noble
Composed in Ashbury, typeface designed by Dieter Hofrichter

24 23 22 21 20 5 4 3 2 1

UNIVERSITY OF WASHINGTON PRESS
uwapress.uw.edu

LIBRARY OF CONGRESS CATALOGING-IN-PUBLICATION DATA
ON FILE
ISBN 978-0-295-74662-3 (hardcover)
ISBN 978-0-295-74660-9 (paperback)
ISBN 978-0-295-74661-6 (ebook)

The paper used in this publication is acid free and meets the
minimum requirements of American National Standard for
Information Sciences—Permanence of Paper for Printed Library
Materials, ANSI Z39.48–1984.∞

Contents

Giitu

Acknowledgments

Our thanks go first to all those people who generously participated in this project through interviews, through granting us permission to quote their words or reproduce images, and by providing feedback that helped us improve our interpretations. Not only did people provide a wealth of information with generosity and alacrity, they also provided encouragement, suggestions, and clarifications that vastly improved our study. We could not have told the story we set out to tell here without the permission and help of people like Britt-Marie Barruk, Mari Boine, Rawdna Carita Eira, Anamaria Fjällgren, Jon Henrik Fjällgren, Katja Gauriloff, Katarina Hällgren, Sofia Jannok, Amanda Kernell, Timimie Märak, Ole Paus, Jeff Schad, Niillas Somby, and many others. Some of the people we thank informed us through person-to-person consultations, others through the inspiring creative works they produced and left behind for future generations. Where appropriate, they are named in the pages that follow; where confidentiality was needed, we thank them here without names. We have endeavored to do justice to these important contributions and we apologize for any failings that arise in our text.

We wish to thank colleagues in the fields of Sámi studies, Indigenous studies, Nordic studies, ethnology and folklore studies, communication studies, and digital studies for their generous and constructive input and help with various aspects of our study. These include: Per Axelsson, Isabelle Brännlund, Susan Brantly, B. Marcus Cederström, Colin Connors, Elizabeth Covington, Tim Frandy, Harald Gaski, Siri

Gaski, Stefan Gelfgren, Lis-Mari Hjortfors, Robert Howard, Ella Johansson, Merrill Kaplan, Lena Kappfjell, Barbro Klein, David Kroik, Dean Krouk, Kristin Kuutma, Patrik Lantto, Jim Leary, Veli-Pekka Lehtola, Evelina Liliequist, Marianne Liliequist, Scott Mellor, Todd Michelson-Ambelang, Lena Maria Nilsson, Ruth Olson, Åsa Össbo, Hanna Outakoski, Tobias Poggats, Jelena Porsanger, John Prusynski, Britt Rajala, Amber Rose, Moa Sandström, Görel Sandström, Kristina Sehlin MacNeil, Hanna Snellman, Peter Steggo, Krister Stoor, Jon Petter Stoor, Charlotta Svonni, Mikael Svonni, Mikael Vinka, Kirsten Wolf, Ekaterina Zmyvalova, and many others. Comments and guidance came also through the feedback we received at academic conferences, including the annual or occasional meetings of the American Folklore Society, the Association for the Advancement of Scandinavian Studies of Canada, the International Society for Folklore and Ethnology, the Native American Indigenous Studies Association, the Nordic Ethnology and Folklore Conference, and the Society for the Advancement of Scandinavian Study. And we thank the two anonymous reviewers of our text for the University of Washington Press, whose feedback and recommendations greatly improved our work. We also wish to thank the Såhkie Umeå Sameföreningen and the Gïelejarnge Samiskt språkcentrum for their enthusiasm and inspirational work.

This book has also benefited from the institutional collegiality and support we encountered along the way. Coppélie wishes to thank Vaartoe–Centre for Sámi research at Umeå University for funding at the initial phase of this work and for the insightful comments and discussions from generous colleagues there. She also thanks her colleagues at Humlab, Umeå university, for making such an intellectually stimulating environment. A special thanks to Ingela Westerlund for her priceless administrative support and kindness along the process. Tom wishes to thank his colleagues and students at the Department of German, Nordic and Slavic at the University of Wisconsin–Madison, and to gratefully acknowledge the crucial funding assistance that came from the University of Wisconsin's Birgit Baldwin Professorship, Halls-Bascom Professorship, Center for European Studies, Graduate School, and Sustaining Scandinavian Folk Arts in the Upper Midwest project. Important fieldwork was also made possible through Tom's time as a fellow of the Swedish Collegium for Advanced Study in Uppsala, Sweden, and through assistance from the Kungl. Gustav Adolfs Akademien för Svensk Folkkultur.

At the University of Washington Press, we thank Larin R. McLaughlin for her unwavering enthusiasm and encouragement of this project, the vital image and quotation rights assistance of Caitlin Tyler-Richards, the production editing of Margaret K. Sullivan, the copyediting of Dale Cotton, and the support we received from the series editor for New Directions in Scandinavian Studies, Andrew Nestingen.

Coppélie addresses her sincere thanks to her brand-new colleagues at the University of Helsinki and Tom addresses his sincere thanks to his longstanding colleagues at the University of Wisconsin–Madison for their patience and goodwill in the hectic period of finalizing this book manuscript.

Čoahkkáigeassu

Sámi Summary

TRANSLATOR: ARLA MAGGA

Dát girji guorahallá dáiddalaš ja aktivisttalaš dáhpáhusaid Sámis 1970-logus dán rádjái ja dat vuojulduvvá gulahallamii ja maiddái govaid ja miellagovaid strategalaš geavaheapmái. Dutkamuša guovddážis lea sámegielat gulahallanvugiid dego gávppálaččat buvttaduvvon lávlagiid, filmmaid, girjjiid, sosiála media forumiid ja čállosiid oktavuohta, ja dat sosiopolitihkalaš fidnu, mainna huksejuvvo sámiid diđolašvuohta ja solidaritehta eamiálbmogin. Min dutkamuš čilge daid vugiid, maid sápmelaš aktivisttat, dáiddárat, kultuvrralaš bargit ja eará čatnašuvvan servodaga lahtut ávkkástallet sámegielat gulahallama bokte. Sii leat atnán dálá lassáneaddji gulahallanteknihkaid gaskaoapmin, maiguin sii meroštallet sámiid kultuvrralaš áššiid ja maiguin sii gaskkustit daid áššiid sihke sámiide ja ii-sámiide. Sin viggamuššan lea leamašan jorgalahttit gielalaš ja kultuvrralaš goarráneami ja gomihit diehtemeahttunvuođa, mii laktása sámiid ealáhusaide ja sámiid iešmearridanvuoigatvuhtii. Sin viggamuššan lea leamašan veahkehit sámiid seailut *sápmelažžan* boahtteáiggis. Nu mo sápmelaš juoigi Jörgen Stenberg cealká 2013 Facebook-čállosisttis: "Kultuvra lea mu vearju, luohti mu ávju." Musihkka, man sáhttá luđet, musihkkafestiválat, filmmat, YouTube videot, Facebook čállosat, Instagram govat ja Twitter civkimat leat dušše oasáš máŋggabealat medias, man bokte Sámi aktivisttat ávjjuineaset jokset iežaset čuozáhagaid: miehis olbmuid váimmuid ja mielaid.

Dán girjji logut gieđahallet dáid beliid sihke buvttaduvvon media (ee. gávppálaččat buvttaduvvon lávlagiid, filmmaid, girjjiid, videoid ja visuála govaid) ja sosiála media bokte. Vuosttaš logut fállet duogášdieđuid sámiid kultuvrras ja árra sápmelaš gova huksemis (Lohku 1 Åppås). Lohku 2 Doalli, geahčada Áltá akšuvnna 1970-logu loahpas. Lohku 3 Tjïekere čuvge Sámi media 1980-logus ja 1990-logu álggus. Lohku 4 Sijvo gieđahallá fas iešguđegelágan ja ovdáneaddji media buktagiid 2000-logus). Girjji nubbi oassi geahčada iešguđege sámi joavkkuid digitála mediageavaheami. Lohku 5 Rahte fátmmasta media ja gulahallama Sámis, nu ahte dat čuvge mo iešguđegelágan gulahallanvugiin lea leamašan jotkkolašvuohta iešguđegelágan mediavuogádagaid bokte ja maiddái dain fuolakeahttá. Lohku 6 Sállat gieđahallá sosiála media árra álgagiid Sámis, earret eará Samenet. Lohku 7 Ruövddietjarvva geahčada eanet dálá ovdamearkkaid, mat geavahuvvojit servoša fámuiduhttimii, giela oinnolašvuođa lasiheapmái ja aktivismii. Loahpahanlohku Fiehta fállá fuomášumiid, main lea loahpaid loahpas optimisttalaš vuoigŋa: Sámi nuppástuvvan ja dan fápmu historjjálaš ja maiddái dálá áiggis.

Sámi Media and Indigenous Agency in the Arctic North

Arvi

Introduction

Dus leat oappát, dus leat vieljat
Lulli–ameriihka arvevuvddiin
Ruonaeatnama geađgerittuin
Itgo don muitte gos don vulget?

You have sisters, you have brothers
In the rainforests of South America
On the stony shores of Greenland
Don't you remember where you're from?

MARI BOINE, *GULA GULA!* (1989)

THE PLAINTIVE, YEARNING VOCALS OF MARI BOINE'S NORTH Sámi single from 1989 *Gula gula!* (Listen, listen!) exhort Sámi listeners to remember they have sisters and brothers in far-off places. Boine's resolute drumming underscores the aural, aesthetic, spiritual, and philosophical commonalities that her song's lyrics suggest, uniting Indigenous people the world over. Similar relationships to lands and resources, and an underlying sense of reverence for the earth lie at the heart of an Indigenous worldview, Boine maintains. And Sámi people, as the Indigenous nation of northern Europe, should take this fact to heart: "Itgo don muitte gos don vulget?" (Don't you remember where you're from?). Remembering that Indigenous origin, Boine's song posits, will result in actions that affirm the sacralization of the earth and its denizens, moving Sámi people—and the wider Nordic societies in which they live—away from the practices of unbridled resource exploitation and environmental damage that came to Sámi country—Sápmi—as part of colonization.

That Boine expresses this pan-Indigenous viewpoint while performing her song in Sámi language underscores and buttresses implicitly but crucially her main point: Sámi people possess a language and a culture of their own, one that encodes, expresses, preserves, and advances Indigenous understandings in a manner wholly different from that of colonial languages and societies, which have forced their way into the lives and minds of Indigenous people in the Nordic region, as elsewhere in the world. Boine sings in Sámi not to limit the audience for her song, but to emphasize the notion of an Indigenous unity lying beneath the words and grammar of Indigenous languages and operating at the level of deep-seated understandings and worldview.

Boine's song appeared on the threshold of the last decade of the twentieth century, in the same year that Sámi people in Norway saw the opening of an official institution for Sámi self-determination and governance—the Sámediggi, Sámi parliament—and the same year that the United Nations International Labour Organization set forth its Indigenous and Tribal Peoples Convention ILO-169, aimed at codifying on an international level the legal rights of Indigenous peoples and the incumbent responsibilities of state authorities toward them (United Nations International Labour Organization 1989; Thuen 1995: 230–36). From the perspective of the history of communications technology, 1989 was also the same year that the Recording Industry Association of America reported that sales of compact discs (CDs) had outstripped sales of vinyl LPs for the first time in the United States, a fact reflecting the burgeoning growth of personalized listening habits in cars and elsewhere that rapidly reduced people's reliance on broadcast radio (Associated Press 1989). And 1989 was also the year that computer scientist Tim Berners-Lee (University of Oxford, MIT) produced the first communication between a Hypertext Transfer Protocol (HTTP) client and a server via the fledgling internet that would come to be called the World Wide Web (Berners-Lee and Fischetti 1999). Boine's message of cultural continuity and memory, of mutual recognition and linkage between Indigenous peoples, despite—or somehow because of—a certain opacity on the level of linguistic lexicon and grammar, was released to the public at a moment of unprecedented technological and economic change in the communication industry that facilitated the distribution of her song to millions of people the world over.

Thirty years later, an attractive home page operated by the United Nations Economic and Social Council announced 2019 as the "International Year of Indigenous Languages" (United Nations Economic and Social Council 2019). Describing Indigenous languages as a "matter for development, peace building and reconciliation," the site's opening statement (tellingly, perhaps, available only in English, French, and Spanish) appears in white lettering floating above a rotating series of vivid photographs depicting Indigenous representatives from around the world participating in the UN's 2018 meeting of the Permanent Forum on Indigenous Issues. The Norwegian Sámediggi's president, Aili Keskitalo, figures prominently in several of the photographs. Available on the site is an Action Plan for the year, as well as a calendar listing events in different countries and times over the course of the year. Choosing to emphasize language in an international discussion of Indigenous people's rights and cultures demonstrates the wider embrace of language among Indigenous communities as a key element of cultural autonomy, maintenance, and development.

Sámi Media and Indigenous Agency in the Arctic North chronicles the series of artistic and activist events that precipitated Sámi songs, like Boine's *Gula gula!* of 1989, and the related or resulting developments in the three decades that followed that continue to unfold today. At the heart of this work is the enduring linkage between Sámi language communications—including commercially produced songs, films, books, and social media platforms and posts—and the evolving sociopolitical project of building Sámi Indigenous awareness and solidarity called for so poignantly in Boine's song. Sámi activists, artists, cultural workers, and other dedicated community members have used Sámi language communication as a vehicle for defining their cultural agenda and for conveying that agenda to both Sámi and non-Sámi audiences through the ever-widening array of modern communications technologies available today. Such actors have aimed to reverse processes of linguistic and cultural erasure, undoing the layers of ignorance surrounding Sámi livelihoods and rights to self-determination, and engaging broader polities in securing support that can help Sámi culture survive *as Sámi* in the future. As the Sámi *joik* singer Jörgen Stenberg (discussed in chapter 4) declares in a 2013 Facebook post: "Culture is my weapon, *joik* my spear." Downloadable tunes, music festivals, films, YouTube videos, Facebook posts, Instagram images, and Twitter tweets are just some of the diverse media through which Sámi activist spears can reach their targets: the hearts and minds of willing audiences.

Definitions

For the international audience of Mari Boine's *Gula gula!* in 1989, neither the terms *Sámi* nor *Indigenous* were necessarily familiar, and the decision of UNESCO to designate 2019 as the International Year of Indigenous Languages suggests that the latter term remains ambiguous to some, if not many, across the world even now. Accordingly, it is important to define what is meant by these terms in this study and more generally in Western societies today.

Defined in the revised constitutions of Norway, Sweden, and Finland as the Indigenous people of the Nordic region, Sámi people possess a unique culture that developed over the course of millennia in the tundra, taiga, and boreal forest environments of Fennoscandia—the

Scandinavian and Kola Peninsulas. Subsisting traditionally on various combinations of hunting, gathering, fishing, and reindeer husbandry, Sámi have resided from time immemorial in areas that are today divided between the countries of Norway, Sweden, Finland, and the Russian Federation. Although statistics vary, it is likely there are between seventy thousand and one hundred thousand people who identify as Sámi today. Over the course of millennia, and with greater or lesser degrees of respect or coercion, they have shared their homeland with Nordic and Russian neighbors. Sámi people today are generally well connected to the rest of the world through broadcast channels and social media. Virtually all are literate in at least one of the majority languages of the four countries in which they live, and most command at least one other world language as well, often English. They may vacation in Spain, Florida, or Thailand, spend idle moments checking their smartphones, and commute to office jobs by car, bus, train, or plane. Despite strong integration into Nordic majority cultures, however, the commitment of many Sámi at least in principle to traditional Sámi livelihoods like reindeer husbandry and a resistance to projects that would threaten or damage the environment often lead Sámi into conflict with other Nordic polities, government agencies, and corporations. These groups are intent on achieving livelihoods and prosperity through extractive industries or through seemingly "green industries" that end up having adverse effects on the local ecosystem, like hydroelectric power plants and dams, wind turbines, and fish farms.

Sámi people speak, or in many cases formerly spoke, one of a set of closely related Sámi languages, somewhat distantly related to Finnish and Estonian but also incorporating many "substrate" terms from a prior language that seems to have been spoken in the Nordic region in the centuries immediately following the last Ice Age, and that was replaced or augmented over time (Aikio 2004). Sámi call their homeland Sápmi, Sábme, Sábmie, or Saepmie, using a root that recurs in the North Sámi derivative term *sápmelaš* (Sámi person) and the English ethonym *Sámi* (also spelled Saami, Same, Sami), a term that replaces an earlier, predominantly pejorative ethonym *Lapp.* In western Scandinavia, Swedes and Norwegians also formerly used the terms *Finne* or *Finn* to refer to Sámi, equating them with, or mistaking them for, the people who make up the majority of the population of modern Finland today and who speak a language called *suomi* (Finnish). Over time, extensive intermarriage between Sámi and neighboring peoples has meant that virtually no one today has an exclusively "Sámi" genealogy, although degrees of intermarriage vary by region, livelihood, and family history. Of the nine extant Sámi languages spoken today, only two have more than a thousand speakers, and many have far fewer. Some Sámi languages are extinct. The language of Mari Boine's *Gula gula!* is the most robust of the current Sámi languages, with some twenty-thousand speakers. Legislation protecting and supporting Sámi languages, particularly through school programs, developed largely in the twentieth century with a goal of reversing assimilationist policies of the past. The public use of Sámi language in media such as popular music, books, and film began only in the twentieth century and at the time of Boine's *Gula gula!* still seemed a novel and surprising musical choice to many Nordic audience members. Despite official recognition of Sámi languages as valid means of communication in Norway, Sweden, and Finland, few non-Sámi majority culture members would be able to greet a Sámi person in Sámi or count to three in the language today.

Definitions of the term *Indigenous* arose out of the same UN process that eventually resulted in the ILO-169 of 1989. A provisional definition was offered by UN Special Rapporteur José Martinez Cobo in 1986 as he endeavored to arrive at a set of policy recommendations regarding populations historically and currently subjected to discrimination in various countries: "Indigenous communities, peoples and nations are those which, having a historical continuity with pre-invasion and pre-colonial societies that developed on their territories, consider themselves distinct from other sectors of the societies now prevailing on those territories, or parts of them. They form at present non-dominant sectors of society and are determined to preserve, develop and transmit to future generations their ancestral territories, and their ethnic identity, as the basis of their continued existence as peoples, in accordance with their own cultural patterns, social institutions and legal system" (Martinez Cobo 1986).

A linchpin of this definition is the notion of a community's longstanding existence in a given territory, often understood as dating from time immemorial, and a decisive process of invasion, economic colonization, or disenfranchisement that ended a community's sovereignty and rendered them "non-dominant sectors." In places like North and South America, this rupture can usually be tied directly to the arrival of European traders, plunderers, or settlers who persuaded or compelled Indigenous communities to cede or vacate their lands, which were then appropriated by arriving settlers. In the Nordic region, in contrast, the rupture occurred more gradually, more insidiously, as Sámi progressively lost more and more control of their lands over the course of centuries. Nordic legal scholars and historians (e.g., Kvist 1992) have chronicled the long process by which Nordic and Russian crowns came to claim Sámi lands and waters for themselves, defining Sámi essentially as interlopers on their ancestral lands. Sámi tracts were turned over to non-Sámi settlers or to Sámi willing to become assimilated into emerging Nordic-dominant societies from the medieval period through the early modern era. As lands came to be used for farming, mining, forestry, or other economic uses, they were no longer available to Sámi for traditional subsistence activities like hunting, fishing, and herding. As the great Sámi intellectual Johan Turi put it in 1910, in the first book ever published in a Sámi language (see chapter 1): "Muhto go lea ruvdna váldán ain sámiin eret ja addán dálolaččaide ja lea sirdon rádji veaháš ain, dassá go lea juo šaddan nu unnin, ahte sámit eai sáhte šat birget" (Turi 2011b: 93; But the Crown has taken these lands away from the Sámi and given them to the settlers, and has shifted the border between the two groups bit by bit, until the part left to the Sámi has become so small that the Sámi can no longer survive on it [translation, Turi 2011a: 87]). Over the course of the nineteenth and early twentieth centuries, Sámi people became viewed as racial others, a topic taken up and decried in later Sámi works, as discussed in chapter 4. Part of the realization that drove Sámi activism in the 1970s and 1980s (detailed in chapter 2), was the fact that the gradual disenfranchisement experienced by the Sámi over the course of centuries was the equivalent in many respects to the more obviously cataclysmic and devastating colonial confrontations characteristic of settler invasions in North and South America. Like other Indigenous peoples elsewhere in the world, Sámi became "non-dominant sectors" of their societies, denied any degree of self-determination regarding culture, education, land use, livelihoods, or other key elements of a nation's life. The process of decolonization promoted by the UN through legislation like the ILO-169 or the Declaration of the Rights of Indigenous Peoples (United Nations General Assembly 2007) involves reversing not only the legal and social elements of this disenfranchisement, but also its cultural and intellectual effects, both on Indigenous communities and on the wider societies within which they live.

A second key element of Martinez Cobo's definition is its description of Indigenous people as "determined to preserve, develop and transmit to future generations their ancestral territories and ethnic identity." Genealogy alone, in other words, is, according to Martinez Cobo's definition, insufficient to qualify for the status of Indigenous. A community must demonstrate a will to exist as a nation, and to transmit that identity and attendant lands, traditions, and culture to future generations. This sense of determination and commitment is precisely what we see the Sámi displaying as they produce, disseminate, and consume Sámi media. Despite centuries of assimilative pressures, racist treatment, and social marginalization, Sámi people demonstrate a strong and enduring commitment to their culture, language, and traditional lands and ways. Rather than viewing themselves as assimilated subpopulations of the states in which they reside, the Sámi discussed here regard and portray themselves as Sámi people first and foremost. To varying degrees this sense of resolve, in the face of long-term discrimination, denigration, or dismissal, characterizes many of the estimated 370 million Indigenous people living in the world today.

Theoretical Background: Sámi and Other Indigenous Communications and Media

Another key concept in this study is *communication*. We seek here to explore and understand not processes of communication in general (a vast task) but rather, of the specific ways that Indigenous communities, and Sámi in particular, make use of communicative technology. Again, definitions are essential. Communication, from the Latin *communis* (common, sharing), finds its key root in *mun* (related to "community," "meaning"). Communication is an act of receiving, and the meaning of the term has evolved from imparting or transmitting tangibles to the more abstract transmission of ideas, knowledge, and information (Peters 2000). Broadly speaking, what we are witnessing today in digital communication is nothing new, as Barbara Kirshenblatt-Gimblett reminds us: "Communication in the absence of face-to-face interaction and at distance is as old as the circulation of objects (gift exchange, commercial transactions, postal service) and the transmission of signals (drumming messages whose sounds carry for several miles down a quiet river, or using smoke to produce visual signs legible from afar)" (Kirshenblatt-Gimblett 1996: 21–22).

The term used in Northern Sámi as a translation for communication—*gulahallan*—derives, in contrast, from the root *gul* meaning both to hear and to understand, thus emphasizing not the materials transferred by acts of communication but the process of meaningful, audible, intelligible interaction between two or more people engaged in intentional conversation. In comparison with the Latin term it glosses, gulahallan connotes more a sense of a negotiated and then mutually shared understanding than of a simple transfer of property or information from one party to another. People come to understand each other through processes of speaking and listening, of performance and reception. The back and forth nature of gulahallan assumes a process of conversation quite unlike that in older forms of Western communication like published books, scripted films, or even produced music. It predicts, however, some of the more iterative tendencies of social media as well as the characteristic processes of receiving and adapting that one can trace in various media products within Sámi culture in the last two centuries. In certain respects, Sámi people are well prepared for the particular affordances and tendencies of modern digital media communication, in part because these resemble normative ideas within Sámi culture about how one goes about communicating with other people in general. The seeming novelty of digital media communication in Sápmi needs to be understood within a broader context of enduring Sámi uses of media in continually evolving historical, cultural, and social circumstances.

The introduction and impact of new technologies entail both social change and technological development. Likewise, the use of a technology cannot be explained by its mere existence. The adoption and adaptation of a specific technology by a group or a community builds on factors that enable the group to take advantage of this new technology in meaningful and effective ways (see, e.g., Castells 2001: 48). Susan Douglas (1987) explains these entwined processes as a "social construction" of technology, that is, of how a technology (e.g., radio broadcasting in Douglas's study) is adapted by individuals and institutions as part of a social and cultural process. These processes shape how these applications of a technology are legitimized in a given social and cultural context. This constructivist view contrasts with a perception of technology as the result of a specific event (an invention). Even though Douglas's view of technological reception and adaptation as a process has been challenged by the exponential rate of development and enormity of change attending new technologies at present (see Ceruzzi 2005), Douglas's perception of the role of technology in social processes is highly relevant when approaching Sámi uses of participatory media. How applications of media technologies are shaped and legitimized by community members must be taken into account in order to further investigate the effects and implications of these technologies within a local culture or community. Further, previous research has emphasized the importance of often neglected cultural perspectives on computer-mediated communication (Bijker and Law 1992; Campbell 2007; Ess et al. 2007). Contextualizing media use in international, Indigenous, and Sámi contexts is a necessary first step in order to understand the implications and effects of contemporary media use.

In Sámi contexts, the first publications of produced media—periodicals and newspapers—began to appear in the late 1800s and early 1900s. Periodicals such as *Sagai Muitalægje* (1873), *Sámi usteb* (1888), and *Nuorttanaste* (1898) afforded Sámi the opportunity of writing in their own language, an opportunity that in turn provided a concrete start for organizing. As noted in chapter 1, Sámi literature and canonized Sámi authors, such as Johan Turi and Elsa Laula Renberg, played significant roles in taking positions on minority-majority relationships. Laula Renberg's *Inför lif eller död? Sanningsord i de Lappska förhållandena* (1904; Facing life or death? Words of truth about the Sámi situation) brings to the fore the injustices that affect her people. Turi's *Muitalus sámiid birra* (1910; An account of the Sámi) addresses issues such as the lack of knowledge about the Sámi situation and denounces the ways in which Swedish and Norwegian authorities have treated the Sámi. An intensification of works and publications by Sámi authors in the 1970s is also commonly linked to political organization, particularly in connection with the ČSV movement (Bjørklund 2000; Cocq 2014; Solbakk 2006), an intellectual awakening and radicalization of viewpoint that mobilized Sámi toward the goals of defining and defending their identity on the principles of self-representation and through markers of identity and vernacular expression.

Alongside the printed word, other technologies have accelerated the pace of communication and circulation of information among Sámi people. The use of wide territories for Sámi livelihoods and the geographic dispersion of the population, combined with the importance of kinship and family relations within the culture, are some of the interwoven aspects that motivate needs and interests in the implementation and application of information and communication technologies. One example of early adoption of modern technologies among Sámi is the NMT (Nordic Mobile Telephony), an analog cellular phone system of the early 1980s that was not only functional in urban environments, but also in rural and mountainous areas, where it became a useful tool for reindeer herders. The NMT system was still in use in the early 2000s and had a far better range than digital cellular systems in remote areas.

Sámi media has continually been developed, to a great extent, with the ambition of making available radio broadcasts of news and other programing in the Sámi languages. These efforts concern mostly the North Sámi language, in part due to its higher number of speakers and thereby listeners, as compared to other Sámi languages. Programs in Sámi have been broadcast on radio since 1946 in Norway, since 1947 in Finland, since 1953 in Sweden, and since 1983 in Russia. The three Nordic broadcasting companies NRK, SR, and YLE cooperate to produce and air joint broadcasts, to some degree also extended to Sámi in Russia. It was, however, only in 2001 that daily news broadcasts in Sámi began to appear on national television throughout Norway and Sweden, and later in Finland. *Ođđasat*, the 15-minute news program in North Sámi, now airs every weekday. Children's programs are aired on a regular basis, often as Nordic Sámi co-productions or as dubbed or subtitled versions of programs in the majority languages. Several Sámi productions make use of traditional storytelling and motifs from legends (Cocq 2014). These include the adaptation of older tales and legends for radio broadcast, digital storytelling portraying central characters from traditional storytelling and mythology, and audio and video resources using joik in an effort to make this traditional form of singing and storytelling accessible and understandable for young children.

Sámi are not alone among Indigenous peoples in possessing sophisticated interest in and control of modern media. In his important study, *Savage Preservation*, Brian Hochman (2014) notes that when in 1890 the white Harvard ethnographer Jesse Walker Fewkes headed to Calais, Maine, in order to experiment with the usefulness of wax cylinder recording equipment for capturing songs and narratives by Passamaquoddy elders, he found that leaders in the community were already quite knowledgeable about the technology and eager to use it to preserve and affirm their local culture. A century after Fewkes's Passamaquoddy experiment, and even with a still highly significant "digital divide" between the likely internet access of Indigenous communities and that of majority-polity members of colonizing societies, Indigenous people have nonetheless made a significant presence for themselves in modern digital media and have used such media as tools for serving local needs as well as reaching broader national and international audiences. Indigenous communities have used media to chronicle processes of social change and as potent tools for questioning power structures, and for gaining more influence in global issues. The growth of technologies such as television, video cassette recorders, video cameras, and satellite video-conferencing were considered in the 1980s and 1990s forms of new media that could, given the right circumstances of funding and access, facilitate self-determination and resistance to cultural domination in Indigenous contexts (Ginsburg 1991; Meadows 1994; Turner 1992). By the 1990s, media use by Indigenous groups was increasing and opened the way for other forms of media production and Indigenous participation. Video and film, for instance, became tools for the construction of identity in Aboriginal Australian communities (Ginsburg 1994). NativeNet, a LISTSERV established in 1991 and used mainly for discussions about Indigenous issues, illustrates the early development of online fora for discussing and furthering Indigenous agendas. Another example of such innovations were CD-ROMs for the digital preservation of American Indian culture in the 1990s, or home pages for education programs, not least in language education (Zimmerman et al. 2000: 72–79).

The use of the internet and digital networks as tools for activism also began in the 1990s. The International Campaign to Ban Landmines in 1996 is one of the early examples that illustrate the use of email and digital communication to facilitate organization and interaction with governments and policy makers beyond national borders (Denning 2000). The Zapatista movement also involved early activist media use: in 1994, "LaNeta," a civil society network, enabled the Zapatista movement to communicate despite the state's restrictions, and played a crucial role in bringing global attention to the rebellion (Sassen 2004: 76; the Zapatista "netwar" and the forms of international solidarity it engendered are discussed in more detail in chapter 3. Other examples can be found in initiatives in other parts of the world—for instance, in multiple uses of BBS (Bulletin Board System) software that allows users to connect to the system through a terminal program and exchange data, information, or messages. The BBS of the 1990s was an important precursor to the World Wide Web as we know it today, and to social media. It is also an early example of a net-based communicative tool subjected to governmental suppression: it was the object of Operation Sundevil, a major crackdown that took place in the United States in 1990 (Sterling 1994).

In activist engagements, and in order to achieve change, media provide a means to educate, raise questions, mobilize, and organize. Scholars have observed and underscored these uses of media as acts of decolonization. As Edward Said put it, "We are beginning to learn that de-colonization was not the termination of imperial relationships but merely the extending of a geo-political web which has been spinning since the Renaissance. The new media have the power to penetrate more deeply into a 'receiving' culture than any previous manifestation of Western terminology" (1994: 353). Seminal early examinations of these decolonizing processes in relation to media include D. R. Browne's *Electronic Media and Indigenous Peoples: A Voice of Our Own?* (1996) and a special issue of the journal *Cultural Survival* devoted to "Aboriginal Media, Aboriginal Control" (1998). From a similar perspective, Maori decolonization researcher Linda Tuhiwai Smith (1999: 147) has described how education, broadcasting, publishing, and other media are developing in tandem as tools for decolonization in a multitude of Indigenous contexts (e.g., Alia 2010), as we discuss in chapter 5.

As the influential volume of essays edited by Kyra Landzelius, *Native on the Net* demonstrates (2006), Indigenous people have increasingly carved a place in a media world that was initially dominated by the voices and viewpoints of majority cultures alone. Where the immensely important Zapatista "netwar" of 1994 consisted largely of Indigenous activists relying on non-Indigenous allies to relay their messages to a wider world through internet channels, Indigenous activists today produce their own media products or work closely with outside media professionals to shape and hone the messages that they wish to share. Landzelius's volume has been followed by a number of important anthologies since, including Laurel Evelyn Dyson, Max Hendriks, and Stephen Grant's *Information Technology and Indigenous People* (2007) and the same team's *Indigenous People and Mobile Technologies* (2016).

On a broader level, the role and potential of Indigenous media has been emphasized in public and political debate, for instance in the context of UNESCO, as expressed in an official statement on the occasion of the International Day of the World's Indigenous People in 2012: "New information and communication technologies play a significant role in enhancing the access to, and quality of, education, science, and culture. Their applications transform the way we share, preserve and transmit knowledge and languages" (UNESCO 2012). Under the theme "Indigenous Media, Empowering Indigenous Voices," UNESCO also underscores the role of Indigenous media "in supporting Indigenous peoples' models of development that are in accordance with their own priorities, cultures and values." Indigenous media are essential because "all voices must not only be heard but listened to," as Irina Bokova, Director-General of UNESCO declared on the occasion of the International Day of the World's Indigenous People.

Noam Chomsky's 2013 lecture in Montreal summarizes these ongoing processes in a comment about mining: "There is resistance: in Canada it's coming from First Nations. But it's worth remembering that that's a world-wide phenomenon. Throughout the world, the Indigenous populations are in the lead. They are actually taking the lead in trying to protect the earth. That's extremely significant" (Keefer 2013a). The statement that Indigenous populations are "taking the lead" has drawn attention on a worldwide level. During the last few years in particular, resistance to mining exploitation by Indigenous groups has led to massive protests in Canada, Australia, South America, Sápmi, and elsewhere. Indigenous populations have also taken the lead in environmental movements more broadly, an engagement that reached new heights at the UN climate conference COP21 in Paris in December 2015 (Liliequist and Cocq 2017; Sandström 2017).

Media, and the discourses they construct and convey, contribute both locally and internationally to shaping and reproducing representations of places, people, and events. Especially in the case of participatory media, the degree of agency open to minority and Indigenous groups offers opportunities for exercising power and control over the framing of reality from local perspectives based on local premises. The rise and growth of new forms of participatory digital media and their uses have generated a broader range of uses and applications, for instance, in the so-called genre of "activist media" (Lievrouw 2011). The term *digital activism* describes situations in which digital technology is used in an effort to engender or further social or political change. Social and political movements in the first decades of the twenty-first century have often been associated with social media, as illustrated in a number of so-called "Twitter revolutions" (Mungiu-Pippidi and Munteanu 2009; Burns and Eltham 2009; Jansen 2010). Instances and applications of digital media in activism, for example, for protest movements, have multiplied since these "Twitter revolutions" of the early 2010s. The media landscape has continued to evolve, yet remains, as it is often characterized, networked, globalized, and potentially democratizing (Rainie et al. 2012; Castells 2001). Participatory media enable minority, Indigenous, marginalized, and alternative groups to become what Rainie, Rainie, and Wellman call "networked actors," employing media as "a form of self-expression." It can also provide individuals an "opportunity to learn," or to find "a space for collaboration or a place to connect with a community," for example, a support group, thereby gaining a sense of empowerment through the support given and received (2012: 217). In terms of globalization, digital media contribute to hastening the pace through which we communicate, and spread information, goods, or ideas (Eriksen 2007: 8).

Today, in the light of the exponential increase of digital media, the potentials, hopes, and expectations that technologies can present for self-determination, empowerment, and democratization have not faded. A number of academic studies and Indigenous initiatives have illustrated how we are witnessing "a powerful international movement that looks both inward and outward, simultaneously helping to preserve ancient languages and cultures and communicating across cultural, political and geographical boundaries" (Alia 2010: xiii). For many Indigenous groups, access to the World Wide Web and, later, to participatory media, has opened the possibility of establishing an active and emancipatory presence online (Nathan 2000; Srinivasan 2006). The same tools, however, can prove equally effective in helping suppress, mislead, or mistreat minority and Indigenous groups. For many Sámi, today's Facebook offers little in the sense of a safe space or intimacy that once characterized the earlier, almost Sámi-exclusive SameNet (see chapter 6). Using contemporary digital technologies effectively for activist ends necessitates keeping on top of trends and developments that are constantly transforming digital media and the norms or potentials they offer.

Inreach

While notably effective as a means of interacting with, and hopefully influencing, majority populations and leaders, digital media can also be used by marginalized groups for *inreach*: services aimed at the community itself and its present members and needs. Minority media provide a multitude of examples and initiatives in which minority language communities strive to "take place" and strengthen their languages and communities through new media products and platforms. Various social media services have been embraced by language communities, including YouTube, Twitter, and Facebook, using these for learning, enhancing language diversity, and performing identity (Haf Gruffydd Jones and Uribe-Jongbloed 2013). The case of Welsh language media use, for instance, has been studied by several scholars, who underscore how Welsh speakers seek and create new language media spaces (Cunliffe and ap Dyfrig 2013; Johnson 2013). By doing so, speakers and learners of the Welsh community articulate linguistic identities. The use of Social Networking Services (SNS) among young people (Cunliffe et al. 2013) indicates that digital media use is not only a way for the language to reach new domains, but also for new groups to engage in language revitalization. Case studies suggest that media use by marginalized communities or linguistic subgroups offer the advantage of developing resources and modes of communication within communities based on the members' interests and needs. Communication accommodation on SNS, for example, on Twitter, allows users to address several audiences in a single message (see, e.g., Johnson 2013; Cocq 2015), illustrating strategies that facilitate bilingualism, code switching, and translanguaging.

New media was not developed with minority languages in mind (compare Cormack 2013), but innovative applications illustrate how people experiment with technology and find new ranges of applications for products they come to use. Barbara Kirshenblatt-Gimblett points out that "the specificity of networked interactive electronic communication becomes especially clear in the unintended consequences of non-instrumental uses of these media, uses for which they were not initially intended" (1996: 22). One example of such unanticipated usage is the smartphone application WeChat, which has become an effective tool for language maintenance and revitalization among minority language speakers in the Tibetan areas of China.[1] In the case of Manegacha in the Henan County, for instance, WeChat enables members of Tibetan language communities living in different areas to communicate in their language on a daily basis despite a lack of face-to-face contact (personal communication with Roche in 2016; Roche 2017). While communicating via text messages can prove challenging for communities in which the language is primarily spoken, WeChat responds to a need and interest in an existing mode of oral communication.

"Indigenous Tweets," created by Kevin Scannell in 2011, used digital media to help endangered languages during the 2010s. A researcher in computational linguistics at Saint Louis University, Missouri, Scannell generated a program that identifies tweets using statistical language recognition based on a data bank of around five hundred languages. It then compiles a database of speakers of minority languages published on the site, along with information about the users, the percentage of Indigenous languages used in the tweets, and a list of trending hashtags. Scannell started his project after receiving a request from a colleague who wanted a tool to gather tweets in Haitian Creole, and then developed it to include Irish, and later other languages as well (Ní Bhroin 2015). It is unclear how the project includes community anchors, which raises questions about its effective use in revitalization purposes. But the site illustrates a remarkable effort to aggregate information on social media activities in order to facilitate communication between speakers of a language community.

We can assume that the needs and interests for such a tool or other kinds of digital products striving for language revitalization are community-specific, and that their implementation and potential success are more dependent on offline communities than on emergent virtual communities. Technologies can carry "culturally and historically contingent assumptions" (Christie 2008) and the production, distribution and consumption of knowledge operate within local and historical contexts (see Kral 2009, 2010; Kral and Schwab 2012). Examinations of Indigenous applications of digital technologies must take into account the cultural aspects these technologies may contain. Similarly, as has been observed in research on Indigenous literacy, there is a need for language-specific tools (Cocq and Sullivan 2019) rather than for general solutions. Where colonization creates recurrent and shared issues for Indigenous peoples around the world, Indigenous communities themselves display considerable and important local differences that condition the form and use of any media.

With the culture-specific development of digital technologies, new methods have been experimented with, for instance, the use of virtual environments to represent Indigenous culture in the *Digital Songlines* project, released in 2006. The goal of the system (a software toolkit) developed by the Australasian Cooperative Research Center for Interaction Design, was to enable Aboriginal communities to "digitally preserve, protect and promote their arts, culture and heritage" (Leavy 2007: 159). The 3D visualization was applied in an effort to reflect the link between the land and Indigenous culture. The project, by its choice of technology, aimed at facilitating the collaborative production and distribution of community-based contributions. The levels of interactivity and accessibility were priorities in the development of the project (168). The toolkit, however, was operational only for a limited time. As is often the case with technology-based infrastructure, efforts and costs for maintenance limit the sustainability of these initiatives.

Globalization: Friend or Foe?

Already in 1990, Arjun Appadurai writes about the dynamics of global cultural flow in a world that "involves interaction of a new order and intensity" (1990: 1). A dimension of this global cultural flow (an approach he developed further later, see Appadurai 1996) is mediascape, "image-centered, narrative-based account of strips of reality" (1990: 9). Today, almost thirty years later, we can observe how these "strips of reality" continued to evolve and have become omnipresent in our smartphones and other mobile devices.

Globalization is also sometimes discussed as a threat to Indigenous languages, cultures, and traditions (Ó Laoire 2008: 204; Smith and Ward 2000; Grenoble and Whaley 2006). For instance, Thomas Hylland Eriksen (2007: 52) links globalization and standardization in formal education, suggesting that a consequence of broader educational access is the eradication of Indigenous languages and a process of "literal genocide" and "cultural genocide." As Smith and Ward (2000: 2–3) point out, globalization can be a threat to Indigenous people by accelerating the process of colonization, increasing the commodification of culture, furthering the entrenchment of inequality, and promoting a loss of identity. These effects arise because, as Smith and Ward contend, globalization "provides access to a smorgasbord of cultural practices that are public property to be 'borrowed' at will. Certainly, globalisation makes Indigenous cultures available to a wider audience, often without that audience ever having to leave home. It deliberately invites the outsiders in," and as a result "Indigenous peoples are having to fight harder on a variety of fronts to ensure their cultural survival and to find means for asserting their rights and autonomy in the face of the new threats posed by globalisation" (2000: 2–3).

On the other hand, as Smith and Ward also note, new media hold the potential for empowerment, as Indigenous communities identify "contemporary forms of communication, particularly expressive media such as film, videos and the internet" as potential tools for "social and political transformations of dominant hegemonies" (2000: 4). Globalization is here perceived as offering new possibilities to preserve heterogeneity and multiple identities. For anthropologist Thomas Hylland Eriksen, "globalization does not entail the production of global uniformity or homogeneity. Rather, it can be seen as a way of organizing heterogeneity" (2007: 10). Globalization, from this perspective, implies the growth of a common global discourse that identifies and makes visible "formal commonalities between ethnic groups struggling for recognition everywhere" (65), calling attention to shared issues of cultural heritage, history of oppression, et cetera. The tension between the beneficial and the disadvantageous effects of the dynamics of globalization taking place through global media play out in Indigenous and Sámi contexts.

To be sure, certain ironies or ambiguities obtain in mediated acts that, on the one hand, underscore an Indigenous rootedness and links to a given locale and, on the other hand, unfold in a global media space that seems to open every nook and cranny of the world to broader scrutiny and that can be accessed from anywhere. Illustrative of the delights and difficulties of this duality was the 2017 Norwegian television program, "slow TV," a minute-by-minute broadcast of the migration of the Finnmark reindeer herd of Josef Mikkel Sara from winter pastures at Iešjávri to summer pastures on the island of Kvalsundet during late April (Bergmo 2017). The broadcast allowed people throughout Norway–and via the internet around the world–to tune in and watch the Sara family and their herd as they made their way step by step, day by day across a snowy tundra. The broadcast footage of landscape, people, dogs, and reindeer was accompanied by recordings of contemporary Sámi music and interspersed with occasional interviews with Sara and members of his family. The broadcast delighted and inspired tens of thousands of viewers worldwide, as it seemed to eliminate the distance and remoteness that separated them from the world of Sámi reindeer herders. At the same time, nature underscored the still considerable limitations of human technology, as the weather played havoc with the television program's intended five-day duration and planned culminating finale. The herd did not move across the landscape in accord with the program's schedule, and in the end, the final swim to the island had to be cancelled because of dangerous waters. (The reindeer were ferried over to the island instead, while the program aired footage of an earlier filmed swimming.) Nature's stern interventions notwithstanding, the program—produced in cooperation with NRK-Sápmi, the branch of the Norwegian broadcasting corporation specifically tasked with producing Sámi-related programing, and involving Sámi media professionals as reporters and commentators—represented a powerful updating and decolonizing of the 1977 *Mutual of Omaha's Wild Kingdom* portrayal of a similar reindeer migration, discussed in chapter 2. It is also illustrative of a process of digital "friend making," in which Indigenous people showcase aspects of their traditions and cultures in order to gain support from international allies and possibly apply pressure on national governments or corporations aiming to exploit Indigenous resources or ignore Indigenous rights. One can find similar trends, for instance, in Mapuche net activism, as Marilyn Andrews (2012) has shown, and in broader Indigenous media in places like the United States, where Native American powwows, music, and filmmaking attract substantial majority-member audiences. As we shall see, particularly in chapter 3, Sámi media artists focused strongly on friend making in the late 1980s, as Sámi rights began to be instated in law.

Alongside friend-making efforts and service within the community, Indigenous activists sometimes use media to shame or embarrass as strategies for leveraging change. We will examine how this strategy materializes in Nordic contexts in a number of coming chapters. Ataya Cespooch (2013: 10–11) discusses the ways that Lakota teenagers used YouTube to talk back to a Diane Sawyer *20/20* American television special entitled "Hidden America: Children of the Plains." The youth challenged the unexamined colonialist viewpoints and sought to replace its stereotypical representations of Native people with fresh and accurate images from their home, Rose Bud reservation. Sheila Bock (2017) has shown how African Americans used Twitter to talk back to white racism in the aftermath of a 2013 racist incident involving a prominent white Southern culinary celebrity. The wry and powerful visual work of activists in Canada's Idle No More movement and the Sámi Suohpanterror (see chapter 7) illustrate the capacity of the internet to serve as a forum for criticizing colonial attitudes and institutions that continue to complicate or hinder Indigenous self-determination.

To illustrate a Sámi version of this talking back to authority, consider Máret Ánne Sara's "Pile o' Sápmi" series, featured in part on a public website (www.pileosapmi.com). Like many counterparts across the contemporary Indigenous art world, Sara's work illustrates the sophistication and sometimes bitter sting of Indigenous activist art, serving both inreach and outreach functions. Her series of art objects made from reindeer skulls plays off both the Cree reverence for buffalo bones—represented by their sacred stockpile of bones near what is today Regina, Saskatchewan, a place called *oskana kâ-asastêki* (where the bones are piled)—and an infamous photograph of discarded buffalo skulls, taken in 1890 at a Michigan glue works, and known widely today as "Pile of Buffalo Skulls." The contrast between these two piles—one sacred, the other markedly profane; one enduring, the other temporary; one respectful of a species that provided life and sustenance to Plains communities for countless generations, the other callously anticipating the near extinction of the species in the course of a few decades—speaks powerfully to the contrasting worldviews of Indigenous and settler polities in North America. Sara's Sámi installations reference these contrasts and direct them to the case of reindeer in Norway. Her installations have both concrete and virtual instantiations, including a website, and in both forms they focus attention on the efforts of her brother Jovsset Ánte Sara to resist a Norwegian state order that he drastically cull his herd. As Sara's art attracts attention in international galleries and newspaper reports, it shines a critical light on the regulatory practices of the Norwegian government, which supports Sámi self-determination in name, but reserves for the state the right to make the most important decisions in nearly every situation. Thirty years after Boine's *Gula gula!*, Sara's

"Pile o' Sápmi" illustrates both the continuities and the changing nature of Sámi media activism as a tool of both inreach and outreach communication.

Frame and Chapter Overview

Within the context of broader scholarly attention to Indigenous presence and activism in modern digital media, our aim is to examine the role Sámi have played in these transnational Indigenous trends and to chronicle the specific ways in which these trends have unfolded within Sápmi and the surrounding Nordic states. How have Sámi—or at least, *some* Sámi—come to see themselves as sharing a common colonial experience with "*oappát, vieljat lulli - ameriihka arvevuvddiin*" (sisters, brothers in the rain forests of South America)? How has this pan-Indigenous identity become articulated in media products and Sámi self-images? And how have these images in turn influenced majority polities as well as Sámi themselves?

Along with Nordic and Sámi counterparts like Trond Thuen (1995) in his important study, *Quest for Equity*, and the various contributors to Anna Lydia Svalastog and Gunlög Fur's 2015 anthology, *Visions of Sápmi/Visjoner av Sápmi*, we argue that in the Álttá dam protests of the late 1970s and early 1980s Sámi built a strategy of image making that proved a powerful tool for gaining attention and redirecting public discourse in directions favorable to Sámi interests. Celebrating a traditional Sámi way of life involving sustainable hunting, fishing, and reindeer husbandry, and displaying and further developing distinctive genres of Sámi oral and material culture—for example, the joik song tradition, *duodji* handicraft made with antler, reindeer leather, and other traditional materials—Sámi have been able to create in the public eye an image of continuity and distinctiveness constructed in part on emblems of alterity, that is, stereotypes. Yet, as we shall demonstrate here, these images are integrally decolonizing in the ways in which Sámi make use of them to serve key ethnopolitical purposes.

Rather than exoticizing Sámi culture in ways that marginalize and stigmatize, the creative image making produced and used by the Sámi surveyed in this study since Álttá, we argue, aims to invite Sámi themselves into greater engagement with their natal culture while simultaneously convincing a non-Sámi audience of Sámi resilience, continuity, and inherent rights to self-determination. In this complex work of making and deploying images, modern media become key tools, demonstrating through their very modernity the persistence of Sámi culture in the present, while also imbuing these hypermodern contexts with visual, narrative, aural, and material content that connotes traditionality, continuity, and persistence. We argue that Sámi image making since Álttá is a process of imagining what it means to be Sámi, in part by looking toward the past, but also by performing takes on traditionality and history in the present in order to secure a Sámi future, one which will be embraced and preserved both by Sámi themselves and by the wider societies in which they live.

We examine these issues in both produced media (e.g., commercially produced music, films, books, videos, and visual images) and in participatory social media. The first chapters, authored primarily by Thomas DuBois, provide a background on Sámi culture and early Sámi image making (chapter 1, *Åppås*), then look at the Álttá dam protests of the late 1970s (chapter 2, *Doalli*), followed by a look at Sámi media in the 1980s and early 1990s (chapter 3, *Tjïekere*), and the varied and thriving media products of the 2000s (chapter 4, *Sijvo*). The second half of the book, authored primarily by Coppélie Cocq, examines uses of digital media by various Sámi groups. Chapter 5, *Rahte*, contextualizes media and communication in Sápmi, illustrating the continuity of patterns of communication through, despite, and thanks to, different forms of media. Chapter 6, *Sállat*, takes its point of departure in early initiatives of social media in Sápmi, reaching forward in chapter 7, *Ruövddietjarvva*, to more recent examples of digital media use for community strengthening, increased language visibility, and activism. The concluding chapter 8, *Fiehta*, ends with an optimistic tone when reflecting on the power and force of change that characterized Sápmi in historical and contemporary times.

It is important to note at the outset that not all Sámi today engage in or advocate the particular Indigenous activist agenda or viewpoints epitomized by Mari Boine's *Gula gula!* and surveyed in this study. Sámi people vary in their views of their culture, their notions of ideal relations between Sámi and the state, and their broader hopes for themselves, their children, and their communities. Just as not all women writers are feminists, so it is that not all Sámi writers or artists are deeply engaged in work aimed at preserving, revitalizing, or valorizing Sámi culture. Differences of viewpoint or strategy are endemic in all human societies and can be seen as a sign of a vital and viable culture. We focus only on one strand of discourse in Sámi communication, one that seeks to celebrate elements of Sámi oral tradition, traditional knowledge, and expressive culture as implements for maintaining and advancing Sámi culture in the present and future. As we shall demonstrate, it is a strand that has built upon itself and evolved over the decades surveyed in very conscious and productive ways. The production, enactment, and dissemination of images of "Sáminess" through various communicative channels is a distinctive and fascinating part of contemporary Sámi culture, and one that has gained a considerable following among Sámi people, young and old, as among non-Sámi audiences and allies. Yet it remains important to point out that it is still only one of a range of attitudes and strategies that coexist or compete within Sámi communities today. Jorunn Eikjok and Ola Røe's *Sámi Images in Modern Times* (2013) includes vignettes of Sámi fishers and herders, handcrafters, dancers, shamans, Laestadian Christians, politicians, doctors, and others, who argue variously and sometimes vehemently for the importance of or the uselessness of Sámi language, Sámi culture, and a Sámi agenda.

We have elected to draw on Sámi snow terminology to describe the developments we examine. Our decision to do so is not meant to trivialize or exoticize this important body of weather terminology in Sámi languages, but rather to acknowledge the vigorous ways in which Sámi scholars have championed Sámi snow terminology as an important topic of study and as an emblem of traditional knowledge and environmental wisdom (Eira 1984; Jernsletten 1994, 1997; Magga 2006, 2014; Ryd 2007; Gaup 2009; Porsanger et al. 2009; Eira et al. 2010, 2012). Scholars have pointed to the nuanced and empirically rigorous nature of these terms, which denote a wide range of snow conditions in relation to traditional Sámi activities like skiing, hunting, tracking, and reindeer husbandry. Sámi educators have also used Sámi snow terminology as a prime example of the kinds of learning that should be included in a decolonized, Sámi-centered educational system.

Each of the coming chapters introduces a snow term from a different Sámi language and discusses its traditional meaning as well as its metaphorical significance in our study. The Lule Sámi term *åppås,* used as the title of the next chapter, refers to fresh, newly fallen snow that has not yet become marked by animal tracks of any kind. We use the term here to signal the initial attempts of Sámi people to present strategic images of themselves and their culture for a surrounding, colonizing audience. The North Sámi term *doalli* refers to fresh snow that has fallen over established tracks or trails, in which the old trail is still discernible beneath the new blanket of snow. We use the term to highlight the fact that the Álttá protests of the late 1970s and early 1980s were built on prior strategies of image making, even when those elements of the protests appeared to a non-Sámi international audience as strikingly novel and unprecedented. The South Sámi *tjïekere* refers to snow that has been pawed up by grazing reindeer, and is used here to describe the process of exploring and lifting up traditions from the past in new ways that Sámi artists engaged in during the early post–Álttá era of Sámi image making. The Inari Sámi term *sijvo* refers to snow conditions that are ideal for skiing and travel. It is used here to describe the remarkable productivity and success of Sámi art and media in recent decades, as Sámi have established a market niche in Nordic and international Indigenous and artistic contexts. The Lule

Sámi term *rahte* refers to a path in the snow resulting from where other people have gone and, like doalli, is meant to signal the continuities within the framework of seeming technological innovation in modern Sámi internet usage and social media. The term *sállat,* in turn, refers to freshly laid tracks in snow, particularly in areas where no one has gone before. We use it here to describe the novelty and remarkable success of early Sámi internet usage, particularly the Sámi forerunner to Facebook, SameNet. The Ume Sámi *ruövddietjarvva* refers to the development of a thick crust of snow capable of supporting even a large animal like a moose or a horse without breaking. We use the term here to describe recent Sámi uses of digital media to strengthen or enhance Sámi identity, and as a tool for activism.

The title of this chapter, *Arvi* (the North Sámi term for rain) differs from those that come after it in that it refers to rain rather than snow. By choosing the term here, we wish to signal the feelings of solidarity with the Indigenous peoples of the Amazon reflected in Boine's "*Lulli-ameriihka arvevuvddiin*" (in the rain forests of South America) quoted at the outset of this chapter. We also wish to highlight the process by which such feelings of common cause with distant Indigenous people have developed among Sámi over the past four decades and the ways in which these feelings become expressed and emblematized in Sámi art and discourse. Likewise, the title of our concluding chapter, *Fiehta*—derived from the Lule Sámi term for the first grazing for reindeer once there is no longer snow on the ground—is meant to signal the sense of optimism and confidence and new beginnings that characterizes the work of many Sámi artists, activists, and involved citizens as they work in novel ways and with new digital tools to ensure a viable status and reality for Sámi language, culture, livelihoods, and people in an unfolding and uncertain future. Where snow terms work well for our study of Sámi Indigenous activism, other bodies of knowledge or systems of lexicon might furnish useful metaphors for other Indigenous communities. We note with appreciation the important anthology of Hawaiian rain terms produced by Collette Leimomi Akana and

Kiele Gonzalez (2015; entitled *Hānau ka ua: Hawaiian Rain Names*) as an excellent example of the rich bodies of insights and metaphors connected with rain in Indigenous Hawaiian culture.

A further element of our text's structure can be seen in the opening vignettes of each chapter, which identify a geographical starting point in a city or village of Sápmi. This choice of place making in our narrative is not only a way of guiding the reader through the vast and varied regions of Sápmi. It is also motivated by the importance of remembering that media are not only global and transnational but also grounded in local communities, where they serve and/or influence local people, who, ideally, connect with broader global communities. Chapter 1, *Åppås*, starts with a juxtaposition of the small Giema (Kemi) lake of Orrejaura/Orrejawre (modern Northern Sámi Oarrejávri; Finnish Orajärvi) and the intellectual center of eighteenth-century Swedish colonization–Uppsala. Here, as the chapter details, one Sirpmá Ovllá sang and wrote down songs that can be regarded as the first instances of Sámi image making shared with an outside, non-Sámi audience. Chapter 2, *Doalli*, similarly pairs the banks of the Álaheaieatnu (Álttá River) of Northern Norway with the lawn outside of the Norwegian parliament building, Stortinget, in downtown Oslo. Here, in 1979, an important protest against the proposed damming of the river drew Sámi and non-Sámi allies into spirited protests against the Norwegian state and led to creative crafting of images to capture the attention of local and distant viewers. Chapter 3, *Tjïekere*, begins with a look at the South Sámi mountain Oulavuolie, located in Norway, where in 1952 Nils Mattias Andersson performed a *vuolle* that has since become a part of the Sámi literary canon. Chapter 4, *Sijvo*, begins in the village of Aanaar/Anár/Inari in the north of Finland, where every year a massive international Indigenous film festival is held, entitled Skábmagovat, pictures of the Arctic night. Chapter 5, *Rahte*, starts in Jåhkåmåhkke, a central meeting place for education, knowledge exchange and, in recent years, activism in the north of Sweden. Chapter 6, *Sállat*, considers the internet as a significant place that, through the early initiative of SameNet, has gained materiality and a physical presence though meetings and social relations. Ubmeje, as a symbol for dedicated work for strengthening threatened languages, is the point of departure in chapter 7, *Ruövddietjarvva*. The book ends in Gállok (concluding chapter, *Fiehta*), a quiet area of reindeer pasture near Jåhkåmåhkke, Sweden, but also the site of a planned open-pit mine that became the focus of Sámi anti-mining activism and concomitant cultural empowerment in recent times.

Just as our choices of snow terms reflect the diversity of Sámi languages, so our choice of places to highlight is meant to underscore the diversity of terrains, ways of life, and hubs of activity that both differentiate various areas of Sápmi and yet contribute together to the notion of Sápmi as a single place, belonging to a single, varied, Sámi nation. That Sámi nation building occurs in part in the virtual world of the internet, as well as in concrete places in four different states, is one of the salient aims and findings of this study.

1

Åppås

Fresh Snow

THE CHARACTERISTIC WAYS IN WHICH SÁMI ARTISTS, ACTIVists, cultural workers, and other dedicated community members use produced and social media to advocate for a Sámi—or broader Indigenous—agenda have their roots in the Álttá dam protests of the late 1970s and early 1980s. At the same time, as both the current chapter and chapter 2 (Doalli) show, the particular image-making strategies employed by Sámi in the Álttá protests did not arise ex nihilo, but rather were built on earlier models and trends. We illustrate that fact through the examination of three important image makers of the Sámi past—Sirpmá Ovllá/Olaf Sirma, Elsa Laula Renberg, and Ovles Juhan/Johan Turi—within their wider cultural and political contexts. While also surveying in broad outline salient trends in Sámi history, the chapter seeks to draw attention to Sámi image making as a powerful, pervasive, and persistent strategy, one that equipped Sámi artist-activists well to take up and embrace the potentials of modern digital media.

In 1672, Sámi divinity student Sirpmá Ovllá wrote down two songs for Johannes Scheffer, a professor at the University of Uppsala (DuBois 2008). Destined to be known by later generations through Latin and

Swedish renderings of his name—Olaus Matthias Sirma/Olof Mattsson Sirma—Ovllá was a native of Giema (Kemi) Sápmi, a region to the northeast of the Bay of Bothnia and today a part of Finland. His songs connect him particularly with the area around the lake that he calls Orrejaura or Orrejawre (modern northern Sámi Oarrejávri; modern Finnish Orajärvi), a small lake about twenty kilometers southeast of the village of Soađegilli (Sodankylä). The region is home today to a community of around two hundred fifty people. The language he spoke was a local variant of closely related Finno-Ugric languages that linguists call Sámi, Sami, Saami, Lappish, or Lapp. The variant that Ovllá spoke, characteristic of the Giema (Kemi) region, is extinct today, a victim of the processes of assimilation and language attrition that have affected all Sámi languages to one degree or another. At the time he wrote down his songs, however, Ovllá was living in Uppsala, where he was studying to become a Lutheran minister in the kingdom of Sweden's prestigious university. Scheffer, for his part, was hard at work in 1672 amassing materials for an encyclopedic overview of Sámi life and lands, a work that was published as *Lapponia* in 1673 (Schefferus 1673). Although he did not travel to Sápmi for materials for his book, Scheffer avidly solicited input from district ministers and Sámi students like Ovllá studying in Uppsala.

Scheffer's book reached a broad and appreciative European readership and eventually was translated into German, Dutch, French, and English. Ovllá's two songs, with Latin translations, were included in Scheffer's volume as samples of Sámi music and courting traditions. The first of these, *Moarsi fávrrot* (Song for a bride) depicts the yearning of a young man for his distant love and his sorrow or guilt at the long delay that has kept him from her side. Describing the landscape in which she lives, alongside the lake Orrejaura/Orrejawre, and listing a series of metaphors for his longing, Ovllá's song ends with evocative and memorable lines that have since passed into world literature. Ovllá wrote them down in Giema Sámi as follows:

Parne miela piägga miela,
noara jorda kockes jorda.
Jos taidä poakaid läm kuldäläm,
luidäm radda wäre radda.

Oucta lie miela oudas waldäman
nute tiedäm pooreponne
oudastan man kauneman.

Harald Gaski, a pivotal scholar of Sámi literature, has rendered these lines in modern northern Sámi thus:

Bártni miella biekka miella
nuora jurdda guhkes jurdda
Jos buot daid guldalan
loaiddan rattái, vearre rattái

Ovtta lea miella mus váldit
vai máhtán buorebut
ovddastan gávdnat
(Gaski 2008b: 16)

In English, they read:

A boy's will is the wind's will
And the thoughts of youth are long, long thoughts
If I listen to them all
I will choose a course, the wrong course

One alone I need to choose
That I may better
Find my way.

Touching in their metaphors and tone of yearning, Ovllá's songs soon captured the hearts and imaginations of European men of letters, none of whom had ever seen the distant and quiet lake Orrejaura/Orrejawre (Kjellstrom et al. 1988: 11; DuBois 2006: 5–13; DuBois 2016). Richard Steele produced an English rendering in 1712, while Hugh Blair, savoring Ovllá's songs in their Latin versions, writes in 1760: "Surely among the wild Laplanders, if any where, barbarity is in its most perfect state. Yet their love songs which Scheffer has given us in his *Lapponia* are proof that natural tenderness of sentiment may be found in a country, into which the least glimmering of science has never penetrated" (quoted in DuBois 2006: 12). Ovllá's songs were translated and republished by Romantic intellectuals the likes of Johann Gottfried von Herder, Johan Runeberg, Johann Goethe, and Ewald Christian von Kleist, while the lines about a boy's thoughts being like the wind were used evocatively in Henry Wadsworth Longfellow's *My Lost Youth* (1855): "And a verse of a Lapland song/Is haunting my memory still:/'A boy's will is the wind's will/And the thoughts of youth are long, long thoughts'" (DuBois 2006: 12). In 1995, the Sámi music group Angelit released their own version of Ovllá's songs in their *Guldnasaš* (Angelin tytöt 1995, tr. 1). Nearly two centuries after Ovllá committed them to writing, his lines continued to emblematize Sámi culture and Sámi "tenderness of sentiment." Ovllá can be regarded as the first Sámi person we know of by name to self-consciously take on the task of representing his culture to an outside audience. He was certainly not the last.

As Yngve Ryd and Johan Rassa detail in their evocative and important study, *Snö* (Snow), the Lule Sámi term *åppås* refers to a stretch of newly fallen, fresh snow that shows no tracks or other disturbance yet (2007: 138). *Åppås* represents a windfall for a reindeer herder, because it signals a new pasture where the reindeer can forage freely once the fodder in their current tract runs low. A herder needed to always be on the lookout for such useable terrain, as Ryd and Rassa discuss, and *åppås* announces a place's freshness and readiness clearly.

In an evocative short poem from 1980, the great Sámi poet and *duodji* artist Paulus Utsi writes of Sámi life as like ski tracks in the snow:

> Min eallin
> lea dego láhttu
> vilges duoddaris
> man guoldu jávista
> juo guovssugeažis
> (Gaski 2008b: 101)
>
> Our life
> is like a ski track
> on the white open plains
> The wind erases it
> before morning dawns
> (Gaski 1996: 115)

With Utsi's poem in mind, we can think of *åppås* as a Sámi equivalent of the graphocentric English expression "clean slate." Ovllá rose to the challenge of representing his culture to an audience in a positive and memorable way, and his poems helped convince Europeans that the Sámi were not as barbarous as they had previously believed.

Ovllá may have been the first Sámi that we know of to represent his culture to an outside audience, but non-Sámi had been writing about the Indigenous population of the far north of Europe for many centuries (Lundmark 1998; Amft and Svonni 2006; Solbakk 2011). The Roman Tacitus includes a description of the "Fenni" in his first-century *Germania* (chapter 46), describing their crude housing, clothing made of skins, and non-agricultural hunting and gathering activities as deplorably primitive and yet somehow deeply satisfying. A Norwegian "Ohthere" (Ottar) informed the English King Alfred concerning the "Fennas" along the north coast of Norway in around 890.

Ottar mentions the income he receives by compelling Sámi to pay him an annual tribute in furs and other animal products, a practice that recurs in Norse saga accounts from later centuries (DuBois 1999: 24–26).

Views of the Sámi began to take on particularly pejorative tones with the arrival of Christianity in the Nordic region around the turn of the second millennium (DuBois 2013). A *Historia Norwegie* account of Sámi from the early thirteenth century deplores their pagan ways and magic practices, including shamanic divinatory and healing rituals. Clerical disapproval of Sámi religious traditions mounts in the thirteenth century and after, and Nordic and European writers more broadly come to describe the Sámi as primitive, untrustworthy, and mysteriously skilled in magic. In 1555, Olaus Magnus, last archbishop of Sweden before the Reformation, describes Sámi as vendors of magic winds, and by the late sixteenth century, Shakespeare quippingly refers to "Lapland sorcerers" in his *Comedy of Errors* (IV: 3) with a fair degree of certainty that his reference will be understood by an English audience. It was in fact in order to dispel these prevalent views that the Swedish Crown had asked Scheffer to write his *Lapponia* (DuBois 2008). In this context, Ovllá's "clean slate" seems more like an act of "wiping the slate clean," or, to employ the metaphor of Sámi-Norwegian writer Aagot Vinterbo-Hohr (1987) and Sámi-American literary scholar Troy Storfjell (2001), to recover a Sámi "palimpsest," overwritten by the prejudices and agendas of colonizing polities. Ovllá may not have set out to refute predominant views and claims about Sámi people point by point, but given his education and training in Uppsala it is certain that he was familiar with them. In this sense, his songs and notes about courtship and singing, and their subsequent dissemination in academic circles throughout Europe and North America, became a highly successful cultural intervention that served to counter the received majority-polity perceptions of Sámi of the time.

Ovllá's seventeenth-century texts entered the world at a time when Sámi were regarded largely as an oddity and an enigma in a Europe firmly centered on agrarian livelihoods. Traditional Sámi life—consisting of seasonal migration between different locales within set home regions with a reliance on hunting, gathering, and reindeer husbandry for subsistence—seemed to tie them to "primitive" peoples elsewhere in the world, peoples of which Europeans were becoming increasingly aware through trade and the development of colonialism in Africa, Asia, and the New World. In the following centuries, government pressures against a Sámi way of life would mount, as Nordic and Russian states sought to replace or assimilate Sámi into the cultures and livelihoods of their majorities (Lundmark 1998; Lehtola 2004; Solbakk 2011). The eventual establishment of farming communities in Sámi traditional areas was facilitated by a state view of Sámi as having no ownership of the lands they used. This interpretation of Sámi ways of life allowed states to sell or award tracts of Sámi lands as agricultural homesteads, creating a situation in which Sámi and their reindeer could come to be viewed as "trespassing" on their own traditional lands. In the nineteenth century, these economic practices became closely tied with assimilationist educational and social policies aimed at putting an end to Sámi language and culture and forcibly drawing Sámi into the majority populations of the Nordic states. The development of racial biology and social Darwinism in the last half of the nineteenth century further buttressed and motivated these practices, portraying the Sámi as racial inferiors of their Scandinavian and Finnish neighbors, destined to die out in a manner parallel to the supposedly "vanishing" Native Americans of North America. As we shall see, all of these injustices become both the topics of Sámi decolonizing history and symbols of Sámi endurance into the present and future.

Aage Solbakk's *Sámit áiggiid čađa 1* (2011) furnishes an apt and interesting history of Sámi activism from the medieval era to the 1970s. Intended for Sámi students in secondary education, it represents a decidedly Sámi-centered chronicle of Sámi history. Solbakk (2011: 240ff.) points out the importance of the Tromsø teachers' college,

Tromsø Seminarium, as a place where many important activists got their start in the late nineteenth century. Educated and then installed in local Sámi communities, Sámi graduates of the college became important local leaders, particularly in matters related to culture and youth. It was one of the graduates from the college, Ánde Jovnnabárdni/Anders Johnsen Bakke (1819–84) who, as a teacher in Návuotna (Kvænangen), set about creating a hymnal in northern Sámi. While serving the spiritual needs of his pupils, Bakke's *Kristalæš Salbmagirji Sabmelæččaidi* (a Christian hymnal for the Sámi) aimed at making Sámi children literate in their own language, instilling a pride in Sámi culture as integral to their spiritual and material lives. Another graduate of the college was Sápp-Issát/Isak Saba (1875–1921), who took up the position of teacher at Unjárga (Nesseby) and worked to instill a sense of pride in Sámi culture among his pupils, as well as their parents. In a letter written in 1903 to Ánde/Anders Larsen, Sápp-Issát writes:

> Oaččut jáhkkit mun sárdnidan mu skuvlamánáide go oahpahan Movssesa historjjá. In máša veardideames egyptalaččaid ja israelaččaid gaskasaš dilálašvuođaide, dasa mii dáhpáhuvvá sámiid ja dáččaid gaskkas. Gean veahkehivččiidet, sápmelačča vai dáčča, jos oannášeiddet sápmelačča ja dášša doarrumin? mun jearan. Ja mun ilosman go álo oaččun vástádusa: Sápmelačča! . . . Dál galggašii maid oažžut ollesolbmuid vástidit seammaláhkai. (Solbakk 2011: 241)

> You can be assured that I preach to my schoolchildren when I teach the history of Moses. I cannot help but compare the relations between the Egyptians and the Israelites with what is happening between the Sámi and Norwegians. "Who would you help, the Sámi or the Norwegians, if you could shorten the struggle between the Sámi and the Norwegians?" I ask. And then I am delighted when I always get the response "The Sámi!" . . . Now if only we would get the adults to answer in the same way.

Saba worked closely with Ánde/Anders Larsen (1870–1949), also a graduate of the college, in founding the first Sámi newspaper, *Sagai Muittalægje,* which ran from 1906–11. In its first issue, Saba published his *Sáme soga laula*, a Sámi national anthem. In part through the activities of the newspaper, Saba was elected to the Norwegian Parliament, where he served two terms, from 1906–12, arguing strongly for Sámi rights, little of which gained traction among his Norwegian colleagues in the parliament, or even within his own party.

While the educators, politicians, and writers mentioned above strongly opposed the assimilationist "Norwegianization" policies of their day, not all Sámi leaders during this period shared these views. Solbakk (2011: 249–52) also discusses leaders of the time who regarded Sámi language and traditions as hindrances to Sámi people and opposed the teaching of Sámi language and culture in schools. These opposing viewpoints remain part of Sámi society down to the present. As in other postcolonial contexts, it becomes part of the task and agenda of Sámi cultural activism—Sámi image making as presented in this study—not only to convince cultural outsiders of the value of Sámi culture but also to convince cultural *insiders* as well. Generations of stigmatized cultural representations and shame must be reversed by decolonizing discourse, and Sámi youth, adults, and elders must be convinced enough of the intrinsic value or advantageousness of Sámi language and culture that they will commit time and energy to their preservation and further development in the present and future.

Two key voices in these efforts at about the same time as Saba and Larsen, were the South Sámi Elsa Laula Renberg (1877–1931) and the North Sámi Ovles Juhan/Johan Turi (1854–1936). Elsa Laula was active in South Sámi communities in both Sweden and Norway (Solbakk 2011: 245–50), and her 1904 pamphlet *Inför lif eller död? Sanningsord i de lappska förhållandena* (Facing life or death? Words of truth about the Sámi situation) seeks first and foremost to convince her readers—colonizers as well as Sámi—of the essential injustice of the present situation for Sámi people. Her work opens thus:

> Långt uppe bland fjällen i öfversta Norrland bor sedan mannaminnes tider vår stam. Svunna tiders häfder tälja dock att vi lappar icke alltid varit hänvisade till att söka lefvebröd bland kala bergstoppar, utan lemningar från forna tider visar att lapparna besuttit rymliga betesmarker under gynnsamma förhållanden. Under seklernas lopp har lappen dock alltjämt fått vika för den jordbruksidkande germanska rasen. Fredlig, lugn, sluten och alltid nöjd med sin lott har lappen utan protester själfmant lemnat hvad han trott vara hans tillhörighet och tum för tum ha de svenska nybyggarna dragit till sig den betesmark, som af lapparne användts. De hafva däraf fått namnet »nomadiserande» d. v. s. ständigt vandrande, men månne icke den omständigheten, att de svagare under alla tider fått gifva vika för de starkare, varit orsaken till denna vandringslusta. (Laula Renberg 1904: 3)

> High up amid the mountains of northernmost Norrland our tribe has lived for as long as people remember. Annals from bygone times however indicate that we Sámi have not always been allotted a life of seeking our daily bread on cold mountaintops; relics from ancient times show that the Sámi populated expansive grazing areas with favorable conditions. Over the course of centuries, however, the Sámi have had to yield to the agriculturalist Germanic race. Peaceful, calm, self-possessed and always contented with his lot, the Sámi has willingly and of his own accord given up what he had thought was his property and inch by inch Swedish settlers have taken over the grazing lands that Sámi had used. Sámi have thus been termed "nomadic"–i.e., perpetually wandering–but the cause of this *Wanderlust* has been the circumstance of the weaker giving way to the stronger.

Laula's tract defends Sámi as a people against the prejudices and criticisms they faced at the time and underscores the economic injustices that deprived Sámi of livable wages, sustainable livelihoods, voting rights, and decent education. It is a powerful corrective of then-current views of the Sámi but also a call to action for Sámi people: "Våra tvister om rätten till jorden måste dagligen bevakas och våra frågor måste stundligen föras fram åt. Men då måste lappen taga saken i sin egen hand" (27; Our disputes about our rights to the land must be monitored daily and our questions must be brought forward at every hour. But then the Sámi must take the matter in his own hands). Laula calls for Sámi to organize local representative bodies and for these to then band together to work for universal rights for Sámi in general through a "en centralstyrelse för hela lappbefolkningen" (28; a centralized government for the entire Sámi population). To this end, Laula helped organize the first international Sámi meeting in 1917. The meeting took place in Trondheim on February 6–9, 1917, and February 6 has since become recognized as the Sámi national day in all the Nordic countries in commemoration of this historic event. Laula's ambitious call for a *centralstyrelse* (centralized government) was not answered until the creation of the Davviriikkaid Sámeráđđi (Nordic Sámi Council) in 1956, and, on a national level, by the eventual creation of national Sámi parliaments in Finland, Norway, and Sweden, as discussed in coming chapters. Laula's program was startlingly ambitious for her day and reveals her visionary qualities. It was also rigorously inclusive. She writes: "Ingen enda lapp får saknas i vår förening" (30; Not a single Sámi must be left out of our organization). It would only be through universal Sámi commitment to the cause of Sámi rights that real progress would be made. More than either Ovllá Sirma or Johan Turi, Elsa Laula's approach was one of decisive inreach. It is little wonder, then, that her portrait has become a favorite element in later Sámi activist works (figure 1.1).

Where Laula began her life on the Swedish side of the border and ended up on the Norwegian side through marriage, Ovles Juhan/Johan Turi began life in the area of Guovdageaidnu (Kautokeino), Norway, and eventually was forced to relocate to Sweden, first living

1.1. Elsa Laula Renberg (1877–1931). Laula's portrait, whole or cropped, figures frequently in later Sámi activist works. Used by permission, Helgeland Museum.

in Gárasavvon (Karesuando) and then in Čohkkeras (Jukkasjärvi). As Nils-Aslak Valkeapää (1994), Kristin Kuutma (2006, 2011) and others have shown (e.g., Cocq 2008; Gaski 1996: 43–56; Storfjell 2001, 2011; Svonni 2011; Sjoholm 2010, 2017), Turi's signature contribution to Sámi image making, his 1910 book *Muitalus sámiid birra* (An account of the Sámi), came about through a complex collaboration with a Danish artist and ethnographer Emilie Demant Hatt (1873–1958). Although he originally planned to write his book in Finnish, a language which Turi had gained functional command of during his life and travels in Norway, Finland, and Sweden, Demant Hatt urged Turi to write in his native language and then worked to produce a bilingual North Sámi-Danish edition of his book. Writing in Sámi allowed Turi's subtle rhetoric and argumentation to shine forth. Turi's opening states:

> Mon lean okta sápmelaš, guhte lean bargan visot sámi bargguid ja mon dovddan visot sámi dili. Ja mon lean ipmirdan, ahte Ruoŧŧa hállehus háliida min veahkehit nu olu go sáhttá, muhto sii eai oaččo riekta čielgasa, jur got dat lea min eallin ja dilli, dainna go sápmelaš ii sáhte jur juste čilget nu go lea. . . . Mon lean jurddašan, ahte dat livččii buoremus, jos livččii dakkár girji, masa lea visot čállojuvvon bajás sámi eallin ja dilli, vai eai dárbbaš jearrat got lea sámi dilli ja eai beasa botnjat nuppe ládje—dakkárat guđet háliidit sámiid ala gielistit—ja botnjat visot beare sámiid sivalažžan, go leat riiddut dálolaččaid ja sámiid gaskkas Norggas ja Ruoŧas. Ja dasa ferte čállit visot dáhpáhusaid ja čilgehusaid, vai boađášii čielggas nu ahte ipmirda juohke olmmos—ja lea dat nuppiide sámiide nai hávski gullat sámi dili birra. (Turi 2011b: 11).

> I am a Sámi who has done all sorts of Sámi work and I know all about Sámi conditions. I have come to understand that the Swedish government wants to help us as much as it can, but they don't get things right regarding our lives and conditions, because no Sámi can explain to them exactly how things are. . . . I have been thinking that it would be best if there was a book in which everything was written about Sámi life and conditions, so that people wouldn't have to ask how Sámi conditions are, and so that people wouldn't misconstrue things, particularly those who want to lie about the Sámi and claim that only the Sámi are at fault when disputes arise between settlers and Sámi in Norway and Sweden. And there one ought to write about all the events and furnish explanations so clearly that anyone could understand. And it would be pleasant also for other Sámi to hear about Sámi conditions as well. (Turi 2011a: 11)

Turi makes his intent and textual strategy clear. He first establishes his authority to speak knowledgeably about the subject because of both his cultural identity and his extensive first-hand experience. He then

1.2. One of Johan Turi's illustrations for his *Muitalus Sámiid birra* (An account of the Sámi) of 1910. Turi (1854–1936) drew the image in 1908 when preparing his book, the first Sámi-language work ever published. Executed in pen and ink on paper, the picture depicts a wide variety of typical activities connected with the autumn reindeer rut season, including lassoing, milking, and slaughtering, as well as social visiting, wood chopping, and residence in *lávvu* tents. Turi explained its contents in detail to Emilie Demant (1873–1958), the Danish artist and ethnographer who translated and helped publish his book. Demant's summary of Turi's explanations was included in the book (for full details, see Turi 2011: 38–90). Used by permission, Nordiska Museet.

castigates extant Swedish understandings of Sámi culture as deficient due to ignorance or deliberate malfeasance. Finally, he also identifies Sámi themselves as a potential audience for his book, noting "ja lea dat nuppiide sámiide nai hávski gullat sámi dili birra" (and it would be pleasant also for other Sámi to hear about Sámi conditions as well), a statement that seems to imagine the Sámi as at least a *listening* audience if not necessarily also a *reading* one. Throughout his work, Turi seeks to inform readers and also persuade them, replacing the prior prejudices or misunderstandings they may have had with clearer and more accurate understandings, ones that recognize the wisdom, ingenuity, endurance, and merit of Sámi people. Like Ovllá Sirma and Elsa

Laula before him, Johan Turi attempts to correct his audience's misunderstandings with a goal of improving the lot of Sámi people.

In addition to its combination of texts of various kinds–history, tales, songs (Cocq 2008)–Turi's work also contained visual art (e.g., figure 1.2), a feature that makes his book a forerunner of the kinds of multimedia works that later Sámi intellectuals like Nils-Aslak Valkeapää (1943–2001) would produce (Gaski 2011b). A willingness to create hybrid art of various kinds characterizes the work of modern Sámi artist-activists like Anders Sunna (Bydler 2010) and many others (Hansen 2007; Lundström 2015). This openness to hybridity can be seen as an important factor in the Sámi embrace of digital media, as surveyed in coming chapters.

Sirpma Ovllá's *Moarsi fávrro*t describes the difficulties of a young man making choices when contemplating the future and the importance of coming up with a single and solid path or plan: "Ovtta lea miella mus váldit" (One alone I need to choose). The quandary depicted in Sirpmá Ovllá's seventeenth-century poem parallels in some ways the quandary facing modern Sámi artists and activists: what is the right path to undertake in the present for Sámi individuals, for their community, and for their descendants? There is an uncertainty regarding which path is best to take, but also of the mechanisms and processes that will occur once a path is selected. In order for success to be achieved, we argue, one must first choose the right path (as Ovllá states), then commit to it with unanimity and force (as Laula exhorts), and finally present it to the colonizers in a persuasive, intriguing, and authoritative manner (as Turi demonstrates). These are the tasks of Sámi image making as it has unfolded in public discourse, media products, and social media communication over the past decades. The tracing of that path taken is the focus of what follows.

2

Doalli

A Strategy Develops

On October 8, 1979, a group of seven Sámi men and women, protesters belonging to the Sámi Action Group (Samisk Aksjonsgruppe), hoping to thwart Norwegian government plans to dam the Álaheaieatnu (Álttá/Alta River), brought their message of resistance in physical and imagistic form to the very heart of the Norwegian state. Erecting a *lávvu* on the lawn outside the Norwegian parliament building, Stortinget, in downtown Oslo, the protesters embarked on a hunger strike they documented through photographs (figure 2.1) (Michael 1981: 13; Jones-Bamman 1993: 305–6; Thuen 1995: 210–12; NRK 2010).

Among the five male and two female strikers were visual artists, performers, and writers, including Mikkel Gaup, Synnøve Persen, and Niillas Aslaksen Somby. They made speeches, invited the public to join in joik singing, and proudly wore traditional Sámi clothing. The strike continued until October 15, when the government announced that it would temporarily halt construction on the dam. During this remarkable week, the Sámi Action Group protest attracted thousands, even tens of thousands, of interested Oslo supporters and was covered in

2.1. One of the iconic photographs of the Sámi protesters during the October 1979 Oslo protests. Sámi protesters occupy a lávvu in downtown Oslo while locals look on. The protesters' sign reads "Mi várjilit Sámi Vi Vil Verge Vårt Land Sameland" (We will protect our country, Sápmi). Photograph by Niillas Somby, used by permission.

newspapers and radio broadcasts around the world. Immediately thereafter, and in the several years of protest that followed, the Sámi Action Group worked closely with anthropologists and human rights activists from, among other places, the Copenhagen-based International Work Group for Indigenous Affairs (IWGIA), to provide expert testimony to interested readers and viewers regarding the predicted negative effects of the dam (Michael 1981; Paine 1982). They also cooperated with the Norwegian anarchist/provocateur filmmaker Bredo Greve in his semifictionalized documentary/narrative film *La elva leve!* (Let the river live!), released in 1980 (Greve 1980).

The group published articles of their own under the title *Charta 79,* an allusion to the Czechoslovakian Charta 77, well known for its defiant stance on Czechoslovakian human rights violations. As the newspaper's chief editor Máret Sárá relates, during the Oslo demonstrations the first ten thousand copies of the first issue of the newspaper were distributed in just two hours and two further printings of ten thousand copies each were necessary to meet the readers' demand for information (ČálliidLágádus 2016). Simultaneous and subsequent protests included Sámi and environmentalist activists chaining themselves together and blocking the access road and construction site in Álttá, a second hunger strike in 1981, an occupation of the offices of Norwegian Prime Minister Gro Harlem Brundtland, a delegation sent to the Vatican, and a failed attempt to blow up a bridge near Álttá in the dead of night (Thuen 1995; NRK 2010; Solbakk 2010; N. Somby 2016). In order to present the situation at hand in a wider historical context, the group commissioned and published an updated Norwegian (*nynorsk*) translation of Nils-Aslak Valkeapää's wry *Terveisiä Lapista* (1971, 1979), as well as, eventually, an English translation of the same work (1983).

As Trond Thuen and others have shown, journalists and members of the wider public were fascinated by the Oslo lávvu scene in particular: the imagistic juxtaposition of the stately Norwegian parliament building and the seeming simplicity of the lávvu occupied by the protesters created interest throughout the West and swayed public opinion strongly toward the pleas of the Sámi protesters, in Norway, as elsewhere. As Thuen explains:

> [The] concrete transfer of specific Saami symbols to the Norwegian geographical centre of political institutions . . . bridged a gap in the public opinion between the geographical remoteness of the Saami population and the peripheral place afforded their existence by the Norwegian political commentators. The existence of a Fourth World minority in Norway had hardly been noticed before. Secondly, the most prominent metonymic sign of the Norwegian political system, the Parliament building, was rendered a new signification of power by the contrasting effect of the small tent. This recodification of power was a simple and fundamental transformation from legitimacy to illegitimacy. Since the crux of

> the matter was the parliamentary decision to start the construction works on the Álttá river, the protest directed against the legitimacy of the decision-making process which had codified the issue as a question of the procuring of energy, and not of ethnic rights and cultural survival. (210–11)

The lávvu protest, that Thuen describes as a "turning point in the process" (210), reinscribed the Norwegian state not as an inclusive, communally achieved nation-state but instead a colonial regime, intent on maintaining control over the resources and society of a distinct Indigenous people. No longer were the Sámi a half-noticed minority, existing in the distant tracts of Finnmark; now they were a vociferous Indigenous nation, defiantly encamped right under politicians' noses, underfoot and insistent. And the images they presented were not of Sámi in suits, conforming to majority tastes and customs in order to be taken seriously within settler society. Instead, their tent, their speeches, the joik music that they shared with passersby, and their dress announced resolutely their intention to remain distinctively Sámi in the present world.

Although the river was eventually dammed, the Álttá protests led to important concessions by the Norwegian government: specifically, in the Sámi Act of 1987 and recognition of Sámi status as the country's Indigenous population, a status that carried with it specific rights eventually codified in the Norwegian constitution as well as in the United Nations International Labour Organization's Indigenous and Tribal Peoples Convention 169 (1990). As a result, in 1989, Sámi in Norway acquired a representative organ, Sámediggi, the Sámi parliament, while Norway ratified the ILO-169 in 1990, the year after Norwegian UN representatives assisted in its drafting (Thuen 1995: 230–36). Sweden followed suit with a Sámi parliament for Swedish Sámi in 1993, and Finland revised the role and authority of its existing Sámi parliament in 1996. Both Sweden and Finland adjusted their constitutions to recognize Sámi indigeneity, but neither Sweden nor Finland have to date ratified ILO-169: a fact that stood as a focus of activism among Sámi in these countries into the 2000s (Smith et al. 1987; Henriksen 1999).

In a study of Sámi uses of media in the work of decolonization, it is valuable to examine the background and events leading up to and surrounding the Álttá dam protest, noting in particular the strategies of self-representation that Sámi activists used to appeal to the public, both Sámi and non-Sámi. In the following, we first look at the protests in a broad Western context of late-twentieth-century cultural and political activism, then in the specific context of emerging Indigenous rights activism during this same period, and finally in light of the local Sámi developments that contributed to, and found new inspiration in, the Álttá protests. We argue that it is in connection with the Álttá dam protests of the late 1970s and early 1980s that a distinctive Sámi strategy arose for using media as a device of decolonization, a strategy that built on models developed by earlier artist-activists, as discussed in the last chapter, but that became more focused and more intentional in the context of the Álttá protests' international image making.

In North Sámi, the term *doalli* denotes an established and hardened trail or track in the snow when it has become blanketed by a fresh coating of new snow. The old trail remains visible but it is now covered by a new layer, one that can initially make travel slower but that in the long run provides an excellent surface for skiing or sledding across large areas. We posit that the image deployment undertaken in connection with the Álttá protests can be metaphorically understood as doalli: What looked new to outsiders was actually built on strategies established by earlier Sámi artists and activists in the past but was given a fresh context and new meaning in the crisis situation of the Álttá dam protests.

International Contexts

In many ways, the Álttá protests drew on an established repertoire of protest actions that were familiar to government officials and the broader public throughout the West. It can be noted first that hunger strikes were not a particularly Sámi method of protest. Hunger strikes by both men and women had become widely recognized activist strategies in India, the United Kingdom, Ireland, and the United States from the mid-nineteenth century onward, directed particularly against states that sought to maintain inequities or the status quo of colonial power structures. The technique had been used by Mahatma Gandhi in the mid-nineteenth century in support of Indian independence (Pratt and Vernon 2005), as well as by English and American suffragettes at the beginning of the twentieth century (Mayhall 2003). Imprisoned Irish nationalists used the method repeatedly during the twentieth century (Meehan 2006). Later protests would repeat the method long after, as the IdleNoMore protests of Canadian First Nations illustrates (see chapter 5). By embarking on a hunger strike, the Samisk Aksjonsgruppe implicitly placed the Norwegian government into the company of colonial regimes with poor human rights records, effectively shaming the government, while also identifying the dam protest as a cause for which one might well risk one's health or even life.

The coming together of Sámi and non-Sámi protesters in defense of the Álttá river also had parallels internationally, particularly in the coalitions of workers and intellectuals that grew out of the 1968 strikes in France and elsewhere, that became known as the New Left movement. Europeans of the New Left found inspiration in the struggle of African Americans in the American civil rights movement and in the writings of philosophers like Antonio Gramsci and Herbert Marcuse. As Thomas Hilder notes (2015: 44), they also drew on the anticolonialist discourse of the philosopher of Martinique Frantz Fanon, whose *Les damnés de la terre* (Wretched of the earth) had become an international bestseller already in 1961. The anti-imperialist interests and activities of the time focused on a wide array of international events, including the Algerian independence movement of the 1950s and early 1960s, the Biafran independence movement of 1967–68, Prague Spring of 1968, and widespread outrage toward the conduct of the military in the US-dominated war in Vietnam. The revolutionary and idealistic spirit of youth culture of the time created a cultural context that would support the Álttá protest as an important act of resistance against the machinery and dictates of a repressive state.

The creation of surprising or memorable images—like a lávvu erected in front of Norway's Stortinget—had also become familiar in an era increasingly captured and processed by journalistic photography and film. Media professionals employed by both Allied and Axis powers during World War II had made ample use of photographs—usually seemingly candid, although often carefully staged—to shock, enrage, convince, or inspire. Yevgeni Khaldei's image of Russian troops raising the Soviet flag over the Berlin Reichstag (a reenacted image; Antill and Dennis 2005: 76), Joseph Rosenthal's image of Marines raising the US flag at Iwo Jima (a reenacted image; Leary 2006), Robert F. Sargent's on-the-scene image of the Allied invasion of Normandy ("Into the Jaws of Death," Young 2013), and Alfred Eisenstaedt's image of a Marine kissing a nurse in New York City's Times Square in celebration of Victory over Japan Day in 1945 (Cosgrove 2014) became iconic depictions of turning points in the war. Such images were often published in magazines that specialized in photojournalism, such as the American *Life*, the French *L'Express*, or Nordic counterparts like the Finnish *Suomen kuvalehti*.

During the lead-up to the Vietnam War in 1963, Buddhist monks in the city of Saigon planned and facilitated the self-immolation of an elderly monk, Thích Quảng Đức, as a means of calling attention to the discrimination they felt under the US-backed regime of South Vietnam's leader Ngô Đình Diệm, a Catholic. The scene, photographed by US journalist Malcolm Browne for the Associated Press, sent shock waves throughout the West and earned Browne a Pulitzer Prize. President J. F. Kennedy said of the image, "No news picture has generated so much emotion around the world as that one" (Jacobs 2006: 149).

Later footage of another self-immolation was included in Ingmar Bergman's 1966 film, *Persona*, as illustrative of the horrors of war (Bergman 1967). Self-immolation was copied as a means of protest in American protests against the Vietnam War, and in Czechoslovakian protests in support of the Prague Spring. Another potent image of the time was US soldier Ronald Haeberle's photo of innocent women and children killed in the March 1968 My Lai massacre. One of Haeberle's gruesome photographs became a potent antiwar image when first released to the world in an issue of *Life* magazine on December 1, 1969. Made into a poster by the Art Workers' Coalition right after its release, it became a ubiquitous part of antiwar protests in the United States and Europe (Oliver 2006). US journalist Joseph Kraft's photograph of Jane Fonda in North Vietnam became known throughout the world in 1972 and became the focus of an important film lecture by Jean-Luc Godard and Jean-Pierre Gorin, appended as a postscript to their film, *Tout va bien*, of the same year (Godard and Gorin 1972). There Godard and Gorin unpack the visual technique and inclusions and exclusions of the image to ask the question of the proper role of intellectuals–be it photographers or actresses–in the work of revolution and what role images can play in creating a better world. In a very concrete sense, potent images had become a mainstay of modern journalism by 1979, and a key device for advancing one's agenda in the public consciousness.

Part of the reason for the ubiquity of images during the era, of course, was the advent of television as a central means of experiencing and sharing news. As Richard Croker argues in his *Boomer Century* (2007), television both shared and leveled experience, providing daily access to events going on in various "trouble spots" of the world with an immediacy and visuality that had not been part of earlier newspaper or radio media. Television took longer to become established in Scandinavia than in North America, but, by the late 1960s, Norway, Sweden, and Finland each had evening programing on several channels. As Nils-Aslak Valkeapää put it, perhaps alluding to the iconic Apollo 8 image, "Earthrise over the Moon," of 1968: "The whole world is coming into people's living rooms, the globe is no longer incomprehensibly great, but a little planet, in a little solar system, in the universe" (1983: 84).

At the same moment that people in North America and Europe were generally becoming aware of the importance of mediated images in their lives, scholars began to devote research to the phenomenon. Roland Barthes had produced his seminal article on journalistic photography, "The Photographic Message" in 1961 (see Barthes 1978). In 1965, Pierre Bourdieu published a study of photography as a medium of particular importance to the rising middle class (1965) and later looked at the ways in which professionals in the expanding media industries affected notions of class and taste through their activities (1979); he would address television as well in a work published later (1996). More influential to a broader readership was Marshall McLuhan's wide-ranging exploration of the effects of media technology on culture, *Understanding Media,* which, when published in 1964, became an international bestseller (McLuhan 1964). Regarding the latter author, Valkeapää writes in his *Terveisiä:* "Many of the idols of the young (like McLuhan, Marcuse, Ho Chi Minh) are beginning to be common property internationally, and many of these point forward towards global thinking. I think the young are becoming more and more aware that they belong to the planet Earth" (1983: 85). Valkeapää's remarks anticipate Benedict Anderson's 1983 contention that nationalism arose historically in part as a product of feelings of simultaneity engendered by media (newspapers) and the standardization of time (2006). Anderson argued that as people developed a sense of common experience, common ground, through reading about each other and through an awareness of simultaneous existence, they began to think of themselves more as members of a unified polity, a nation. Valkeapää's remark suggests also that as that sense of simultaneity and common ground expands, people come to see themselves as part of a single human polity, as members of (to use McLuhan's term) a "global village," interconnected by electronic media like television (McLuhan 1962).

The concrete effects of these tendencies became highly useful for the Álttá protests: viewers came to see the Sámi situation not as a remote issue facing a marginalized community far away, but as a pressing human rights issue facing all humanity. The Sámi use of a familiar vocabulary of recognizable protest acts like the hunger strike, and evocative images like the Oslo lávvu, helped audiences comprehend and embrace the Sámi situation as relevant to their lives. Sámi protesters were soon contacted by representatives of the Irish Republican Army (IRA) as well as the Basque ETA and West German Red Army Faction, who recognized in their actions parallel situations (NRK 2010), clear indications of the fact that other European observers found resonance between their own struggles and those so stirringly presented in the Álttá protests.

Indigenous Contexts

The coalition of young Western intellectuals and local struggles against entrenched state imperialism, so powerfully demonstrated in the African American civil rights movement, eventually inspired similar efforts in connection with the long-struggling Indigenous communities of the world. In the United States, multiple generations of residential boarding schools, beginning in the 1890s, and the equally damaging 1956 Indian Relocation Act, helped spawn a huge polity of frustrated, urbanized Native Americans. Young urban Indians felt separated from their reservation origins and also barred from pathways toward upward mobility by the inherent racism of the dominant society. A direct result of this frustration was the 1968 founding of the American Indian Movement (AIM), in Minneapolis, Minnesota. AIM activists quickly became expert in developing creative images to convey their views and capture media attention: the organization's 1969 occupation of Alcatraz Island, 1970 seizure of a Mayflower replica, 1971 occupation of Mount Rushmore, and 1973 occupation of Wounded

Knee were all events that captured photojournalistic attention and garnered international interest.

In terms of textual activism, Lakota activist and academic Vine Deloria Jr.'s *Custer Died for Your Sins: An Indian Manifesto* (1969) delivered a witty and provocative Native American perspective on the ploys and practices of white America. The librarian Dee Brown's *Bury My Heart at Wounded Knee: An Indian History of the American West* presented the public with an unvarnished overview of nineteenth-century American imperialist oppression against Native peoples in North America (1970). The work proved an instant bestseller, selling more than five million copies and soon becoming translated into a dozen other languages, including Finnish (Brown 1973), Norwegian (Brown 1974a), and Swedish (Brown 1974b). As Hampton Sides notes in his 2007 foreword to a reprint of the now classic study, Brown's work pointed to a grim continuity between the genocidal policies of US Manifest Destiny and the unseemly conduct of military in the Vietnam War: "It came along at the precise moment when the public was ready to receive the full plangency of its message. *Bury My Heart* landed on America's doorstep in the anguished midst of the Vietnam War, shortly after revelation of the My Lai massacre had plunged the nation into gnawing self-doubt. Here was a book filled with a hundred My Lais, a book that explored the dark roots of American arrogance . . ." (Sides 2007: xvi).

In Canada, the 1970 founding of the National Indian Brotherhood (renamed the Assembly of First Nations in the 1980s), built on earlier intertribal and provincial organizations in Canada. When one of its founders and then president of the organization, Shuswap tribal member George Manuel, accompanied Prime Minister Jean Chrétien on a state visit to New Zealand, the idea for an international organization of Indigenous peoples was born. In 1972, the resulting World Council of Indigenous Peoples (WCIP) applied for UN Economic and Social Council observer status. Prior to this time, Indigenous communities had been covered in Article 27 of the UN Covenant on Civilian and

Political Rights, which states: "In those States in which ethnic, religious or linguistic minorities exist, persons belonging to such minorities shall not be denied the right, in community with the other members of their group, to enjoy their own culture, to profess and practice their own religion, or to use their own language" (United Nations General Assembly 1966). The Covenant had been by adopted by the UN General Assembly in 1966 and was due to enter into force in 1976.

It was in part in response to the WCIP's application that the United Nations commissioned a study of Indigenous issues. José Martínez Cobo began research in 1972 and completed his report in 1986. The report included a working definition of "Indigenous communities, peoples and nations" that became foundational to later UN undertakings in the area of Indigenous rights, as discussed in the introduction to this book (Martinez Cobo 1986). The WCIP's request for observer status was granted in 1974. The UN's commitment to investigating Indigenous issues would lead to the creation of the Working Group on Indigenous Populations in 1982 (Thuen 1995: 229), that in turn helped develop the International Labour Organization's Convention 169 of 1990, as well as two decades of official attention to the situation of the world's Indigenous peoples (1995–2004 and 2005–15), the establishment of the UN's Permanent Forum on Indigenous Issues in 2000, and the eventual passing of the UN Declaration on the Rights of Indigenous Peoples in 2007 (United Nations General Assembly 2007).

In 1975, at the beginning of this process, the WCIP organized the first World Conference of Indigenous Peoples, hosted on the reservation of the Sheshaht Band of the Nuu-chah-nulth First Nation, at Port Alberni, British Columbia. Sámi Nils-Aslak Valkeapää and Ole Henrik Magga were among the more than three hundred participants drawn from some nineteen different countries that took part in the conference. In reflecting on the event in the 1983 translation of his *Terveisiä* into English, Valkeapää writes: "It was unforgettable. Strenuous. For me at any rate it was an experience. A privilege. The fate of the Indigenous peoples who were gathered there was so similar, that at the end of the conference the assembly stood up and passed a resolution to found the World Council of Indigenous Peoples (WCIP). The ninth Sami Conference at Inari in 1976 ratified the rules of the council, and thus associated itself officially with the World Council. In summer 1977, the second world conference of Indigenous peoples was held in Samiland, in Kiruna" (1983: 110). Involvement in the WCIP and in other international Indigenous activism proved decisive as a learning experience for Sámi activists, allowing them to recognize, perhaps for the first time, the parallels between colonial experiences in North and South America, New Zealand, Australia, and elsewhere and those that Sámi faced in each of the four countries in which they lived. Valkeapää writes of the 1975 conference: "The fact that the Samis have a light skin, and some of us are quite blond, certainly had no positive associations for people who had learned to equate a white skin with colonialism and the terrible assaults on people which accompanied it. We heard about experiences of this nature, and I think the effect was pretty much of a shock for the Sami delegates who weren't well orientated about these conditions beforehand" (1983: 113). Learning to see the Sámi experience within the broader context of colonization was both revelatory and admonishing for Sámi activists: it convinced them of the importance of marshaling Nordic support wherever possible for Indigenous efforts.

Although Sámi faced similar sorts of racism and discrimination as that directed toward other Indigenous communities, they also enjoyed a far higher standard of living and on the whole much less open hostility or violence. The 1975 Port Alberni conference received funding from the governments of both Norway and Denmark, and the hosting of the second WCIP conference in Kiruna in 1977 entailed substantial funding support from Nordic sources, particularly Sweden. In 1977 Valkeapää and other Sámi musicians received funding to go on a musical tour of Indigenous communities in Canada and Greenland. Valkeapää writes, "these travels of the Indigenous peoples of Northern Scandinavia were intended to be a presentation of Sami culture, first and foremost music.... What urbanized (standardized) culture has to offer today is so enormous that it's difficult for the various cultures to survive it. For that reason it means a lot to get cultural exchange between Indigenous peoples going" (1983: 115). As Sámi activists learned to articulate their situation in terms of Indigenous rights, it became crucial that the Nordic governments recognize Sámi colonial history and nature as well. The Norwegian government, through its UN representatives in the Economic and Social Council, proposed in 1976 a declaration of the World Council to Combat Racism and Racial Discrimination. It called on UN member states to recognize the official status of Indigenous minorities within their borders, respect and employ the use of Indigenous languages in state proceedings, and recognize the right of Indigenous peoples to maintain their traditional ways of life and rights to their traditional lands. One of the key factors motivating outrage and interest in the Álttá protests of 1979 was the fact that the government did not seem willing to follow the lines of its 1976 declaration within its own borders. In fact, to many observers, it appeared that the Norwegian government had no inkling of Sámi people as Indigenous. Certainly the government had made no efforts to conduct separate consultations with the Sámi community of Finnmark before planning the Álttá dam project, a fact that seemed to prove protesters' assertions of colonial disregard for Sámi rights (Michael 1981: 12–13). Thus, part of the Álttá protests and the Sámi activism that led up to it was centered on revealing government actions as instances of colonial oppression. As Valkeapää writes, "there must be some reason for the Samis becoming members of the World Organization of Indigenous Peoples. Because it's not likely that the Samis would set out to support the other Indigenous peoples of the world purely out of humanitarian grounds. No the Samis have good reasons for becoming members of the organization. The Samis want their right to land and water to be accepted, and to have the right to live the way they themselves choose. Let it be said" (1983: 122).

Within this wider global Indigenous movement, Sámi people and Sámi media have played important roles, as coming chapters will demonstrate. One need only consider the fact that the ILO-169 was drafted with Sámi input (Thuen 1995: 230–36), or that the first president of the Permanent Forum on Indigenous Issues, Ole Henrik Magga (who took office in 2004), was Sámi, to realize that Sámi have played pivotal roles in Indigenous rights activism worldwide (Nystad 2016).

The Sámi Contexts

We have shown that Sámi activism of earlier eras has provided inspiration and historical grounding for Sámi activists in the present. At the same time, distinct developments in the Sámi situation during the post–World War II era played important roles in shaping the Álttá protests (Giddens 1991; Hansen 2014). A process of nation building across international boundaries was well underway by the late 1970s, abetted by improvements in Sámi education in the postwar era.

One of the most important steps in Sámi nation building was the creation in 1956 of the Davviriikkaid Sámeráđđi, the Nordic Sámi Council. In a postwar context of Nordic cooperation and integration, Sámi were able to realize Elsa Laula's dream of an international organ for promoting Sámi interests. A preparatory meeting held in Jokkmokk in 1953—the first Sámi Conference—set the grounds for the creation of the council (Solbakk 2011: 276). Similar conferences have been organized every four years since and have addressed in concrete terms the goals and aspirations of the Sámi movement. The Council came to serve as an intergenerational device for advancing Sámi causes over time, even if Sámi policies remained (and still by and large remain) primarily national in scope and detail. As noted above, in 1975, the Council voted to join the World Council of Indigenous Peoples, and hosted the WCIP's second conference in 1977, held in Giron (Kiruna).

Another key development for Sámi in the postwar era was the restructuring of Sámi education. The basic aim of Sámi education prior to the world wars had largely been assimilatory, or at best, aimed at equipping Sámi for entry into the dominant society should they choose to abandon their traditional ways (Kvist 1992; Henrysson 1992). Not only were Sámi taught in a language that was not their own, but the curriculum provided no reference whatsoever to Sámi culture or livelihoods. Residential boarding schools and strict policies regarding content taught in national schools often made schooling a traumatic experience for Sámi children, an assault on their native identity and ambient culture (Kuokkanen 2003). As Krister Stoor (2015) has shown, even when curricula included Sámi materials, these were often far from affirmative of Sámi students' culture or identity. The Forest Sámi educator and activist Karin Stenberg (1884–1969) notes her educational experience in a teachers' training school in Mattisudden, east of Jokkmokk in the early part of the twentieth century: although the school's teachers knew no Sámi themselves, they had received examples of "proper" Sámi from K. B. Wiklund, illustrating a standard language based on the Sámi spoken in and around Jokkmokk. Because Stenberg came from another district (near Aerviesjaevrie), her Sámi was deemed "incorrect" (Stoor 2015: 151). She writes, "vi voro ju inte 'riktiga lappar', då kunde vårt språk ej vara 'riktig lappska'" (151; we were not "proper Lapps," so our language could not be "proper Lappish"). Lappologists like Wiklund shaped the paternalistic educational and cultural policies directed toward Sámi, creating norms that remained in place into the early postwar period (Cocq 2016). Valkeapää, recalling his childhood schooling experience in Enontekiö in the early 1950s writes, "When I started school I learned that I had no mother tongue. Finland has two official languages [Finnish and Swedish] according to the Constitution, but neither of these is Sami" (1983: 81).

Israel Ruong (1903–86) was instrumental in initiating a process of change, at least in Sweden. The first Sámi to earn a PhD (in 1943), he became Inspector of the Swedish Nomad Schools, a post he held from 1946 to 1967. In 1957 he headed the Royal Commission on Sámi Education, which recommended a program that would provide Swedish Sámi pupils with opportunities to learn not only dominant culture subjects and languages, but also Sámi subjects (Henrysson 1992; Kvist

1992). New instructional materials were developed, like Ruong's own basic primer for learning Sámi as a second language, notably entitled *Min sámigiella* (Our Sámi language; Ruong 1976). The Finnish Sámi educator Siri Magga-Miettunen wrote an ABC book for use in Finnish Sámi schools in the early 1970s, and a South Sami primer, *Lohkede saemien,* appeared in 1974.

As these very welcome reforms were implemented during the 1960s and 1970s, Sámi children at last had the opportunity to become literate in their own native or heritage language and to learn at least to some extent about Sámi culture and history. Sámi whose families or communities no longer spoke Sámi could find in the new curricular materials concrete avenues for recovery. Over time, Sámi language and culture became a source of pride and interest for school children. In a Nordic context in which the concept of one's native language has been a longstanding element of cultural nationalism, the dominant polity could not easily take issue with Sámi resolve to maintain and value their native language. In fact, Nordic governments went to efforts to support and promote this act, as can be illustrated for instance by a school textbook on Nordic folk songs sponsored by a consortium of Nordic national radio corporations. Entitled *Avannaamiut erinarsuutit, Davvilávlagat, Nordsange, Nordsanger, Nordsånger, Norðurlendskir sangir, Norðursöngvar, Pohjolan lauluja,* the anthology presents folk songs not only from Danish, Finnish, Norwegian (*bokmål* and *nynorsk*), and Swedish traditions, but also from Fenno-Swedish, Faroese, Icelandic, Greenlandic, and North Sámi (Leijonhufvud 1980). The sections are arranged alphabetically according to the name for the language in the language itself. Sámi songs ("Sámiid lávlagat") are presented alongside songs from other Nordic cultures, with translations and respectful, engaging illustrations. Such curricular materials may have held little significance in the actual working and administrative lives of adult speakers of the Nordic region's minority languages. But the image and discourse of equality—of minority languages enjoying the same esteem and attention as the state majority languages—instilled in children a sense of justice and a measure of entitlement to equal rights that resonated with international trends of the time.

As Sámi children advanced through the new schooling system, they took with them demands and expectations of Sámi curriculum at each subsequent level, so that by the 1970s Sámi were entering universities not solely to receive training in disciplines unrelated to their cultural heritage, but with the expectation of advancing academic knowledge concerning Sámi culture in particular (Keskitalo 1997; Stordahl 1997; Nystad 2016). School reforms had made vocational training in Sámi traditional arts (duodji) possible in several venues, including Jokkmokk, where students not only received training in Sámi textiles, leather, wood, antler, and metal arts, but also came in contact with knowledgeable and often inspirational figures like the duodji instructor Paulus Utsi, whose poems, written in a mix of Lule and North Sámi, put into words many of the Sámi frustrations regarding ecological and administrative wrongs perpetrated against them by Nordic governments (Gaski 1996: 109). Utsi's memorable poem of 1974, "Nu guhká" (As long), could read as a manifesto for the eventual Álttá protests:

Nu guhká go mis lea čáhci, gos guolli vuodjá
Nu guhká go mis leat eatnamat, jos bohccot guhtot ja bálget
Nu guhká go mis leat meahcit, gos ealibat čiehkádallet
De lea mis dorvu dán eatnan alde

Go min ruovttut eai šat gávdno ja min eanan lea billanan
gos mii galgat de orrut

Min duovdagat, min ealáhusat leat gáržon
jávrrit leat dulvan
eanut leat goikan
jogažat morašmielain lávlot
meahcit čáhpodit ja rásit goldnet
lottážat jaskkodit ja báhtarit

Buot buriid maid mii leat ožžon
eai leat midjiide váimmoláččat
Buot álki maid mii vuostá váldit
Leat duššálussan min eallimii

Garra geađgegeainnut bavččistahttet min lihkastagaid
Luondduolbmo jaskavuohta
Čierru iežas váimmu siste

Dan johtilis ággi siste
njárbu min varra
min suopman ii šat šuva
ii ge luonddu čáhci šoava. (Gaski 2008b: 100)

Roland Thorstensson's translation reads:

As long as we have waters where the fish can swim
As long as we have land where the reindeer can graze
As long as we have woods where wild animals can hide
we are safe on this earth

When our homes are gone and our land destroyed
–then where are we to be?

Our own land, our lives' bread, has shrunk
the mountain lakes have risen
rivers have become dry
the streams sing in sorrowful voices
the land grows dark, the grass is dying
the birds grow silent and leave

The good gifts we have received
no longer move our hearts

Things meant to make life easier
have made life less

Painful is the walk
on rough roads of stone
Silent cry the people of the mountains

While time rushes on
our blood becomes thin
our language no longer resounds
the water no longer speaks (Gaski 1996: 116–17)

The active role students played in the protests of this era, of course, had parallels in places like France, Germany, and the United States, where university-aged activists were central for driving revolutionary movements of the time. In a Nordic context, the Sámi embrace of higher education during this period also reflected an important era in the history of mature Nordic welfare states, in which young persons of talent were drawn into public sector careers—like education, health, and the arts—as ways to contribute to the betterment of society while securing a meaningful wage and career. Individuals like Ole Henrik Magga and Nils Jernsletten set out to become scholars of Sámi linguistics, receiving training that would equip them to make substantive contributions to the establishment of Sámi as an official language used in public places and documents (Michael 1981: 140–42; Nystad 2016). Liv Østmo received training in political science that helped her work with IWGIA and later to teach and research at Sámi University College (Michael 1981: 123–26). For young Sámi, education offered avenues for making a difference in a situation that held great significance for them: the very survival of their culture. And they strove to ensure that educational institutions would rise to the challenge and contribute meaningfully to the struggle for Sámi rights.

A sense of growing outrage as well as empowerment among Sámi was evident in the first Álttá dam protests of 1968, in which the Sámi community of the village, Máze/Masi, successfully prevented the Norwegian government from submerging their town in a man-made lake (Michael 1981: 8). It was also evident in the 1973 letter writing of a nine-year-old, Åsa Maria Gabriella Simma, who would eventually go on to a major career in Sámi performing arts. Concerned about her difficulties in getting to school without an adequate bridge connecting her part of the village of Idivuoma with the rest of the town, she wrote to Crown Prince Carl Gustaf of Sweden. Her request for a bridge was fulfilled, much to the delight of local villagers and journalists covering the event (Sternlund 2015). The same year saw the formation of a musical group, Deatnogátte Nuorat/Tanabreddens Ungdom (Youth of the Deatnu River Bank), comprising Irene Pettersen, Leif Wigelius, Ingvald Guttorm, and Hartvik Hansen. Their 1974 album included Sámi-language songs sung in US country music style, modern adaptations of joik, and musical renderings of the poetry of Paulus Utsi (Deatnogátte Nuorat 1974).

In a 1977 Finnish television program aired as part of the series, *Luillaako?* (One sings la-la?), Nils Aslak Valkeapää references both the Máze protests and welcomes as his co-host the young Åsa Simma in a program aimed at encouraging Sámi children to embrace and perform joik (Yleisradio 1977). The program, conducted entirely in northern Sámi, introduces the child viewer to joik and enunciates clearly a linkage between cultural maintenance and activism, one in which young people are expected to play important roles in reclaiming and advancing Sámi culture and rights. Valkeapää's message to children in this program was one of empowerment: letting children know that performing joik was an enjoyable and meaningful activity that they could embrace. The program featured children singing joik, both in traditional fashion and in conjunction with an electric organ. Earlier presentations of joik, like the Swedish radio documentation project of the early 1950s, had portrayed the musical tradition as static and moribund, performed mostly by elderly Sámi in remote settings, a remnant of a vanishing culture (Arnberg et al. 1997). Among Laestadians, and many other Sámi, the joik tradition prior to the 1970s had been regarded as backward and even sinful (Hilder 2015: 41). The decision of the Guovdageaidnu Sámi Searvi to stage a joik concert on Easter Sunday, 1972, was thus both provocative and revolutionary. The concert came to be an annual event and eventually (in 1990) evolved into the Sámi Grand Prix. As Hilder writes: "[W]hile joik was still largely considered sinful by a majority of the local population, the concerts became an increasingly popular event, and articulated the urge to revive and publicly promote a Sámi musical tradition" (41). In his own musical endeavors, Valkeapää made it a point to innovate on the joik tradition, combining it with other genres of popular music as well as visual arts (Jones-Bamman 1993; Dana 2003). Writing against a preservationist approach to joik that would freeze its contents and style into a historical snapshot, Valkeapää writes in his English version of *Terveisiä*: "It seems as though the adherents of preservation want to press our culture the way one presses plants, in order to admire them later in an herbarium" (57–58); "When I hear talk of conserving the culture, I see an investigator of folklore in my mind's eye, and interpret their activities quite literally: cataloguing a dead culture" (104).

During the year after making the children's program (1978), Valkeapää teamed up with Finnish jazz flutist Seppo (Paroni) Paakkunainen to explore jazz renditions of joik (Jones-Bamman 1993: 323). A 1978 Yleisradio TV 2 program (Yleisradio 1978) provides a sample of the kind of musical experimentation Valkeapää was engaging in at the time. In an interview as part of the program, Valkeapää responds to the question of whether he is exoticizing the Sámi in performing joik in *gákti*. He states: "Toisaalta ei olisi niin kauhean paha asia sekään . . . jos se on eksoottinen, jos me sillä tavalla saattaisiin vähän meidän asiamme parenemaan—meidän olojemme tunnetummaksi, meidän vaikeuksiamme myöskin enemmän julkisuuteen" (330; On the other hand, it wouldn't be such a terrible thing . . . if it is exotic, if we can in this way improve our situation a little, make our conditions better known and also draw attention to our difficulties as well.) In his English version of *Terveisiä,* Valkeapää states: "Today I'm doing fine. The young Sámi support me. They have accepted me and my way of yoiking, they have accepted new ideas. I would have finished with anything related to yoik long ago if I had to function like a tape recorder or a gramophone record. Sheer reproduction would feel like a straightjacket to me. . . . I am genuine, but I don't want to be genuine in the sense of petrification. I want to create new things, I want to live in the culture I was born into, and I shall let myself be influenced by the currents of the times" (57).

What Valkeapää sought to achieve for joik, other artist activists aimed to accomplish for other branches of art. Following in the footsteps of Deatnogátte Nuorat, the Sámi girl group Máze Nieiddat (Girls of Máze) recorded two albums of country/folk/pop-inspired Sámi dance music in 1977 and 1978 (Jones-Bamman 1993: 294). The group's original members—Marit Elisabeth Hætta, Rávdná Sara Hætta, Karen Maria Hætta, Marit Tornensis, Berit Solbritt Eira, Inger Marie Eira, and male joik soloist Ole Hendrik Hætta—were able to release their albums through the newly founded Deatnu/Tana-based book and media company Jårgalæđđji (Jårgalæđđji 2016). Their upbeat and affirmative songs remain fond memories for Sámi today, even a generation later, although at the time the young performers' parents were careful to prevent their daughters from performing lyrics that took too strident or defiant a political stance (Pulk and Eira 2009). In 1978, a group of Sámi artists trained in southern Nordic institutions formed the Mázejoavku, an artist group that came to be centered, like Máze Nieiddat, in the village of Máze. As Hanna Horsberg Hansen has shown (2014), these artists—Aage Gaup, Synnøve Persen, Josef Halse, Hans Ragnar Mathisen, Trygve Lund Guttormsen, Ranveig Persen, Berit Marit Hætta, and in 1980 Britta Marakatt-Labba—differed from figures like Valkeapää or Magga in that they were of coastal Sámi background and had less active command of Sámi language. Yet they were strongly engaged in issues of Sámi identity and rights, and sought to make a place for Sámi artists engaged in high art genres like painting. Together with Nils-Aslak Valkeapää, they helped found Sámi Dáidócehppid Searvi (SDS; Sámi Artists' Union) in 1979, seeking to advance the status and career opportunities of Sámi artists as equal to those from the other Nordic nations (Hansen 2014: 97). Synnøve Persen not only participated actively in the group, but also became the second president of the new union (after Valkeapää); she was one of two women to participate in the 1979 Oslo hunger strike.

Among young Sámi of the time, the anagram ČSV became a watchword. Consisting of letters often used in Sámi words, and taken variously to mean Čájehehkot Sámi Vuoiŋŋa (Show Sámi Spirit) or Čohkkejehket Sámiid Vuitui (Sámi Unite for Victory) (Brantenberg 2014: 47) the term came to mean the conscious and engaged performance of Sámi identity in all aspects of life. Hans Ragnar Mathisen, Keviselie, a member of the Mázejoavku, attributes the slogan to Johan Jernsletten, who, during the 1970 Máze protests, had glossed it as Čiegus Sámi Viehka (Secret Sámi Helper) (Mathisen 2019). Mathisen notes that part of the point of the anagram was to devise different plausible meanings for it: "The symbol was very flexible, and it was up to the users' fantasy and creativity to make slogans from these three letters" (2019), thereby demonstrating the creativity and adaptability of Sámi people and their enjoyment of, and commitment to, their language and culture. Solbakk traces the slogan's first appearance to a seminar held in 1970, the ideas from which were to circulate and gain momentum throughout the 1970s (2011: 292–97). As Vigdis Stordahl writes, "The ČSVs were recognizable, not only because of their strong and revolutionary opinions, but also by virtue of their style of dress. Even though they did not wear the Sámi dress daily, they always wore some cultural emblems that signalled that they were Sámi: Sámi boots, pewter embroidered watch straps, ČSV pins and buttons, sweaters and caps with Sámi colors and patterns. Their use of Sámi handicraft and folk music was also part of this cultural repertoire" (1997: 145). For many idealistic young Sámi, working to use and develop Sámi language, along with embracing elements of performed Sámi ethnicity (dress, duodji, joik), became acts of personal activism, akin to those of the Black Power and Red Power movements underway in North America (Stordahl 1997: 144; Cocq 2014).

Alongside these important cultural developments, the decades leading up to the Álttá protests were significant for inspiring new national as well as pan-Sámi international organizations. These institutions would give ČSV youth a forum in which to share and cultivate their Sámi interests, both within their own countries and across Nordic borders. They would also furnish a platform for turning personal opinions into lasting policies and institutional change. As noted above, a central institution was the Sámi Council—Sámiráđđi. The Nordic Council was founded in 1952 as a inter-parliamentary vehicle for cooperation and mutual support between the various Nordic countries and subsidiary states, Denmark, the Faeroes, Finland, Greenland, Iceland, Norway, Sweden, and Åland (Nordic Council 2016). Following this model, in 1953, Sámi organizations in Finland, Norway, and Sweden cooperated to organize a first Sámi Conference, which immediately began to explore the possibilities of creating a Sámiráđđi representing the interests of Sámi in those countries. At the second Sámi Conference, held at Kárášjohka in 1956, these plans were brought into reality and a new organization was established. During the 1990s its membership would come to include representatives of Russian Sámi as well, with specific rules for the number of delegates accorded to each of the four countries in which Sámi live (Seurujärvi-Kari 2005). Significantly, this pan-Sámi organization emerged well before Sámi parliaments had become established in any of the Nordic countries. It served as a vehicle for promoting Sámi institution building on the local and national levels, reversing the local-to-national-to-supranational sequence of development presumed in most grass-roots movements.

In Norway, the student- and intellectual-dominated Oslo Sámi Searvi merged with other more northerly Sámi organizations in 1968 to form the Norgga Sámiid Riikkasearvvi/Norske Samers Riksforbund (NSR; Association of Norwegian Sámi; Solbakk 2011: 288–91), with Johan M. Klemetsen of Guovdageaidnu as its first chair. This organization would eventually serve as one of the prime institutional platforms for Sámi representatives to speak in a united manner with the Norwegian government (Thuen 1995: 41; Brantenberg 2014: 44). It was eventually (in 1978) opposed by a rival organization—Samenes Landsforbund (SLF; Norwegian Saami Union; Thuen 1995: 42)—which advocated for a more conciliatory approach and was linked more closely to the goals and philosophies of the ruling Labor Party, particularly as represented in Finnmark. But the NSR's attention to questions of media and message had a clear and unmistakable influence on the tactics Sámi would adopt in the Álttá protests. As mentioned above, it was through the NSR and the Sámiráđđi that young intellectuals like Valkeapää, Magga, and Østmo could begin the work of positioning Sámi into the category of nation, even going so far as to join the WCIP. By 1980, the Sámiráđđi could adopt a truly challenging political platform, reflecting the viewpoints of Sámi activists energized by the Álttá protests. As Thuen quotes the Sámiráđđi 's 1980 platform:

1. We Saami are one people, and the national borders shall not break up the community of our people.
2. We have our own history, or traditions, our own culture and our own language. From our ancestors we have inherited rights to land and water and to our ways of livelihood.
3. It is our inalienable right to protect and develop our ways of living and our societies, in accordance with our own common conditions, and we will in common take care of our lands, our natural resources and our national inheritance for the benefit of coming generations. (41–42)

The Council also enumerated seven basic rights:

1. that the Saami should have a legal protection as an aboriginal people in each country;
2. that the Saami's inherited rights to land and water should have legal protection within the national states;
3. that the traditional Saami ways of living should be protected by law, and that the legislation of each country should be adapted to this principle;
4. that the Saami language should have legal status as an official language;
5. that the Saami social organization and the representative associations of the Saami should be officially recognized;
6. that the Saami language and culture should be protected and allowed to develop as a living language and culture;
7. that we should be allowed to live in peaceful coexistence with our neighboring peoples and to support the work for peace in the world, in accordance with our own traditions. (42)

These goals became realized for Sámi people in each of the Nordic countries to a great extent in the decades following the Álttá protests, although some goals remain unrealized, particularly the Council's second goal, the recognition and acceptance of Sámi rights over lands and waters.

In closing this snapshot of the late 1970s and mediated images of Sámi, we look at five media products that all appear around the same time as the Álttá lávvu protest. Together they indicate the extensive interest the wider world took in Sámi culture and the cogent ways Sámi found of using this interest to advance their political and cultural goals.

In 1975, amid the growing embrace of Sámi culture evinced by the ČSV generation, Norwegian television aired a television series entitled *Ante*. Subtitled "*et år i en samegutts liv*" (a year in the life of a Sámi boy), the series, and its 1976 feature film adaptation, explored the personal experiences of a Sámi boy trying to fit in while attending a Norwegian residential boarding school in Guovdageaidnu (Dokka 2015). Its screenplay was written by Norwegian Tor Edvin Dahl, who spent time living in Sápmi to gain insights into his story. The film presents the legacy of Norwegianization policies in a negative light and focuses sympathy on the predicament of the film's main character, forced to leave his family and familiar surroundings for life in a hostile residential school environment. As Ingrid Dokka writes: "The series attracted enormous attention—and initiated an extremely important and far-reaching social debate on how the Norwegian state dealt with its Indigenous population" (2015: 116). It may be said that *Ante* helped create a broader Norway public interest in Sámi issues while convincing a Sámi audience that the dominant society might become interested in and even supportive of Sámi rights.

In 1977, the government of Norway invited the American television program, *Mutual of Omaha's Wild Kingdom*, to film and present the spring migration of Guovdageaidnu Sámi herders from their winter grounds near the village to their spring and summer pasturage on the coastal island of Kågan. In the resulting two-part documentary aired that same year, host Marlin Perkins accompanies the family of Johan Låggja on the family's trek. The film includes abundant images of Sámi traditional dress, shoe grass, dogs, reindeer, ear marking, lassoing, *goahti* construction, and other elements of traditional Sámi life. It also includes warm images of tea drinking, Easter-time reindeer races at Guovdageaidnu, and intense depictions of a two-day blizzard that besets the herders on their way. The Sámi are depicted in traditional dress and using reindeer sleds for transport, while the American observer, dressed in a bright red synthetic parka, is shown observing from the side astride a snowmobile. The film builds to a dramatic swimming of the herd from the mainland to the island, after which the cows begin to drop their calves. Typical of the program is the close attention paid to the conduct of the reindeer and dogs, and the tender depiction of a reindeer cow vigorously licking her newborn calf. The closing narration of the second installment of the two-part program states:

> There's an element of sorrow in seeing a tradition of centuries ending. The annual overland trek of the Lapps with their herds is changing. Now, with so much modern technology, the difficulties and dangers of the overland reindeer drive from Kautokeino northward are being largely eliminated. And it is now becoming simpler for the Lapps to reach the strait and cross to Kågan island. Perhaps drives like the one we participated in may be undertaken a few more times in the future but almost surely with less primitive equipment and less hazard. It is fortunate we could witness what might well have been the last primitive reindeer drive in the Wild Kingdom. (Meier 1977)

It would have been clear to any person knowing something about Sámi reindeer herding at the time that the documentary takes some liberties: snowmobiles were certainly commonplace among Sámi herders by then, and the migration to Kågan would continue much as always after 1977, albeit with the added convenience of a new ferry to bring the reindeer, and other visitors, to the island with greater ease. But it remains clear that the Sámi participating in the documentary seem willing and even enthusiastic to do so. They demonstrate lassoing, ear-marking, and other traditional herders' skills with willingness and interest. Perhaps they felt, as Valkeapää put it in his interview in 1978, that some exoticism is fine so long as it accomplishes the end of highlighting Sámi issues and difficulties.

Also in 1977, Valkeapää participated in a joint Soviet Estonian-Finnish documentary, entitled *Linnutee tuuled* (Winds of the Milky Way; Meri 1977). The film was the work of Estonian filmmaker (and eventual president) Lennart Meri, whose 1970 documentary *Veelinnurahvas* (People of the Waterfowl) had explored in evocative manner the Finno-Ugric cultures in the Soviet Union and Finland. While the earlier film makes no mention of Sámi, the 1977 sequel certainly does. As with the American documentary, here we see traditional Sámi dress, shoe grass, and skis, but also a discussion of Sámi shamanic traditions and drums (a central interest of Meri's). The joik singing of Nils Piera Labba is featured, and a stirring interview with Valkeapää is included. Speaking directly to the camera in minutes 30–36 of the 50-minute film, Valkeapää explains, in Sámi, why small cultures should be respected and how Sámi wish to continue to exist as a distinct and valuable people. Meri, as the narrator, speaks on behalf of the Sámi and his Soviet and Western audience: "Meie tuhandeaastane kultuur on jätnud tundra puutumata ja muutnud üksi meid. Meil on üksainus tundur, meil kõigil üksainus maailm. Vahest tulekski šamanistlikust elukäsitlusest õppida ökoloogiat" (Our thousand-year-old culture has left the tundra untouched and changed only us. We have only one tundra. We have only one world. Perhaps we should learn ecology from the shamanic way of living). The film was released in Denmark, Sweden, and Finland in 1978, after some delays from Soviet authorities. It was a finely crafted and evocative product that received an award when first shown in the United States in 1979 (Lõhmus 2010).

In late 1979, in the immediate aftermath of the Oslo lávvu demonstration, well-known Norwegian pop star Sverre Kjelsberg collaborated with the Sámi joiker Mattis Hætta of Máze to produce "Sámiid Ædnan," a dramatic pop song that narrated the events of the Álttá protests, intercut with Hætta's evocative joiking. With lyrics written by Norwegian writer, composer, and theater professional Ragnar Olsen, the song became Norway's selection for the Eurovision Grand Prix contest (Jones-Bamman 1993: 304–6; Hilder 2015: 10). In the Eurovision performance (EscLIVEmusic1 2012), a full orchestra conducted by Sigurd Jansen introduces the piece with a lilting combination of woodwind, percussion, and brass. Above the orchestra stands Sverre Kjelsberg, center stage and spotlighted, clothed in white, with an electrified acoustic guitar. In slow dramatic cadence Kjelsberg sings:

Enkel tone, to små ord: Sámiid Ædnan, samisk jord.
Kom som vindpust ifra nord, ifra nord Sámiid Ædnan

Kan et krav få mjukar form: Sámiid Ædnan, Sameland
Vokste sæ fra bris tel storm, bris tel storm, Sámiid Ædnan

Framførr tinget der dem satt, oh!
Hørtes joiken dag og natt, Sámiid Ædnan!

A simple tune, two small words: Sámiid Ædnan, Sámi earth
Came as a burst of wind from the north, from the north
Sámiid Ædnan
Can a demand take a meeker form: Sámiid Ædnan, Sámi
land
Grew from a breeze into a storm, breeze into a storm, Sámiid
Ædnan
In front of the parliament they sat, oh!
Joik was heard day and night, Sámiid Ædnan

At this point the spotlight goes out on Kjelsberg and the music stops. Then quietly from stage right, Hætta takes the stage, spotlighted and singing the joik *Máze nieiddat* a cappella. He is dressed in a bright traditional gákti with leather boots that match Kjelsberg's. As he approaches Kjelsberg singing and smiling, the Norwegian begins to nod and strum along with the joik on his guitar. As Hætta reaches center stage, the two men turn toward the audience and continue the joik as a duet, with orchestra accompaniment gradually rising. The joik now sounds bold and confident. As Hætta continues the joik, Kjelsberg interjects melodic commentary:

Joik har større kraft enn krutt, oh! Sámiid Ædnan
Førr en joik tar aldri slutt, hej . . . Sámiid Ædnan
Førr en joik tar aldri slutt, oh! Sámiid Ædnan

Joik has greater power than gunpowder, oh! Sámiid Ædnan
Because a joik never ends, hej, Sámiid Ædnan
Because a joik never ends, oh! Sámiid Ædnan]

The song finishes with Hætta again being given the opportunity to sing alone, after which the orchestra sounds dramatic ending notes.

Musically, the song enacts the Norwegian majority's experience of the Álttá lávvu protest. The Sámi man, brightly clad and exotic, emerges onto the Oslo stage like a fresh wind from the north, gradually pulling the Norwegian public, embodied in Kjelsberg, into the performance of an appealing and simple Sámi melody. Inspired by the song, the Norwegian cannot help but assent to the mild and reasonable request of the Sámi for control of their homeland, Sámiid Ædnan. That the two men finish the song with a warm handshake symbolizes the new feelings of friendship and respect that the song suggests will prevail. As Richard Jones-Bamman writes: "In late 1979, the Oslo occupation was still very much in the minds of most Norwegians, thanks largely to the media coverage which had primarily presented the protest in a positive manner" (307).

In 1982, Nils-Aslak Valkeapää and Ingor Ántte Áilu Gaup produced their own musical narration of the protests, an album entitled *Sápmi, vuoi Sápmi* (Jones-Bamman 1993: 327). Using the ČSV preferred term *Sápmi*, the album laments the loss of control over waters and lands that the Álttá defeat entails. With the protests now over and the building of the dam a certainty, the album makes exclusive use of Sámi, encapsulating the events and reminding listeners to continue the battle for Sámi rights. That the album makes no attempt to reach a non-Sámi audience is a clear artistic choice, one aimed at articulating a Sámi perspective for a Sámi audience without the simplifications and gestures of inclusion that are evident in Kjelsberg and Hætta's Eurovision song. Nonetheless, it is no preservationist performance of traditional joik. The two singers continue the creative innovation and stylistic experimentation that, Valkeapää argued, was the essence of a Sámi approach to tradition.

Five moments performed over modern media for any audience to see and hear: a sympathetic television series, a nostalgic foreign documentary, a politically charged Soviet documentary, a glitzy Eurovision Song Contest entry, and a pensive Sámi-language-only album. The late 1970s were a time during which Sámi artists and activists perfected techniques of communicating a message of Sámi rights, both to broad international audiences and to Sámi themselves. In his analysis of Sámi media, John Solbakk concurs with the argument of this chapter, that is, that the Álttá protests were a transformative moment, not only for Sámi activists but for all Sámi media professionals. Solbakk points to "a remarkable change in attitude and practice . . . among many Norwegian journalists with regard to their reporting on Sámi conditions" (Solbakk 1997: 178). Perhaps this change in attitude occurred in part because Sámi artists and activists had learned how to effectively use media images—so central in protest and thought of the era (and ever after, as we shall argue)—to communicate Sámi interests in a convincing and appealing manner. As Valkeapää writes in his English version of *Terveisiä*, "[a] successful culture battle can only be fought if we adopt the same weapons as those others already have [radio, television], and at the same time take care to use them in our own way" (1971: 60).

3

Tjïekere

The Recovery of Sámi Continuity

IN 1952, MATTS ARNBERG AND HÅKAN UNSGAARD OF THE Swedish Radio Corporation joined Sámi scholar Israel Ruong to collect joik from different Sámi communities across Swedish Sápmi (Arnberg et al. 1997). In the South Sámi region of Tärnaby, the collectors met with and recorded vuolle renditions from Nils Mattias Andersson (1887–1974), a retired reindeer herder who was seventy-two at the time. Andersson had relocated to the area of Mount Oulavuolie, after spending his boyhood in Vilhelmina and then moving with his father to Tärnaby. As a newly married adult, he applied for permission to herd and was granted grazing pastures on Oulavuolie. The authorities obliged him to take up residence on the Norwegian side of the border in order to access the mountain, where he kept a small tame herd of reindeer that he milked regularly. In the living room of Ejnar Grundström, the head of the local residential boarding school for the children of Sámi herders, *nomadskola*, Andersson performed two extended vuolle for the team, one lasting 4:19 minutes, the other 9:33 minutes. The latter, an extended poetic reminiscence of the Mount Oulavuolie, has been called by Harald Gaski "one of the most beautiful epic poetic pieces we know within Sámi impressionistic poetry" (2000b: 193). *Åvlavuelien råantjoeh* (Reindeer herd on Oulavuolie; Andersson 2005) encapsulated the mountain, Andersson's once impressive reindeer herd, a dangerous ice fissure that ran across the mountain's glacier and that occasionally swallowed up traversing reindeer, memories of a wife blowing embers to stir up a fire, children intimidated by a great fish they had caught, and closed with reflections on the aging and loneliness of the singer and his wife. It has become a key work in not only Sámi joik research but also in the construction of a pan-Sámi literary canon (Gaski and Kappfjell 2005). Some twelve years after the original performance, Arnberg, Nilsson, and Öhrström returned to Tärnaby to film Andersson listening to the recording and to create an evocative short film that combines the original sound recording with Israel Ruong's voice-over translation into Swedish (Arnberg et al., n.d.). The text of Andersson's vuolle was printed in 1965 in a supplement issue to the newspaper *Samefolket*, and presented in English translation in Ruong's 1967 *The Lapps in Sweden*, and has been repeatedly republished and anthologized since. The text, audio recording, and filmed reading of Andersson's vuolle constitute a unique treasure in an emergent Sámi literary history, one extending back into earlier eras and encompassing the collecting efforts of ethnographers, musicologists, and archivists. A single performative event of the 1950s becomes a monument to Sámi expressive artistry, as enduring and imposing as the great mountain, Oulavuolie, featured in the vuolle.

The South Sámi term *tjïekere* denotes an area of light, deep, relatively dry snow that has been pawed up by reindeer. Light, powdery snow poses little challenge to reindeer grazing, especially in the early winter, or in birch forests. The reindeer easily paw through the snow as they search for lichen or other food. At the same time, the process of pawing occupies the reindeer's energies and attention so that they remain in a relatively confined area rather than ranging more widely. Tjïekere provides a clear record of where the reindeer have been, which herders can use to monitor the herd and its status. As Ole Henrik Magga points out in his study of South Sámi snow terminology (2014: 42), the term has cognates in all the Sámi languages as well as in the more distant Uralic languages Khanty, Mansi, and Kamassian (see also Ruong 1969: 98, 166; Álgu database: search term "Čiegar"). Magga suggests that the term probably originated in practices of tracking and hunting wild reindeer and then became incorporated into the vocabulary of herders with the development of reindeer husbandry. We use the term here to suggest the creative and industrious ways that Sámi artists and activists have sought to unearth antecedents of the modern Sámi movement in the works and ideas of past Sámi. DuBois (2018) refers to this process as "recovered continuity," as it reflects a conscious attempt to learn about the Sámi past and reconnect with its artistic, spiritual, and ecological norms in the present, despite the sometimes sizeable disjunctures and lapses that have occurred as a result of colonization. Viewing cultural changes as driven by processes of colonial oppression, Sámi artists sought to recover past traditions as acts of conscious decolonization. Digging industriously and concertedly, Sámi artists have sought to make use of past Sámi insights and statements in their efforts to establish and disseminate discourse on Sámi culture and rights for the present and future.

Contexts and Controversies

The "Tjïekere era" of Sámi media picks up in the aftermath of the Álttá dam protests of the early 1980s and continues through the 1990s. This was a period of remarkable legal and political progress for Sámi and for Indigenous peoples internationally. With significant Norwegian participation, the UN's Working Group on Indigenous Populations formed in 1982 and eventually drafted in 1989 the United Nations International Labour Organization's Indigenous and Tribal Peoples Convention (ILO-169; United Nations 1990), which Norway was the first country to ratify (Thuen 1995: 230–36). As noted in previous chapters, in the Sámi Act of 1987, Norway formally recognized that status of Sámi as the country's Indigenous population, a status that carried with it specific rights eventually codified in the Norwegian constitution. As a result, in 1989, Sámi in Norway acquired a representative organ, Sámediggi, the Sámi parliament. Sweden followed suit with a Sámi parliament for Swedish Sámi in 1993 (albeit with a less programmatic role in attaining Sámi self-determination), and Finland revised the role and authority of its existing Sámi parliament in 1996. Both Sweden and Finland adjusted their constitutions to recognize Sámi Indigeneity. A broader UN initiative to frame a Declaration of the Rights of Indigenous Peoples (UNDRIP) was finalized in 2006.

Alongside these legal developments, Sámi in the 1980s and 1990s made strides in the areas of media and entertainment. Where a Sámi press history can be traced back to the nineteenth century (Ijäs 2011), and regular radio news broadcasts in Sámi date to the immediate post–World War II era (Lehtola and Vest 2001; Pietikäinen 2008), the production of Sámi-language entertainment got underway as a widespread enterprise only in the 1970s. The founding of the Sámi Našunálateáhter Beaivváš (Sámi National Theater) in 1981 (Lehtola 2008) created a key performative venue for the integration of Sámi writers, actors, and musicians, with the aim of producing entertaining and thought-provoking dramatic pieces for a Sámi-language audience as well as for members of the Nordic majority cultures. Continuing the longstanding Nordic tradition of theater as a platform for discussion and debate, as well as the "everyman" orientation that differentiates Nordic theater culture from that of the United States, Beaivváš soon became an important vehicle for Sámi artists and collaborations.

Internationally, the 1980s was an era of optimism concerning the increased mobility and cultural sharing of globalizing trends. The first World of Music, Arts and Dance festival (WOMAD) took place in 1982, the brainchild of Peter Gabriel and other leaders of what would become known as world music. Indigenous artists like Buffy Sainte Marie were now joined by other Indigenous and roots musicians who mounted their own careers, or, more often, were invited into collaborations with white musicians. Peter Gabriel's "In Your Eyes," on the *So* album of 1986, featured Senegalese percussionist and singer Youssou N'Dour. Paul Simon's *Graceland* album of the same year incorporated South African and American roots musicians, rhythms, and sounds melded into eclectic creations through the wonders of newly emerging digital editing. While mentions of co-option and suggestions of colonialism were at times expressed regarding various of these recording projects, and led to efforts to protect intangible cultural heritage and copyright (Hafstein 2018), the overall response from the public was upbeat and affirmative: hungry for new sounds and styles, consumers embraced the world's diverse musical traditions–now made accessible, familiar, and approachable through commercially produced syntheses. Indigenous artists could find a place in the international spotlight if they got lucky and played well, as Sámi artists would discover. Their otherness became a positive attribute as well as a commodity to be traded in the global village, and economic success in the international marketplace often translated into perceptions of intrinsic worth in local contexts. In each of the four Sámi media projects described in this chapter, the fact of broader economic success proved crucial as a means of reversing the persistent marginalization and stigmatization of how Sámi culture was perceived among Sámi and their Nordic neighbors in the late twentieth century.

It is noteworthy that this economic strategy for celebrating and commodifying cultural otherness arises for Indigenous artists like Sámi at the same time that Swedish and Norwegian groups were having their greatest economic success mimicking the sounds and whiteness of America: the Swedish group ABBA dominated the charts internationally for the whole of the 1970s, and the Norwegian pop band A-ha's *Take On Me* (1985), gave no hint of the group's Norwegian makeup. Singing in American English, with sounds and rhythms derived from international pop music norms, Scandinavian pop singers adopted a completely different approach to stardom than Sámi. In the case of Finland, one can contrast the strategies of Hanoi Rocks with that of Värttinä: whereas the lead vocalists of Hanoi Rocks of the early 1980s—Matti Fagerholm and Antti Hulko—adopted the Scandinavian performance model, disguising their Finnish identities under the English pseudonyms Michael Monroe and Andy McCoy, the leaders of the folk-pop fusion band Värttinä, sisters Sari and Kari Kaasinen, made every effort to emphasize their Finnish and Karelian roots. As otherness became emblematized in sound, Nordic performers could opt to either stand out or blend in.

It was perhaps in response to these competing trends in Nordic popular music that Nils-Aslak Valkeapää and associates opted to establish the Sámi Grand Prix in 1990. Here, the international leveling, pageantry, and glitz of the Eurovision Song Contest—with its emphasis on youth, beauty, and fun—was meshed artfully with a competition featuring traditional joik and distinctively Sámi performance traditions. Sámi artists were welcome to compete in either category, and both were seen as important in serving the cause of modern Sámi identity. Norwegian embrace of Valkeapää's leadership was signaled by the decision of the planners of the Olympic Games, held in Lillehammer in 1994, to have Valkeapää joik in the games' opening ceremony. Other festivals, like Riddu Riđđu (1991–) and Márkomeannu (1999–) followed, as festival stages, Sámi radio, and other venues created opportunities for Sámi to perform and to be seen and heard. Of another kind, but also important, is the international contest, Liet International—a song contest for linguistic minorities in Europe. Hosted in Sweden in 2006 and 2008 as "Liet Lavlut," the event offers a Eurovision Song Contest platform for the continent's minority language singers and musicians. The artists profiled in this chapter illustrate the achievements and the strategies employed by Sámi in this new context of optimism and self-assertion. Independent, entrepreneurial, and self-directed, these artists made performing Sámi culture a heroic and creative act, one that would aid a new generation of Sámi in working toward self-determination, helping convince subsequent generations to embrace rather than shun their Sámi cultural heritage.

Nils Gaup's *Ofelaš* (1987–1988)

Perhaps no other media product since the Álttá demonstrations accomplished the goals of enhancing Sámi cultural visibility and affirmation as powerfully and effectively as Nils Gaup's acclaimed and successful *Ofelaš* (Pathfinder) of 1987. Written and directed by Gaup, an actor and veteran member of the Beaivváš Sámi Našunálateáhter, and produced by Norwegian John M. Jacobsen, *Ofelaš* bucked film industry norms by employing northern Sámi as its language, emphasizing the essential Sámi nature of its plot and images. The film included a cast of talented Sámi actors—including the young and appealing Mikkel Gaup and Sara Máret Gaup as the film's romantic couple, Nils Utsi as the film's heroic *noaidi,* and Nils-Aslak Valkeapää as the good-willed head of the beset Sámi *siida.* With joiking contributed by Valkeapää and artful use of Sámi oral tradition, the film created a presence for Sámi in the international imagination that expunged and replaced the pejorative colonial stereotypes of the past. Building on a premise of Sámi cultural continuity, adaptation to a harsh but beautiful environment, and close relation to nature (partly embodied in shamanic religious traditions), the film asserted a uniquely Sámi claim to the lands of Sápmi and a narrative of cultural survival and persistence that depicted colonial deprivations and challenges as already beginning in the Iron Age. In the filmic world of *Ofelaš,* Sámi are survivors, and their intrinsic right to cultural maintenance is summed up by the film's final words: "Mis lea álo ofelaš" (We will always have a pathfinder), in which attendance to cultural traditions and cultural leaders ensures continuity in the present and future.

The combination of Indigenous content and viewer accessibility of *Ofelaš* proved paradigmatic for the development of Indigenous filmmaking in the late 1990s and early 2000s (Ginsburg 1991, 2002; Kilpatrick 1999; DuBois 2000; Singer 2001; Wood 2008; Skarðhamar 2008; Christensen 2015; Dokka 2015), an international movement among Indigenous artists that seeks to dismantle earlier stereotypes of Indigenous people and replace them with more nuanced, affirmative, and decolonizing images. Sámi contributions to this wider development are discussed in detail in the next chapter. In the context of 1987, however, when *Ofelaš* first reached the screen, it was one of a plethora of international and Hollywood movies exploring cross-cultural encounters more broadly, including Stephen Spielberg's harrowing depiction of a British child's experiences as a prisoner of war in World-War-II Japan, *Empire of the Sun*; Bernardo Bertolucci's grand chronicle of the end of the Chinese empire, *The Last Emperor*; Norman Jewison's wistful exoticism of New York Italian-American culture, *Moonstruck*; Gabriel Axel's warm portrayal of Danish-French culinary encounters in his adaptation of an Isak Dinesen/Karen Blixen story, *Babettes gæstebud* (Babette's feast); and Percy Adlon's mystical portrayal of American multiculturalism and German xenophobia, *Bagdad Café*. It was also the year of Oliver Stone's grim, Faustian *Wall Street,* and its villainous character's evil but alluring adage, "greed is good," a sound bite that would eventually become momentous in the anti–Wall Street movements of the 2010s. But where most of these films adopt an outsider's exoticizing gaze toward the cultures depicted, as perceptively discussed by Streese and Shea (1992) and Mennel and Ongiri (2000) in connection with *Bagdad Café*, *Ofelaš* presents an unabashedly insider's view of Sámi culture, one in which Sámi language, cultural traditions, and struggle for survival are presented in sympathetic and complex detail. In *Ofelaš* one senses a dual attention to both an insider audience of Sámi and an international outsider audience of non-Sámi (DuBois 2000), making it analogous in important ways to the films of the African-American filmmaker Spike Lee, whose *She's Gotta Have It* came out in 1986 and *Do the Right Thing* in 1989. Gaup was on the forefront of the international feature film transformation from a bastion of white colonial viewpoints to a canvas for the portrayal of other cultures and understandings in appealing but challenging ways. *Ofelaš* was the winner of two 1988 Norwegian Amanda awards (for best film and best director), and, as the first Norwegian film ever to be selected for distribution in the United States and England, became a nominee for the 1988 American Academy Award for Best Foreign Language Film, winner of the Sutherland trophy of 1989 awarded by the British Film Institute, nominee for a 1988 European Film Award, winner of a special mention award for the 1988 Sitges Catalonian International Film Festival, and winner of the jury grand prize in the 1990 Yubari International Fantastic Film Festival. Even thirty years after its début, the film figured prominently in festivals such as the 2018 Maoriland Film Festival of New Zealand.

The film's opening is both atmospheric and mysterious. A bleak wintry landscape is shown at night, its snows shifting in the winds. The moon appears just above the snowy horizon. Off-camera, a wolf's howl is added to the forceful sound of the wind, creating an impression of a cold and dangerous world. A voice-over of the noaidi character, Raste (Nils Utsi), begins relating his having seen a vision of a reindeer bull. This is the third time he has seen such a vision: the first time in his youth, the second in his prime, and now today. Partway through this narration, the film cuts to a close-up of Raste's face, as he speaks directly to the camera in what is clearly a lávvu, illuminated by flickering firelight. The audience is given no clues as to whom he is addressing or what his statements mean until significantly later in the film. But the audience is prepared in this way to be on the lookout for both the character Raste and the meanings of this mysterious monologue. Like the film's main character, Aigin, the audience is tasked with trying to make sense of a reality that is clear to Raste but which remains hidden from anyone else at this point in the film. And quintessentially, the audience is inserted into the heart of the natural and cultural environment of Sámi people in an unspecified but clearly ancient past. The opening title sequence features the powerful joik singing of Nils-Aslak Valkeapää and animated images that imitate noaidi drum figures. It ends with the statement written in a medieval script: "Dát máinnas lea vadjolan buolvvas bulvii lagabui 1000 jagi" (This story has passed from generation to generation for a thousand years). A continuity of oral tradition and culture more generally is asserted, one that includes storytelling, joik, and shamanic beliefs, with the ensuing narrative furnishing proof of the vitality and persistence of this tradition to the present.

With this mysterious but also ambitious opening, Gaup's film proceeds to build a suspenseful and exciting filmic narrative, with artful cuts, literal cliff-hangers, an underdog hero (a teenager named Aigin, played by Mikkel Gaup), a nascent romance (between Aigin and Sahve, played by Sara Máret Gaup), repeated acts of heroic altruism, and all the elements that make for an exciting Hollywood Western. The film introduces as villains a troop of grim, black-clad marauders—the Čuđit—and depicts their greed and brutality. Seemingly nothing can stop their trudging advance, as they kill the entire family of the film's main character, Aigin. Aigin himself is wounded, but manages to escape thanks to his skill in skiing. In contrast to the Čuđit, the Sámi are shown as bright, beautiful, and peace-loving—skiing across the arctic landscape, living in close relation to nature, and showing no proclivity for violence, although, when pushed by necessity, they will act to protect their community.

An early sequence of scenes portraying a traditional Sámi bear ceremonial is important in conveying a Sámi relationship to nature. With the community hungry at what is clearly an advanced stage of winter, the men of the siida discover the den of a bear and determine to hunt it. Here is where Raste makes his first actual appearance in the narrative, as he performs a divinatory ritual using his drum to determine which of the men should lead the coming hunt. The *siida isit,* or chief, played by Nils-Aslak Valkeapää, is shown commanding the respect of the other men as he authorizes the hunt and leads the men to consult with Raste. The bear is referred to by its nickname, Darffot, and the audience is informed of the importance of this act through the questions and answers of a small boy in the scene. The audience is schooled in the worldview and beliefs of traditional Sámi, as we see the matriarch of the siida, Varia, explaining the sacred meaning of the bear hunt to the boy. Throughout the scene, the lavish attention to the characters' clothing is evident: in this premodern era, we see no fabric in their leather and fur clothing, which instead features different colors and patterns achieved by sewing together furs of different types. The film goes to lengths to place its story in a medieval context, before the development of trade goods like woven fabric and other staples of later Sámi life. Strongly reminiscent of modern Sámi clothing, the characters' fur attire suggests a continuity between the medieval past and the modern present, one in which Sámi worldview, aesthetics, and livelihoods remain surprisingly intact over time.

The bear hunting sequence allows Gaup to portray a culture in which the activities of daily life are accompanied by elaborate and honored rituals, ones that make nature sacred and reflect a Sámi dependence on the various animals of their arctic environment. Gaup also uses the sequence to set up key conflicts in his film, particularly between young and headstrong men like Orbes (and eventually Aigin) and more mature, but sometimes somewhat cowardly, men like Sierge. Aigin, orphaned by the Čuđit and anxious to stop their advance, will learn the value of cleverness and trickery in defeating the menacing threat represented by the Čuđit, but he will also gain the assistance of noaidi powers in the process.

The closing of the bear hunt sequence allows Gaup to complete his depiction of Sámi ritual traditions while also setting up the underlying shamanic narrative in the film. When Sierge's fear prevents him from killing the bear, Raste must do the act. His necklace of bear claws shows that he is an accomplished hunter, but his killing of the bear also allows for his absence from coming scenes. When the other men arrive at the siida camp without Raste, the curious boy character again asks questions, leading Varia to explain to him (and of course, also to the audience) that the hunter must absent himself for a time due to the power gained from killing the bear. He may be viewed safely only through looking through a metal ring. As Varia relates: "Dat goddá goddima vuoimmi ja luoihtá eallima vuoimmi eallit" (This kills the power of killing and lets the power of life live). The image encapsulates one of the key messages of the film, as Aigin will eventually come to recognize the power of the circle, of connectedness, over the power of senseless death and destruction.

While separated from the siida in this way, Raste has a mystical vision of a reindeer bull. Filmic suture between the eyes of Raste and those of the reindeer indicate supernatural communication, and Raste is shown busily beating his drum and joiking afterward, as he seeks to understand the significance of the vision and the actions he will need to take as a result. Meanwhile, the wounded Aigin arrives at the camp, informs them of the nearing Čuđit, and urges the siida to prepare to battle them. Instead, wisely, the community opts to flee to the coast, where they can hopefully gain the assistance of other Sámi. Varia sends Sahve to seek out Raste so that he can heal Aigin, and we see Sahve use the metal ring to protect her eyes. When Aigin awakens from his healing treatment, he refuses to flee with the others but instead spends the night in the deserted camp. There he is awakened first by a vision of his deceased sister, then by a small dog, and finally by Raste, who urges him to follow the others to the coast, while he also tells Aigin of his vision of the reindeer bull. Presaged as it is by the repetition of elements of the scene at the opening of the film, the lávvu conference scene—in which Raste instructs the young Aigin on the interconnectedness all things, united in a single "stuorra oktavuohta" (great unity)—stands at the center and heart of the film. It not only provides essential characterization of both Raste and Aigin, but also hints at Raste's full cognizance at what will occur in the rest of the narrative. For if we assume that Raste subscribes to the beliefs about the ring and the power gained by hunting and killing the bear, we must realize that his decision to appear to Aigin without offering him a protective ring to shield his eyes from harm signals Raste's awareness of Aigin's supernatural power. When Aigin withstands the encounter with Raste unharmed, it confirms his destiny as Raste's eventual replacement as the siida's intermediary with the supernatural. Raste's words hint at the stratagem Aigin will eventually use to defeat the Čuđit, as he warns Aigin not to lose track of his connectedness with creation and become like the Čuđit, stumbling blindly in the darkness of their self-centeredness and greed. Raste disappears as suddenly as he appeared, leaving Aigin—and the audience—still bewildered about the meaning of the reindeer vision.

In scenes that follow, we see some of the men of the siida, badly outnumbered, futilely attempt to battle the Čuđit, with only Aigin managing to escape. Raste, too, dies at their hands, despite Aigin's attempt to save him by agreeing to show the Čuđit the way to the Sámi's coastal camp. He must serve as their ofelaš, pathfinder, a role that Gaup fuses narratively in his film with that of a noaidi. The vulnerability of the peaceful Sámi camp on the coast is shown through warm depictions of community members sharing an evening bath in the sauna, children laughing and playing, and other scenes of harmony and goodwill. These are intercut with tense scenes of the Čuđit advancing toward the camp, led by Aigin on a circuitous trail through jagged snow-clad mountains. At the climax of the film, when it looks like the Čuđit will soon be able to descend from the mountains to attack and destroy the Sámi community, it becomes clear that Aigin has hatched a clever plot to defeat the Čuđit, leading them over a cliff where they are swept away to their deaths by a sudden and dramatic avalanche. His acts are witnessed by the men of the siida, particularly the *isit* and Sierge, who return to the camp to share the news with the rest of the community.

Miraculously, however, as a following scene shows, the avalanche has left Aigin alive and well, as he scrambles up the now barren cliff under the flickering northern lights. It is now that he sees the reindeer bull vision himself, in a scene that harkens back to Raste's vision early in the film. The suture of the reindeer's and Aigin's eyes again indicates the unstated but evident supernatural communication that occurs.

The scene cuts back to the camp, where the community's mourning for Aigin is abruptly interrupted by his entry. The astonished siida members watch as Aigin explains that the Čuđit will never threaten them again. When he hands Raste's drum to Varia, with the sorrowful information that the community has lost its "ofelaš" (pathfinder), Varia receives the drum gravely, and then after glancing at the isit for his confirmation, returns the drum to Aigin, stating "Mis lea álo ofelaš" (We will always have a pathfinder). As Aigin settles into the company of people around the fire, evidently as a now-valued member and budding noaidi, we see the fire from above, mimicking the rhomboid sun figures on many traditional Sámi drums. A close-up on the drum held in Aigin's lap underscores the imagistic link and drum figures once again appear on the screen, above the characters that they seem to represent: a noaidi above Aigin; images of the Sámi goddesses above Varia, Sahve, and another prominent female character; and images of a leader and a warrior above the isit and Sierge. All have roles in the community's future, one that possesses both natural and supernatural allies.

As Siv Ellen Kraft (2007) and Cato Christensen (2015) detail, the film's positive portrayal of shamanism ties in with broader trends in international popular culture of the time, which imagine Indigenous peoples as having a special regard for nature, embodied in their ancient beliefs and rituals. The details of shamanism in the film, in combination with the careful depiction of the bear ceremonial, suggest a past Sámi culture closely tied to nature through both rituals and worldview. At the same time, continuities suggested by oral tradition, costume, and language link this past religious sensibility to the present, suggesting that the Sámi of today are heirs and continuers of these ancient traditions. To be sure, the details of Sámi shamanism included in the film are noticeably streamlined and simplified, particularly in comparison with the lavishly detailed depiction of the bear ceremonial. The film's shamanic calling features only a single animal spirit guide (the reindeer bull), in keeping with notions of "core shamanism" put forward in Michael Harner's *Way of the Shaman* (1980), and differing markedly from the more complex array of tutelary spirits and animal spirit guides reported in missionary accounts of eighteenth-century Sámi practice (Bäckman and Hulkrantz 1977). In an era when many Sámi, particularly those of Laestadian background, still strongly disapproved of past Sámi religious traditions as demonic and backward, the film seems intent at suggesting only just enough of the old religion to capture the mystique and allure of a past Sámi "nature religion" that can serve to further tie Sámi to the environment and an identity as Indigenous people. By situating the film in a pre-Christian past, the film further avoids taking any position on Christianity as an element of modern Sámi identity, or as a factor in the historical colonization of Sámi people. This positive portrayal of shamanic traditions, and assertion of a continuity from the past to the present, is echoed and furthered in works like Valkeapää's *Beaivi, áhčážan* (The sun, my father).

Nils-Aslak Valkeapää's *Beaivi, áhčážan* (1989)

The years around the time of the début of *Ofelaš* were momentous in more ways than one for the field of Sámi literature. In 1987, Sámi writers, along with their Faroese and Greenlandic counterparts, successfully lobbied the Nordic Council to permit separate nominations of Sámi, Faroese, and Greenlandic literature to the Council's prestigious Nordic Prize for Literature (Gaski 2010: 158). This change in policy promised to raise the profile of literature in the Nordic region's smaller languages, the writers of which had previously been obliged to compete for nominations with writers producing work in the majority languages of each writer's home country. In order to win the prize, a literary work would still have to be recognized as superior to anything else written in any of the Nordic languages during the previous year. Yet with the new policy, at least entry into consideration for that honor had been eased. As a result, Valkeapää's collection of poetry,

Ruoktu váimmus (Home in the heart), was nominated, a work that had appeared in 1985 and had recently come out in Scandinavian-language translation. The collection did not win, but was warmly received by the jury. Even more significant, however, was the publication in 1989 of a new collection of Valkeapää's poetry, entitled *Beaivi, áhčážan*. The collection was a stunningly sensitive and powerful melding of poetry, line art, photography, and typography, all meticulously laid out by Valkeapää himself and published in the Sámi press he helped found (DAT). *Beaivi, áhčážan* would eventually win the Nordic Prize for Literature in 1991, the year that a Scandinavian-language translation of the work appeared. In its haunting and evocative poetry, striking black-and-white ink artworks, accompanying joik and recitation soundtrack, and incorporation of a cavalcade of historical photographs of Sámi people, *Beaivi, áhčážan* served as a visual and verbal testament to the enduring culture of Sámi people and their unique identity as a nation. After receiving the prize, Valkeapää's poetry was translated into a wide array of other languages, including all of the Nordic national languages along with English, French, German, Hungarian, Japanese, Russian, and Spanish. The full multimedia version of *Beaivi, áhčážan,* however, complete with its artful and strategic use of images, has never been reproduced in any other language other than its Sámi original. Even within its verbal translation, one of the collection's poems was left untranslated (poem 272; see below). *Beaivi, áhčážan* marked a milestone in Sámi culture, one that confirmed the assertion of Sámi cultural activists that their people possess unique and nuanced artistic works of value not only to Sámi people themselves—for whom they are the lifeblood and building blocks of a Sámi national identity—but also for world literature and a sense of art and culture that incorporates and respects the artistry of Indigenous peoples.

Coming out as it did in 1989, Valkeapää's work participated centrally in the enterprise we term here as *tjïekere.* Given Valkeapää's importance in the cultural awakening that had served to inspire the Álttá protests, and the centrality of his viewpoints in the protests themselves, and given his prominence in the film *Ofelaš* from the previous year (where he was wryly cast as the siida's head), it would seem natural that a new work by him would receive much notice among Sámi readers. Yet in *Beaivi, áhčážan,* Valkeapää does much more than simply author a new collection of poems. He steps forward into the international literary limelight to propel Sámi literature, and by extension, Sámi people, to new heights through creating a literary and artistic masterpiece.

It is beyond the scope of this study to offer a comprehensive interpretation of this rich and complex work, other than to acknowledge and introduce some of the prominent scholars who have contributed readings and insights on it, particularly Harald Gaski (2008, 2015), Kathleen Dana (2003), and Anne Heith (2014). Looking specifically at Sámi media, we focus particularly on the substantive and concrete ways in which Valkeapää addresses the concept of image making and the extensive body of archival images included in his book. Building on the insights of Gaski, Dana, and Heith, we suggest that Valkeapää seeks to repurpose the images he uses in his text: decolonizing their colonial intent and replacing it with uses that uplift and affirm Sámi identity and worth, particularly as Indigenous people who have persevered against longstanding and nearly continual colonial pressures. The volume offers strategies for confronting and instrumentalizing past racism, disenfranchisement, and marginalization, which later artists and works adopt and extend, as we note in the coming chapters. We argue that *Beaivi, áhčážan* becomes a seminal text in the ongoing Sámi struggle toward Sámi identity and self-determination.

Longtime friend of Valkeapää and expert on his poetry, Harald Gaski has this to say about Valkeapää's multiple artistic channels:

> Especially important to Nils-Aslak Valkeapää's art is its holistic nature; he expresses himself in a range of media and modes. A poem can be read in isolation but it is best understood when it is read in relation to his other poems and, perhaps just as importantly, in relation to a yoik on the same theme or an image that

> accompanies the poem in the form of a photograph, a pencil drawing or a painting. It is in the totality of his expression that one understands Nils-Aslak best, but one can also readily enjoy the works of art individually. (Gaski 2008a: 157)

In considering Valkeapää's use of these multiple artistic modes and resources, Dana writes, "[i]n effect, Valkeapää's oeuvre is a Sámi shaman drum, complete with the natural and mythical images that comprise the Sámi world, replete with the images and totems that signify Sámi identity" (2003: 49). Regarding Valkeapää's use of photographs in particular, she writes: "The storytelling power of images is one that Áillohaš uses with considerable flair in *Beaivi, áhčážan*. While he leaves the 'official' archival captions with all the photographs, and gives full credit to the researchers in the final pages of the book, the scope and sequence of the photos is the poet's alone. Each sequence echoes or anticipates the poems that precede or follow" (2003: 133). Anne Heith suggests that Valkeapää not only quotes such past uses of Sámi images, but does so in order to problematize them: "Valkeapää's book functions as a specimen of Sámi metahistory which exposes the conceptual strategies used in nineteenth and twentieth century production of knowledge about the Sámi" (2014: 45). Drawing on both Ashcroft, Griffins, and Tiffin (2000) and Hooper-Greenhill (2000), Heith writes: "Through the reframing of photographs from the second half of the nineteenth century in a book from 1988 in Northern Sámi . . . *Beaivi áhčážan* exemplifies a contemporary deconstruction of the meanings produced by ethnographic exhibitions" (2014: 56). That he does so while repurposing the images to create a narrative affirmative of Sámi identity is what we hope to suggest below.

One of the first things one notices about *Beaivi, áhčážan* is that its dust jacket—its removable cover—is an essential and indispensable element of the book's content (figure 3.1). With its black format and white lettering listing title, author, and publisher on the spine, the dust jacket announces boldly that this book will reverse the norms of

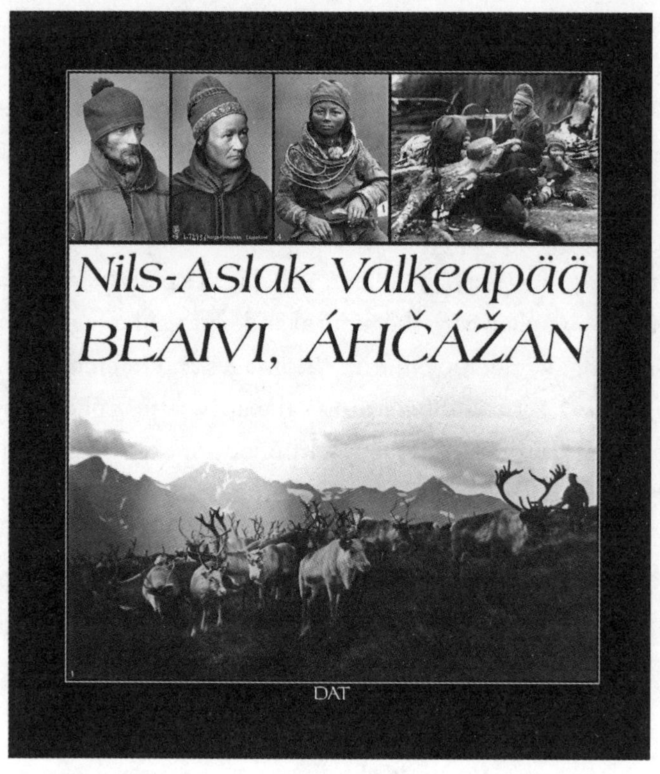

3.1. The cover and opening images of Nils-Aslak Valkeapää's multimedia work *Beaivi áhčážan* (1989). Used by permission, DAT.

representation that have long controlled images of Sámi in colonial discourse. It will not be a white book with black letters, in other words, but, the cover seems to suggest, a black one with white letters. As one examines the cover further, it becomes clear that the images of the work begin here. They are numbered in sequence, along with the volume's poems, from the front of the dust jacket through the entirety of the text to the back of the dust jacket, so that the total work contains some 575 items, 386 of which are images and 189 of which are poems of varying lengths.

To a non-Sámi viewer accustomed to seeing unnamed images of Indigenous people as curiosities or exotics in colonial works, the images of the front cover of Valkeapää's text can seem at first expectable, even mundane. We see reindeer, Sámi in traditional dress, and images of traditional livelihoods and dwellings. Yet it soon becomes clear that for Valkeapää, and a Sámi audience, these images have deeper meanings. They are photographs of *people* and *places*, with names and identities, and they are arranged in a manner that is carefully thought out. On the front cover, in the center, Valkeapää places his image 1, a photograph of a reindeer herd and herder with a backdrop of snow-speckled mountains. The reindeer vary in color and markings and sport large antlers, a sign that the photograph is taken in the autumn. On the inside flap of the dust jacket, the photo is identified as having been produced by Annie Giaver and conserved at the Tromsø Museum, and is captioned "Reinflokk på Uløy" (Reindeer herd on Uløya). The Giaver family owned the main trading settlement on the island, which formed the summer grazing grounds for the herd of Valkeapää's mother's family. In the gray expanse of sky at the top of the photo, Valkeapää has placed, in black letters, his name and the title of the book. Above this photo, he has placed four smaller images: images 2, 3, 4, and 5. The first two, identified as possibly the work of Jörgen Wikström and conserved at the Norsk Folkemuseum in Oslo, depict a woman and a man in partial profile, wearing traditional dress. Their somber expressions and the fact that they do not look at the camera indicate that these are not photographs taken at the subjects' request, for example, as photographs to share with other family members or friends. Instead, as becomes clear when comparing them with other images in Valkeapää's work, they appear as documentary photographs aimed at recording the traditional dress of the photographed Sámi, as well as their racial features. This is also the case with image 4, which was produced by Prince Roland Bonaparte during his expedition to Norway in 1884, an expedition in which the prince aimed to investigate the racial biology as well as the traditional livelihoods of Sámi people. In contrast to images 2 and 3, however, here the pictured individual, a boy, is identified by name as Mikel Nielsen Ommar. He looks out at the viewer with a seemingly self-assured, almost defiant gaze, as he clutches his knife. The photograph repeats as image 157 in Valkeapää's book, and there, the photographer's placement of an identifying number 14 can be plainly seen behind the boy's left elbow. In this larger-format image, the boy looks somewhat less confident than on the front cover, and one can see that he is looking intently at the camera apparatus in front of him, appraising its operator with a reserved, suspicious eye. His clutching of the knife takes on new meaning. His leather gákti, fur-lined collar, felt hat, and coil of rope are visible in vivid detail. They are well-worn, even somewhat tattered. The final, right-hand image at the top of the dust jacket, image 5, is a photograph of a Sámi woman and her children and dog, produced by Borg Mesch. Mesch took a great number of such quasi-ethnographic, quasi-touristic photographs during his long career in Kiruna, selling them as postcards and as contributions to publications like *National Geographic* (DuBois 2014). The exoticizing and racializing practices of colonial discourse are illustrated here, but in a manner that does not initially call attention to itself. Instead, the gaze of the adults in images 2, 3, and 5 seem trained on the boy of image 4, who looks out at the viewer, much as do the reindeer of image 1. As elsewhere in his volume (see below), Valkeapää has constructed a family portrait of sorts here: one that gestures outward toward the Sámi viewer in a thoughtful, friendly, inclusive way.

The inside front flap of the dust jacket reproduces poems 31–33 of the collection, identifying them tacitly as important for understanding the collection as a whole. It is convenient for their placement on the dust jacket that these poems avoid the expressive placement of words on the page which Valkeapää employs so abundantly in many of the other poems of the volume. With lineation following an orderly and simple flush-left array, the flap reads:

31. govva
gova
govaid

govvái
govadasa govat
girjái
govvás máilbmi

32. mun sárggun dáid govaid áigái
geađgái, gárrái

álbmogiid
eallin
loktana
luoitá

go beaivi,
biegga

33. mun dearppan dáid govaid
geađgái, gárrái

dat lea fal nu hiđis

go lean dearpan bottaža
jámálgan, rohttásan

oainnuid oaidnit

In their English translation/adaptation of *Beaivi, áhčážan,* Ralph Salisbury, Lars Nordström, and Harald Gaski render these poems as follows:

31. image
the symbols
of the image

symbolize
the images of the image
varied
world full of images

32. I inscribe these images to time
on the stone, on the drum

peoples'
life
rising
falling

like the sun,
the wind

33. I beat these images
on the stone, on the drum

it is so slow

after drumming for a while
I am pulled into another world

to visions

The notion of creating images in stone and then on drums ties with photographs in the early portions of the work, particularly images 9, 10, 24, 25, 26, 27, 28, 29, and 30, which include stone *sieiddit,* shamanic drums and drum symbols, close-ups of rock carvings from the shores of Alta fjord (today a UNESCO World Heritage site), and a trove of carvings that first came to scholarly and popular notice with their archaeological discovery in the early 1970s. Through artful juxtaposition and ordering, Valkeapää suggests a unity between these varying works, suggesting a continuity in Sámi culture that reaches ten thousand years into the past.

As Gaski discusses elsewhere (2015: 252, 260), and as Dana notes in relation to poems 31–33 in particular (2003: 152–53), the lines of Valkeapää's poems reflect the poet's technique of elaborating the semantic range of lexemes he employs, a technique that Gaski relates to joik performance traditions (2015: 255). Here, the various meanings of the root *govva* are explored, in ways that relate to the ancient practice of image carving and painting—as detailed in the poetic context of the poems as they appear in the overall volume—but also here, on the dust jacket, as a sort of author's statement for Valkeapää's volume as a whole. In the volume, poem 31 suggests, Valkeapää creates images out of images, making or finding them *girjái*, a term that the English translators interpret as the adjective "varied" but a word that also can be read as the illative form of *girji*, meaning "into a book," a polysemy that takes on particular nuance when appearing on the volume's dust jacket. The poems seem to suggest that Valkeapää has made images of images, and placed them in a book, so as both to carry on an ancient Sámi practice of image making, and to propel himself, and with him, his audience, into worlds of the imagination, like a noaidi entering other worlds through drumming, joik, and trance. Coming out the year after *Ofelaš*, and following upon themes established in earlier anthologies of his poems, Valkeapää's text seems to echo and further the recovery of *noaidevuohta*, Sámi shamanism, as an heroic and valued past religious practice and a potent symbol of Sámi identity to be deployed metaphorically, strategically, in the present day.

Throughout the volume, Valkeapää alternates between page spreads that have a black background overlaid with photographs, white borders, and letters, and those employing a white background with black and gray images. And if the bulk of his poems are set in black font on white pages, some stand out in white font on black pages. Such is the case, for instance, with poem 562, near the very end of the collection, set alongside image 563, a shamanic drum with split drumhead, acquired by Prince Roland Bonaparte in 1884 and now conserved in Paris. The poem reads:

562. nu mun sárggun dáid govaid
geađgái garrái
áigái
munnje,
munnje iežanii
sárgu

dát govat
iežan govat
mu eara hámit
iežá bealit
mun

ja dál,
dál de dearppan
iežan sárggun
ollisin, easka
čavddisin

ja dan govas
in boađe ruoktot
šahten

dan govas
in boađe

in

562. this is how I inscribe these images
on the stone on the drum
in time
to me
to myself
is revealed
these images
my images
my other shapes
other sides
I

and now,
now I drum
draw myself
whole, finally
complete

and from this image
I will not return
again

from this image
I will not leave

ever

The echoes of the work's earlier poems, and the colonial implications of the defaced drum are evident and tie in disquieting ways to the disturbing visual reminders of Nordic race studies found in items 408–12 and intermittently throughout the collection. A Sámi audience is invited to consider the confusion, frustration, and disempowerment undoubtedly occasioned by such intrusive, reifying photographs, which transform the images of naked Sámi, or Sámi alongside strings of numerical formulas detailing the length of their heads, shape of the foreheads, and character of their noses, from putative evidence of outdated but lingering racial theories into evidence of the concrete mental and spiritual harm done by such colonial scholarly practices. The Sámi audience is invited to consider the human situations of the people subjected to these dehumanizing regimens and the abuse of power that made it possible for scientists of the Nordic majority cultures to compel Sámi to submit to such degradation. These are themes that will later be taken up again in Simma's *Give Us Our Skeletons* (1999), as well as Kernell's *Sameblod* (2017), as detailed below and in the coming chapter. Other later Sámi artists, such as Anders Sunna, have also taken up these topics, suggested obliquely and hauntingly in the tone of loss and finality inherent in poem 562.

Images 77–80 embody a technique of standing in solidarity with past Sámi subjected to such racialization, as Valkeapää inserts his own image from the film *Ofelaš* into a sequence of pictures of Sámi taken by Prince Roland Bonaparte in 1884 as part of his race biological investigations. But whereas the pictures of Kristine Andersdatter Gunnar (77), Anders Henriksen Valgiaberg (78), and Niels Nielsen Valgiaberg (80), all relatives of the poet, are depicted in somber front and profile "mug" shots, aimed at displaying fully their racial characteristics, Valkeapää's own images (79), although also two in number, both show a smiling and confident Nils-Áslat [*sic*] staring confidently out at the viewer. The space below these images is taken up by further photographs of Kristine and Anders with their family in front of their goahti in Tromsdalen, Norway (76; an image taken by Knud Knudsen and eventually conserved in Bergen), and of family members beside a lávvu during the summer in the Finnish arm (81; conserved in Helsinki). Valkeapää has in essence created a family album in these two pages out of disparate images produced for other purposes: the scientific goals of late nineteenth-century French race biology, the documentary ethnography of twentieth-century Norwegian and Finnish fieldworkers, and the feature film of Valkeapää's Sámi friend and collaborator Nils Gaup. It is an act of repatriation and decolonization, in which the images can now play entirely different roles, serving as markers of Sámi perseverance and intrinsic worth. The fact that the image of Valkeapää, where he is dressed in his Iron Age Sámi clothing for a feature film concerning legendary threats, conveys both the notion of looking to the past to recover continuity, and the essentially creative enterprise of such decolonizing work. When viewing this page spread, it is easy to understand what Valkeapää meant when he characterized his book as a family album for the Sámi people (Kulonen et al. 2005: 423).

As vivid and evocative as Valkeapää's strategic use of images, his poetry is even more effective to a reader conversant in Sámi language and culture. Gaski (2008) has written in detail about Valkeapää's "untranslatable" poem 272, a concrete poem where terms for varying behaviors and tendencies of a reindeer herd are placed on the page in imitation of the form and look of a herd. The words are situated in relation to where a reindeer of such gender, age, or behavioral tendency would be located as the herd moves across the landscape. Some reindeer lead, others follow; some stay close to the middle of the herd, some stray away at the edges. Valkeapää's placement of the terms transforms the book medium from a narrative to a *mapping* and represents in tangible form the deep wealth of traditional knowledge that surrounds reindeer husbandry among Sámi herders. In his examination of poem 558, Gaski (2015) has shown the elaborate and overarching thematic choices that Valkeapää incorporates into his poems, ones that link the various poems of the work into recurrent themes and motifs surrounding key symbols like the sun, the earth, the wind, noaidevuohta, images, and cultural continuity. These intricacies make reading *Beaivi, áhčážan* an endlessly rewarding and thought-provoking process, reminding the Sámi reader of the rich oral and cultural traditions that Sámi share, and that they must work to preserve and pass on to coming generations. Like a family album, *Beaivi, áhčážan* reminds its Sámi audience of its common past and the importance of working toward a positive common future.

Mari Boine's *Gula gula!* (1989)

Where Nils-Aslak Valkeapää stands out as the single most important figure for the recovery and transformation of Sámi joik, Mari Boine is recognized as perhaps the best known Sámi musician of her day. The overview below draws on the work of Richard Jones-Bamman (1993) as well as Thomas R. Hilder (2015) and barely scratches the surface of the abundant popular and scholarly writing on Boine's persona and career. In 1989, in the aftermath of *Ofelaš* and alongside Nils-Aslak Valkeapää's important but by then still obscure *Beaivi, áhčážan*, Boine's *Gula gula!* album helped stoke the interest of the Nordic majority populace in contemporary Sámi culture and inspired numerous Sámi artists to begin musical careers of their own.

The hard-hitting lyrics of Boine's debut album, *Jaskatvuođa maŋŋá/Etter stillheten* (1985; After the silence), had put into words the frustrations and outrage of young Sámi who had suffered under the assimilationist schooling and culture of their youth and were now hungering for a visibility and acceptance that seemed thwarted by a Nordic insistence on conformity. With spirited rock songs sung in vigorous northern Sámi, Boine set about to single-handedly reverse the erasure of Sámi voices and cultural expressions in pop media. She played off familiar styles and songs of the time: the album's first track, "Alla Hearra guhkkin Oslos" (Our High Lord off in Oslo), for instance, parodies Sr. Janet Mead's 1973 rock setting of the *Our Father* prayer, underscoring the high-handed control of Sámi culture evinced by Norwegian authorities in the distant capital. Her album called attention to the hypocrisy, complacency, and enduring racism of Norwegian society, challenging them to live up to commitments toward cultural inclusiveness and Indigenous rights that were being formulated in both Norwegian and UN legislation at the time.

As inspiring as Boine's first album was for a Sámi audience, it was her second release, *Gula gula!*, from 1989, that truly brought Boine into the limelight. The album bore a dual Sámi-Norwegian title: *Gula, gula! Hør stammmødrenes stemme* (Listen, listen! Hear the voice of ancestral women) and contained liner notes with the songs' lyrics in both Sámi and Norwegian translation. One of the tracks (no. 7, "Oppskrift for Herrefolk" [Recipe for a Master Race]) was written and performed entirely in Norwegian. Boine wanted her audience to understand her messages regardless of whether they spoke Sámi, but she also wanted to expose them to the sounds and power of her native language, in this album fused innovatively with the sounds of other Indigenous musical traditions and the eclectic, far-reaching styles of the emerging world music genre. Boine produced the album herself under her own label, IĐUT, but the album was also acquired by Peter Gabriel, whose label Realworld produced English translations for the songs and marketed the album internationally. Gabriel was also instrumental in inviting Boine to the 1991 WOMAD festival, which vastly enhanced her international exposure and contributed to her stardom in the Nordic countries.

Where *Jaskatvuođa maŋŋá* adopted whole the electric guitar/drum set sounds and techniques of international rock—even including a cut sung to the tune of John Lennon's "Working Class Hero" (Na darvanii jahkku)—*Gula gula!* incorporated the talents of immigrant and international musicians, like the woodwind artist Peruvian-Norwegian Carlos Z. Quispe, and offered a sound that fused diverse Indigenous musical styles and aesthetics into performances that were slow, at times nearly hypnotic, and full of distinctive instrumental backup and innovation. Raised in a Laestadian household in the small village of Gámehisnjárga, outside of Kárášjohka, Boine had little childhood experience of joik or other music outside of hymns. Yet in *Gula gula!*, she aimed to create her own brand of joik, fusing it with Native American styles while addressing questions of significance to Indigenous people worldwide, including the importance of protecting a threatened environment.

These aspects of her new sound are evident in her album's title track, "Gula, gula." Relatively lengthy at 3:43 minutes, the piece starts slowly, with Boine singing vocables, with yearning tones, augmented by an echo effect. After a little more than twenty seconds, she brings in her own rhythmic beating of a small hand drum, a new element in her performances that replaced her electric guitar. Her lyrics begin about a half-minute into the performance:

> Gula gula, nieida, gánda
> Gula máttut dál du čurvot
> Manin attát eatnama duolvat
> Mirkkoduvvot, guoriduvvot?
> Mirkkoduvvot, guoriduvvot?
> Gula jiena, nieida, gánda
> Gula máttaráhkuid jiena
> Eana lea min buohkaid eadni
> dan jos goddit ieža jápmit
> dan jos goddit ieža jápmit
>
> Listen, listen, girl, boy,
> Listen, as the forefathers call to you—
> "Why have you polluted the land,
> Poisoned, exploited it?
> Poisoned, exploited it?"
> Listen to the voice, girl, boy
> Listen to the voice of goddesses—
> "The earth is mother to us all
> If you kill her, we all die.
> If you kill her, we all die."

Part way through the verses, Boine's drumming is subtly backed by the unobtrusive sounds of a bass, emphasizing the pulsing, repeated rhythm of the melody and drumming. Boine's lines, steeped in images of ancestral wisdom and spirituality, are followed by a return to her singing vocables, allowing a Sámi-language audience to reflect on the pleading, scolding content of the two verses. The vocables are now accompanied with progressively more instrumentation, as the piece begins to acquire the weight and force of the full band. About a minute and three-quarters into the song, Boine returns to her lyrics with an additional two verses, sung with heightened, almost tearful, intensity:

> Leatgo diktán iežat báinnot
> Leatgo iešge mielde gilvvus
> Gula máttut dál dus jerret:
> "Itgo don muitte gos don vulget?"
> "Itgo don muitte gos don vulget?"
> Dus leat oappát, dus leat vieljat
> Lulli–ameriihka arvevuvddiin
> Ruonaeatnama geađgerittuin
> Itgo don muitte gos don vulget?
> Itgo don muitte gos don vulget?
>
> Have you let yourself become sullied,
> Are you playing along in the game,
> Listen as the forefathers ask you
> "Don't you remember where you're from?"
> "Don't you remember where you're from?"
> You have sisters, you have brothers
> In the rainforests of South America
> On the stony shores of Greenland
> Don't you remember where you're from?
> Don't you remember where you're from?

Boine sings another chorus of vocables before returning to a reprise of her original two verses and additional vocables as the background instrumentation grows progressively in volume and intensity. At last the entire piece fades into just Boine's plaintive solo voice repeating the vocables that had opened the performance.

The words of Boine's song reflect her programmatic aims. Addressing Sámi youth ("Gula gula, nieida, gánda" [Listen, listen, girl, boy]), Boine, in her early thirties at the time, adopts the authoritative tone of a concerned elder, joining her voice to beings personified in the song as ancestors and ancient goddesses, who are watching, in apparent dismay, the reckless environmental destructiveness of modern people, Sámi included. The scolding questions of the ancestors, and the stern warnings of the goddesses, aim to discomfort and chasten the listener, as the goddesses deliver the warning, "dan jos goddit ieža jápmit" (if you kill her [i.e., the Earth], we all die). If these words sound accusatory, they seem tame compared with the second two verses, which directly confront and interrogate the listener. The line "Leatgo iešge mielde gilvvus?" (Are you in on the game?) switches register from the elevated discourse of the ancients to the confiding tone of a contemporary, accusing the listener of complicity in the acts of destruction threatening the earth's survival. Here, the singer's persona rises to the fore, melding with the voice of the ancestors in the repeated question "Itgo don muitte gos don vulget?" (Don't you remember where you came from?). The verses inform the listener that brothers and sisters exist in the rainforests of South America and the rocky shores of Greenland, articulating an overarching Indigenous family whose other members have better preserved an awareness of the environment, its importance, and its sacrality. The past tense of the verb *vulget* suggests separation from the past, a loss of connection that now renders Sámi distant from their mother earth. Here, the message aimed at Sámi also applies to non-Sámi, as all Westerners are reminded of the essential truths we have forgotten: "Eana lea min buohkaid eadni/Dan jos goddit ieža jápmit" (The earth is mother to us all/If you kill her, we all die). In musical style and lyrical content, Boine adopts the voice of the Indigenous environmentalist, familiar from words attributed to nineteenth-century Suquamish Chief Seattle and important in environmental discourse of the day. At the same time, to a Sámi audience, she underscores an essential disjunction: Sámi have forgotten their Indigenous roots and values, which they should now, Boine's persona urges, recover and restore. In essence, *Gula gula!* is an invitation to Sámi youth to join in the process of recovering continuity paralleled and advanced by both *Ofelaš* and *Beaivi, áhčážan*. With the intensity of a revivalist sermon, Boine calls her audience to awareness and reform.

The success and personal momentum created for Mari Boine by her breakthrough album *Gula gula!* never subsides. In the decades that followed, Boine toured the world giving concerts, produced (as of 2018) some fourteen albums, compilations, and soundtracks, and became a cultural ambassador for Sámi people in relation to the Norwegian state. We discuss her Sámi version of "Mitt lille land" in the coming chapter and note her melancholic title track for the film *Guovdageainnu stuimmit/Kautokeino opprøret* (Kautokeino uprising). Boine sings at royal weddings and somber state memorials, speaks out on Sámi issues, and seemingly embodies in her presence and engagement the Sámi nation as a whole. In 2003, she was awarded the Nordic Council's Music Prize, the first Sámi artist so honored. In 2017, she released her first album in English, *See the Woman*, where the singer's concern for feminist issues, and connection to Indigenous writers from elsewhere in the world, comes to the fore. Boine continues to respond to current trends and to evolve as an artist. At the same time, this development does not lessen the singular iconicity and endurance of her 1989 album, *Gula gula!*, which continues to call out to its audience, Sámi and non-Sámi alike.

Aŋŋel Nieiddat/Angelin Tytöt/Angelit's *Dolla* (1992)

The meteoric rise of the girl group, Aŋŋel Nieiddat/Angelin Tytöt/Angelit, reflects the ways in which this sudden "Sámi boom" reached into the lives and careers of talented Sámi artists of the period. Born in the small community of Aŋŋel/Angeli in the early 1970s, sisters

Ursula and Tuuni Länsman and their friend Ulla Pirttijärvi were raised in a Laestadian Lutheran community that regarded joik as sinful. In a retrospective interview in 2015 (Ahvenniemi 2015), Ursula Länsman notes that the only music allowed in the Länsman home in her childhood were cassettes of Christian hymns that the girls' grandmother listened to. Ursula notes that her grandmother's singing style was reminiscent of joiks, but that no one dared mention such a thing at the time. Attending residential school some fifty kilometers away in Riutula, the girls watched programs like the American television series, *Dynasty,* and were eventually encouraged by their Finnish teacher to sing at a Sámi cultural gathering in Utsjoki in 1982. They made their first recording in 1987, a Christmas song with Mari Boine, but their real breakthrough came in 1992 with their first solo album, *Dolla* (Fire). Intended as a sort of parting event as the girls prepared to leave for college, *Dolla* catapulted the girls into fame. In the following seven years, their band played more than 350 gigs and attracted attention throughout the Nordic region, Europe, and Japan. Ursula Länsman states: "Kaikki alkoi yhtäkkiä oikein isosti. Minusta olimme aina enemmän saamelaiskultuurin lähettiläitä kuin muusikoita" (Ahvenniemi 2015; It all started in a big way all of the sudden. To me, we were always more ambassadors of Sámi culture than musicians). Band members came and went: Ulla Pirttijärvi went on to form her own group (Ulda), while guitarist Jonne Järvelä formed his own heavy metal band, Shaman, in 1996, later broadening to a more Finnish-focused folk-heavy Korpiklaani in 2003. Eventually, the enterprise grew tiresome to the Länsman sisters: as Tuuni Länsman-Partti reflects "Siinä vaiheessa kun Lapinpuku alkoi tuntua työhaalarilta oli aika lopettaa" (Heiska 2011; When Sámi dress began to seem like a work uniform, that's when it was time to quit).

Instrumental in the production of *Dolla* was Sari Kaasinen, part of the Sari and Mari Kaasinen duo at the center of the Finnish Karelian folk pop group Värttinä, whose breakthrough album *Oi Dai!* had appeared in 1991 to stupendous national and international acclaim.

Sari did the mixing on the *Dolla* album, which was recorded in Helsinki and released by Mipu Music, Sari's newly formed label. Mipu Music produced the subsequent three albums of Angelin tytöt as well: *Giitu* (Thanks, 1993), *Skeaikit* (Laugh, 1995), and *Girls of Angeli: The New Voice of the Earth* (1997). As Angelit, the Länsman sisters produced two further albums for Finlandia Records: *Mánnu* (Moon, 1999) and *Reasons* (2003). Like the Kaasinens' Värttinä albums, the albums of Angelin tytöt would front the energetic and powerful voices of the band's female vocalists, eventually backed by eclectic mixtures of traditional and contemporary sounds, played by a varying ensemble of Sámi and Finnish musicians that generally go unnamed on the albums.

Vivid cover art by Sámi artist Merja Aletta Ranttila depicts three naked women riding a reindeer, with the album's title *Dolla* (Fire) overset in simple white letters and the band's name in purple and white letters in the lower corner. Executed in orange and black, Ranttila's drawing appears in other colors as *Neitsyiden iltapäivä* (Maidens' afternoon) and conveys the lively and confident tone of the album, as well as its links to Sámi tradition and mythology (Ranttila 2019). Inset photos on the album cover and jacket show Ulla Pirttijärvi, Ursula Länsman, and Tuuni Länsman smiling in identical red and silver Sámi dresses, adorned with ample silver brooches and tassels; they are holding the drums they play in the album's cuts.

The album consists of sixteen pieces, some under a minute in length, others approaching three and a half minutes in duration. Of them, nine are listed as traditional, while four are composed by Ulla Pirttijärvi and one each by Ingor Ántte Áilu Gaup and Sara Máret Gaup. Ursula is credited with lyrics and/or composition on four cuts, and Tuuni as the composer of one. The album contains no liner notes or lyrics, leaving the materials contained, and their relation to traditional joik, unglossed. Illustrative of the traditional pieces in the collection is "Inguna gánda" (the Boy Inguna), cut no. 11. The 1:49 minute piece opens with syncopated drumming on the hand drums pictured on the album cover, the piece's sole instrumental accompaniment, which runs throughout the performance. After establishing a lively repeated rhythm, the three women enter the song, singing with clear enunciation and obvious verve: "Váiban čearbmat go njolgalastii Go Ohcejoganjálmái . . ." (The tired yearling trotted along toward the mouth of the Ohcejohka river . . .). These lines are followed by several additional lines of vocables repeating the melodic phrase over and over again, in which the women's voices diverge from unison singing to create harmonies and depth, alternating between solo and choral interludes. The same pattern of textual verse followed by vocables occurs for two more verses, the third a repetition of the first:

Gákcavárri lei báhcan čierrut
Go Inguna Gánda lei vuolgán . . .
Váiban čearbmat go njolgalastii
Go Ohcejoganjálmái . . .

Gákcavárri mountain was left behind to cry
When the boy Inguna departed . . .
The tired yearling trotted along
Toward the mouth of the Ohcejohka river . . .)

The piece ends with a return to the lone drumming that opened the cut, intimating a sense of a joik melody that continues without stopping while also introducing into the song a signal of closure and finality. As a traditional joik, the piece makes specific mention of several concrete places: the mouth of the Ohcejohka river and the mountain Gákcavárri. The town of Ohcejohka (Utsjoki) lies near the mouth of the river by the same name, where it joins the Deatnu (Tana) river forming the border between Finland and Norway. The town and river mouth lie some two hundred kilometers to the north of the village of Angeli. Gákcavárri (Kahcâvääri) lies roughly midway between the two villages, in an area of mountains, birch forests, and marshland at the northern border of the Muotkeduoddara (Muotkatunturi) wilderness area. The character of the boy Inguna is unglossed in either the song and album liner, although the implications are that he is an eligible and accomplished man who is making the journey to Ohcejohka with marked success, possibly leaving some broken hearts behind. The same recording is repeated in the band's later album, *Girls of Angeli: The New Voice of the Earth* (1997). There, as signaled by the album's English title, greater efforts are made to introduce the songs, and the piece (no. 8 on that album) is provided with a transcription of the Sámi text, along with a loose translation into Finnish, and a close translation of the Finnish into English. The piece is included as track 9 in a much reworked longer rendition (3:31 minutes) on the *Mánnu* album (1999), where the instrumental backup is expanded to include a standard drum set, electric guitar, electric bass, saxophone, synthesizer, echo effects, female voice backup, and a funky beat.

The band's explorations of modern rhythms and styles is illustrated by a cut from the group's fourth album, *Girls of Angeli*. Here, with a text credited to Pedar Jalvi and Tuuni Länsman, and musical arrangement credited to both Länsman sisters and Kimmo Kajasto, Pedar Jalvi's classic poem from 1915, *Muohtačalmmit* (Snowflakes), is quoted nearly verbatim for the first verse, followed by lines composed by Tuuni Länsman, all set to an appealing, danceable beat. The song opens with a catchy percussive rhythm backed by bass guitar, as Tuuni Länsman intones in rhythmic speaking voice Jalvi's famous lines:

Sattahallet áimmuid čađa
Hiljit gahččet muohtačalmmit
Gahččet geđggiid, skiriid ala
Vielgadin dan gokčá

Whirling through the air
Snowflakes softly fall
On stones and rocky ground
Covering them with white.

As the spoken words end, the women begin a spirited chorus of vocables ("Hei lo loilaa") that continues for several lines until being interrupted once again by Tuuni's recitation, this time with lines of her own creation. Tuuni repeats words or lines coyly in time with the backup percussion, sometimes speaking, sometimes whispering, with her text reproduced in the album liner notes as follows. (The liner notes again provide a loose translation into Finnish and a close translation of the Finnish into English, resulting in a text different from the translation presented below.)

Nohkas dál
Vuoinnas dál
Na eai dat gille roggat
Mehciid, eatnamiid roggat
Na eaihan dat gille boltut.
Eai dat beasa boltut
Vuoinnas dál.

Nohkas dál
Veajat fas morihit
Ja eana šaddá nanasabbon.
Eana šaddá nanasabbon.

Sleep now
Rest now
They cannot paw,
Paw in forests, lands
They don't have the strength to dig
They cannot manage to dig
Rest now.

Sleep now
So that you can awaken

And the earth will become stronger
The earth will become stronger.

The text supplied by Tuuni turns the poem into a lullaby, one in which the listener is assured that "eai dat gille roggat" (they will not be able to paw) while the listener sleeps: lines that imply a herder resting along with tired reindeer, who are unable to reach lichen or other grazing materials due to the fresh fallen snow. At the same time, *roggat* can refer to digging in the sense of mining, leading to the Finnish translation of the verb with *kaivata*, and the English as "quarrying." The final verse urges the listener to rest so that "Veajat fas morihit/ja eana šaddá nana-sabbon" (You can awaken/and the earth will become stronger). Where the lines appear at first homespun and simple, they also imply a symbolism that is left ambiguous, a message of strengthening the earth that ties in with the environmental and cultural agendas of much Sámi activism of the day. The practice of using lines from past Sámi writers, as Tuuni does here with the poetry of Pedar Jalvi, is one that Mari Boine takes up both in her *Goaskinviellja* album (1993) as well as *Bálvvoslatnja* (1998) and marks the fervent interest Sámi artists and activists have taken in their predecessors by pawing through the past. While presenting a light and danceable song, one emulated by later Sámi artists like Sofia Jannok and Anna Kärrstadt in their early recording *Du čalmmit* (Your eyes), Angelit creates a work that allows its Sámi audience members to take it as seriously and as philosophically as they wish.

The musical creations of Angelit perfected a winning combination of careful reproduction of past, traditional joiks, and creative composition of new ones. Sometimes songs are performed in a wholly traditional manner, without instrumental accompaniment and with the strong joik voices of the singers. At other times, the group plays with traditional materials, adding unexpected backup rhythms or instrumental backup and also changing the quality or tenor of their voices. In other numbers, the group offers entirely new creations, ones that nonetheless recall elements of traditional *luohti* enough to remind the listener of the group's emphatically Sámi identity. Sámi tradition is a joyful resource, to be used avidly by young and talented performers.

Characterizing Sámi cultural products of the recent past, Harald Gaski writes: "The new Sami art takes tradition seriously, looking back in order to find the way forward, at the same time helping to give a small group of people in the Arctic north a voice that can be heard much further than their numbers would seem to justify" (2011b: 52). The late 1980s and early 1990s were a time of optimism and experimentation for Sámi, as new recognition, expanding rights, and broader public support and interest for their culture seemed to suddenly emerge. Constitutions were emended, people cheered for Sámi film heroes, flocked to Sámi-language concerts, bought and played Sámi recordings, and read and relished Sámi literature. These positive developments occurred not only among the majority cultures of the Nordic countries (and occasionally the wider world, including continental Europe, the United States, and Japan), but also among Sámi themselves, who began to throw off the sense of shame and embarrassment that they had long ago internalized regarding their language and culture. It became exciting to be Sámi. With so much obvious goodwill, and so many marks of progress, it is not surprising that Sámi artists like Nils Gaup, Nils-Aslak Valkeapää, Mari Boine, and Aŋŋel Nieiddat sometimes downplay conflicts, locating them in the past, or referring to them metaphorically, while asserting a positive and productive present and future, when all the deprivations and wrongs of colonization would be put behind.

Of course, as the Álttá dam protest shows, achievements in dismantling Nordic colonialism had not occurred by chance or without fierce struggle, nor was the pathway to real self-determination for Sámi as clear and open as it may have sometimes seemed to Sámi of the late 1980s. Soon enough, Nordic state majorities began to grow less enamored of the Sámi, characterizing them as whiny and presumptuous and rekindling in subtle or overt ways the stereotypes and prejudices of the past. Internationally, white majority culture members in various Western nations grew tired of "multiculturalism" and "political correctness," projects they asserted had somehow "failed." Support for ratification of ILO-169 declined in Sweden and Finland, and even in Norway support for Sámi rights dwindled in the decades after 2000. In each of the Nordic countries, right-wing populist movements grew in popularity during the late 1990s and after, often capitalizing on negative images of the Sámi and ethnic or linguistic minorities as tools for mobilizing majority-member supporters. Sámi became (again) an unwanted Other, clinging to environmental safeguards that should be swept away in the interest of progress, or jobs, or profits. Yet despite these setbacks, the confident, playful, insightful, and strong musical, literary, and filmic creations of the Tjïekere era remained, as milestones of Sámi artistic achievements, and as sources and symbols upon which to build further, more strident works of Sámi artistic activism in the future.

4

Sijvo

The Momentum Underway

IN LATE JANUARY 2017, FINAL PREPARATIONS ARE UNDERWAY in the snow-cloaked town of Aanaar/Anár/Inari, Finland, located on the shores of the great lake Inari and home to native speakers of Northern Sámi, Inari Sámi, Skolt Sámi, and Finnish. In the town's streets, churches, hotels, tourist shops, grocery stores, and gas stations, anticipation runs high for the town's biggest annual event: a massive international Indigenous film festival entitled Skábmagovat (Pictures of the Arctic Night). The year is a momentous one. Billed jubilantly throughout Finland as the one-hundredth anniversary of Finnish independence, it is also the centennial anniversary of the first international Sámi meeting, held at Trondheim in February 1917, the nineteenth anniversary of the Skábmagovat festival, as well as the thirtieth anniversary of the début of *Ofelaš,* the singular Sámi film that propelled Sámi into the filmic limelight and helped establish a place for Indigenous filmmaking in the modern media market. The festival's website promises showings of Sámi and international Indigenous films at three different sites within the town: the Sámi Cultural Center Sajos (home to Finland's Sámi parliament and a prized venue for Sámi cultural events), the Siida Sámi museum (Finland's most prominent Sámi museum and Sámi tourist attraction), and the atmospheric Northern Lights Theater, built from snow to accommodate the festival's film screenings each winter. Amid promises of various documentary and feature films, the website lists an array of cultural institutions involved in organizing and financing the festival: the Friends of Sámi Art, the Siida Museum, the Sajos Cultural Center, the Skábma Indigenous Film Center, the Sámi Education Institute, the International Sámi Film Institute, and the Finnish Broadcasting company YLE. Of this impressive list, perhaps only YLE existed in quite the same way thirty years earlier, when *Ofelaš* first took the world by storm. Sámi filmmaking, film consumption, and film promotion have come of age.

And Skábmagovat, which began in 1999, is not alone: Indigenous film has become the focus of popular festivals at Sundance (1994–), the Toronto ImagineNATIVE film festival (1998–), among many others. In Sápmi, Skábmagovat is augmented by the activities of the International Sámi Film Centre/Institute (2007–/2014–) and the Dellie maa Indigenous Film and Art Festival (2014–). Films like Chris Eyre and Sherman Alexie's *Smoke Signals* (1998), Zacharias Kunuk's *Atanarjuat: The Fast Runner* (2001), Phillip Noyce's *Rabbit-Proof Fence* (2002), and Niki Caro's *Whale Rider* (2002), have made Indigenous films and topics common in art house and independent film circles, and have increased awareness of Indigenous issues and attracted both wider audiences and talented new filmmakers to the field.

In Aanaar (Inari) Sámi, the term *sijvo* denotes a good snow crust able to support skis, reindeer, or other animals. It most often develops in the late winter or early spring, when the snow has been on the ground for some time, warming, partly melting, and then refreezing. Sijvo is a positive term and is used here to describe the remarkable productivity and success of Sámi artists in the areas of commercial music and film since the 1980s. With the development of the Sámi Grand Prix as a musical showcase and professional threshold, and a variety of other Sámi music festivals, as well as the development of a high-profile, internationally recognized Sámi film industry, Sámi artists have found institutional and artistic support for their experiments and contributions. The rise of YouTube as a major venue for produced videos has allowed Sámi artists to reach the larger world in new ways, combining popular music, visual images, and dramatizations in sophisticated, sometimes ironizing manner. These stand alongside images and messages disseminated in public or private circles through social media. Sámi use technical, musical, and visual products to call attention to Sámi issues and to continue the activist spirit that melded music, image, and public demonstrations in the Álttá conflict of 1979. In comparison with earlier decades, Sámi artists today enjoy a well-established media visibility and market, one receptive to activist interventions. It is in this sense that we describe the 2000s as the "Sijvo era."

Contexts and Controversies

The "Sijvo era" of Sámi media coincides with a period of mounting international recognition for Indigenous rights alongside a continued or even intensified industrial push to exploit resources found in the lands and waters that sustain Indigenous communities. It is a time when the internet has become commonplace among affluent Westerners, and also among canny Indigenous activists. In understanding these trends in Sápmi, we acknowledge trends arising among Indigenous communities in Greenland, the United States, Mexico, Canada, New Zealand, Australia, and elsewhere in the world, trends that Sámi can learn about in ever speedier and more complete ways, as the internet has expanded in the lives of Nordic peoples.

Repatriation is an important development in the rise of Indigenous rights during this period. In the United States, the protracted struggle of American Indian activists to compel government-funded museums and institutions of higher education to return human remains and other sacred objects to the communities from which they were taken revealed the inherent racism of state-supported science, whose practitioners labored throughout the nineteenth and twentieth century to justify colonization and exoticize and marginalize Indigenous people. The activism of Maria Darlene Pearson (Hai-Mecha Eunka), a Yankton Dakota woman, led to the Iowa Burials Protection Act of 1976, building momentum for the eventual passage of the landmark Native American Graves Protection and Repatriation Act (NAGPRA) of 1990, which set forth a framework for dismantling state collections of human remains and inappropriately acquired sacred objects in all US public institutions. The act created a new focus for Indigenous communities to develop frameworks to receive and honor returned remains, and signaled a legal context of nation-to-nation negotiation between the US federal government and Native American nations that honored the country's historical treaties with native communities but contrasted with federal and state policies of earlier eras of the twentieth century. Meetings mandated by NAGPRA obligated museum curators and directors of institutes holding Native American remains to sit down at the bargaining table with tribal representatives to listen to and respect native decisions regarding artifacts and articles. The American legislation and the expected pushback it initially received from archaeologists and museum curators became familiar in Europe through Danielle Peck and Alex Seaborne's 1995 BBC documentary, *Bones of Contention,* a program that influenced Simma's film, *Oaivveskaldjut* (1999; Give us our skeletons) and helped lead to a movement among Sámi more broadly to compel Nordic states to enter into similar processes of repatriation.

The legacy of museums as colonial institutions received substantive response in the Nordic countries through changes in museum institutions. In the nineteenth century and first half of the twentieth century, Sámi materials were collected and displayed in various Nordic national museums, for example, the Swedish Historical Museum, the National Museum of Finland, the Norwegian Folk Museum, and Stockholm's Nordic Museum. During the Tjïekere period, more attention began to be paid to the idea of creating Sámi museum collections in areas close to Sámi populations, and ensuring that exhibits reflected the interests and understandings of Sámi people rather than colonial or national views. A Sámi museum opened in Inari already in 1963, and in 1986 the Saamelaismuseosäätiö (Sámi Museum Society) formed to help further develop the institution, which became known as Siida (Siida 2017). A new building was constructed in 1998, and close contact between Siida and the National Museum of Finland has ensured that more and more of extant Sámi materials are conserved and displayed in Inari. A similar process occurred in Sweden, where the Nordic Museum and Swedish Historical Museum permanently loaned artifacts to the Ájtte Museum (opened 1989) in Jåhkåmåhkke (Jokkmokk), particularly sacred artifacts like noaidi drums and stone sieiddit that had been acquired and displayed as part of the Swedish colonial project (Silvén 2016). Museums like the Várjját Sami Musea in Unjárga (Nesseby; opened 1983), the Saemien Sijte South Sami Museum and Cultural Center in Trøndelag Snåsa, the Sámiid Vuorká-Dávvirat Sámi Collections in Kárášjohka (Karasjok), and Ä′vv Saa′mi Mu′zei in Njauddâm (Neiden; opened 2017) provide distinctively local presentations of Sámi cultures and livelihoods, while revised exhibits in museums like the Nordic Museum, Norwegian Folk Museum, and Tromsø University Museum endeavor to better respond to Sámi viewpoints and preferences. Numerous local Sámi cultural centers supplement and further localize these important acts of Sámi self-representation and self-definition. Where earlier museum exhibitions depicted Sámi as racially distinct and historically declining, more recent exhibits emphasize the evolving, dynamic nature of Sámi culture and the place of Sámi in present and future Nordic societies.

On the wider international plane, the passage and ratification of the UN ILO-169, in which Norway played a leading role, and the formation of a Permanent Forum on Indigenous Issues in 2002—in which Norwegian Sámi leader Ole Henrik Magga served as the organization's first chair—marked new international attention to Indigenous rights, and led to the development of the UN Declaration of the Rights of Indigenous Peoples (UNDRIP). The momentum established in Nordic legal contexts, and symbolized so intriguingly by the artistic works of the Tjïekere era, had ripple effects internationally. Progress in Indigenous self-determination occurred in Greenland, which achieved home rule in 1979 and further elements of self-rule in 2009. In northern Canada, a part of the Canadian Northwest Territories became separated into its own territory, Nunavut, allowing for Inuit autonomy. Similar movements among Inuit in northern Québec and Labrador ensued. Often begrudgingly, states began to acknowledge the legal rights of Indigenous communities to shape their futures themselves, even when that might entail breaks with colonial states. Notions of regional autonomy and home rule began to suggest pathways for control over local lands and waters unlike any achieved at this point in Sápmi.

At the same time, processes of globalization and neoliberal economic consolidation, facilitated by the growth of the EU and international free trade agreements in various parts of the world, such as NAFTA (the North American Free Trade Agreement), began to shift decision-making power from states to transnational authorities, economic organizations, and industries, creating a framework in which national policies became subject to adjudicative processes aimed at serving the goals of optimized cross-border commerce. These conflicting trends became vividly juxtaposed in the public imagination through the "Zapatista netwar" of 1994 (Denning 2000; Sassen 2004: 76). Commencing on the very day that NAFTA went into effect, Indigenous farmers and villagers of Chiapas formed the Ejercito Zapatista de Liberación National (EZLN, or the Zapatista National Liberation Army), staging insurrections against the Mexican government and calling for local autonomy. As government-controlled media sought to isolate and malign the movement, Zapatistas funneled their own reports of events and positions to sympathetic allies in Mexico and across the world, who uploaded them to websites, LISTSERVs, and other internet venues, creating what became known as "LaNeta." The counternarrative created by the posting of Zapatista viewpoints was soon supplemented by the words and images of observers who flocked to the region to engage with the Zapatistas and document and disseminate their accounts of the events. The internet became a forum for debating and resisting neoliberal institutions, attracting thousands of supporters internationally and leading to broader anticapitalist movements and actions elsewhere (Ronfeldt et al. 1998; Belausteguigoitia 2006; Alonso 2014). As the term "globalization" began to take on more unseemly connotations among intellectuals throughout the West in the years that followed, the internet became a place to speak out about what seemed insidious processes of consolidation and disenfranchisement at work in the world.

Emboldened by international attention to Indigenous issues and growing access to digital products and networks, Indigenous activists have made abundant use of the internet to focus attention on local situations and mount protests. Often their activities are directed internally at Indigenous community members themselves, but frequently, the internet is used to call out to potential allies elsewhere, galvanizing support against national or corporate forces aiming to disempower or coerce Indigenous communities, as the various articles of the edited volume *Indigenous People and Mobile Technologies* (Dyson et al. 2016) show. The Canadian Indigenous movement Idle No More and the Sámi Suohpanterror have supplemented in-person protest and resistance with online meme- and gif-based activism that can be readily shared and disseminated through social media.

One of the challenges of providing an overview of Sámi activist media in the "Sijvo era," is the prodigious array of talented artists and works emerging in each of the Nordic countries. In order to provide an overview of the main features of recent Sámi film and music in relation to activism more generally, our discussion is limited to a selection of four films and four music videos, reflecting some (but by no means all) of the leading figures in the enterprise during this period. Two of the artists profiled–Nils Gaup and Mari Boine–have been selected in part because their work carries over from the period discussed earlier, but in new ways. The other six artists vary in age and background but reflect some of the prominent directions Sámi image making has gone since the late 1990s.

Paul-Anders Simma's *Oaivveskaldjut* (1999)

Simma's 1999 film *Oaivveskaldjut* (Give us our skeletons) furnishes a good example of the ways in which past injustices to the Sámi can be unearthed, interrogated, and rectified as a process of decolonization. The film centers of the crusade of Nillas Somby as he endeavors to recover and repatriate the skull of his ancestor Mons Somby, executed in the aftermath of the Guovdageaidnu uprising of 1852. Narrated by Somby, a key participant in the Álttá demonstrations, the film's narrative recounts the details of the 1852 event, the Álttá dam demonstrations, Nordic participation in race biology, eugenic policies and forced sterilization practices in the early twentieth century, and the resistance of majority member scientists to relinquish their collections of human remains or fully comprehend the colonial implications of their scholarly practices. Archival footage and interwar era racist propaganda films are interspersed with the bleak narrative of modern colonial realities in Norway and the hard work of repatriating even two of the thousands of Sámi remains currently housed in anatomical institutes in each of the Nordic countries.

Somby's attempts to recover his ancestor's remains were successful only after a 1996 television program exposed his efforts to a wider public, which led the Norwegian Sámi Parliament to formally petition for the return of the skulls. The University of Oslo returned the skulls in November 1997, and they were buried in the Kåfjord cemetery, an event that forms the outset and finale of Simma's film. Interviews included in Simma's documentary predate the University of Oslo's decision and reflect the scholarly controversy regarding calls for repatriation during the 1990s. The project won prizes at the Lübeck Nordic

Film Days of 1999 and the Tampere International Short Film Festival of 1999, and represents Simma's most successful film to date, eclipsing his earlier films, including *Let's Dance* (1992), *Duoddara árbi* (1994a; Legacy of the tundra), *Guovza* (1994b; Bear), and *Sagojoga Minister* (1997; Minister of state).

The film opens on a wintry day in the Kåfjord cemetery, cutting immediately to archival footage of the Álttá demonstrations, and then a slow pan up the body of Niillas Somby, in which his artificial arm is evident. Somby declares that he will not enter the church, which he identifies as part of the domain of the colonizers. The film shows a small casket, containing the skull of Mons Somby, being lowered into a grave, as numerous journalists' cameras capture the moment. Eerie background music makes the scene seem unsettling, even macabre.

After a further sequence military and police force scenes at the Álttá demonstrations, the film cuts to a domestic scene of Niillas Somby dressing his small child. Somby introduces himself and explains that he lost an arm and eye but does not regret his actions. The scene fades to a black background featuring the skull of Mons Somby, with the title "Give Us Our Skeletons!"

The film uses the testimonies of elderly Sámi, direct descendants of Aslak Hætta and Mons Somby, as well as Somby's narration and a series of evocative cartoons, to relate the painful story of the 1852 Guovdageaidnu uprising. With a soundtrack of drumming and the joiking of Wimme Saari, the sequence recounts the events as remembered in Sámi legends, with Norwegian officials toasting and laughing, God crying at the injustice, and the soul of Aslak Hætta rising into the sky as a willow grouse after his execution. Somby's narration ends with the skulls of the two executed men being caught up by a soldier and transported to Oslo to be deposited in the basement of the Anatomical Institute. The scene cuts to a close-up of Mons Somby's skull, missing a tooth, and marked with the number 46 on the forehead.

The scene cuts to an interview with Niillas Somby at home, in which we learn that he strongly identifies with the executed men and even wonders sometimes if he is a reincarnation of Mons Somby. He recounts having sent a letter to the Norwegian government and University of Oslo requesting the return of Mons Somby's skull already in 1985, but that he did not receive an official reply until late August 1995. In the reproduced and quoted letter, University of Oslo Professor Per Holck rejects the request, characterizing Somby's ancestor in passing as more "en brutal morder enn en martir for samenes sak" (a brutal murderer rather than a martyr for the Sami cause). Holck's animosity toward the premise of repatriation, and more broadly toward Sámi assertions of Indigeneity, become evident later in the film, as he, unidentified, matter-of-factly discusses the collection at the Anatomical Institute, the importance of not returning human remains, and his doubts about the actual Indigeneity of the Sámi, doubts that he had expressed in written scholarship in 1991 (Holck 1991: 199). A stark face-off is presented between the sorrowing Sámi descendants of Mons and Aslak, epitomized by Niilas as well as the executed men's elderly grandchildren and other descendants, and the callous and facetious Norwegian professor, who rejects their pleas offhandedly as he sits in a white lab coat at his desk, surrounded by human skulls. This conflict becomes developed further in following scenes, which contain archival footage of past Sámi life and troubling depictions of the experiences of the Sámi protagonists. Repeated slow pans of some of the three thousand Sámi skulls stored at the institute punctuate the narrative of captivity and intransigence. The film depicts Niillas Somby in Oslo learning of the extent of Norwegian race biological research and cuts to a Finnish archeologist in Aanaar, recounting the regrettable way in which people raided unearthed Sámi bodies from a local cemetery and made away with bones as souvenirs. The narrator recounts Nordic skull collection as a tool for asserting the racial superiority of Norwegians, Swedes, and Finns over their Sámi neighbors.

Niillas's presence in Oslo furnishes the opportunity for a flashback recounting of the events of the Álttá dam protests and Nillas's pivotal role in them. News footage of the protests depicts the horses, dogs, police cars, helicopters, and policemen arrayed against the protesters, as the soundtrack captures the sounds of the conflict and the chanted slogan "Elva skal leva" (Let the river live). Niillas's role in the failed explosion of a bridge that led to the loss of his arm and eye, and imprisonment in solitary confinement, are detailed in his own words. Niillas's flight to Canada, where he was given asylum by a Canadian First Nation, is detailed with footage of the event. Somby relates that he learned the importance of honoring one's ancestors during his two years with the tribe, and his quip—that he would rather lose an arm and eye than a head—closes the sequence, as the film shows a scientist in white gloves fondly stroking a preserved skeletal hand. By referring to the Álttá protests as the "second Sámi revolt," and tying the events to physical body parts and bones, the film suggests a direct link between the Guovdageaidnu uprising, the confiscation of the skull of Mons Somby, the Álttá dam protests, and Niillas Somby's efforts to recover the skull from the collection in Oslo.

Rather than focusing solely on the nineteenth-century context of the Guovdageaidnu uprising and the story of the skulls' repatriation in the film's present, the documentary devotes considerable attention to the institutionalized racism of the era leading up to World War II. Cuts from German propaganda films advocating eugenic sterilization and newsreel footage of sporting events and beauty pageants during the late 1930s illustrate the deep and openly racist discourse of the era. Intercut with images of Nordic race scholars like Anders Retzius and Valdemar Lundborg and further interview footage from Holck, the documentary underscores the nationalist and racist motivations behind the Nordic collection of Sámi remains and the ongoing maintenance of collections like that of the Anatomical Institute. The Sámi experience of these scholarly practices is demonstrated by footage of Somby sharing racist images with his child as they flip through pages of Nils Aslak Valkeapää's *Beaivi, áhčážan*. An interview with Skolt Sámi Sinaida Feodoroff conveys the confusion and fear Sámi experienced as racial studies researchers descended upon the village of Inari and forced its women to submit to nude photography in the 1930s. An interview with Maj-Britt Faggi of Jåhkåmåhkke illustrates the sorrow and regrets of women subjected to forced sterilizations and electroshock therapy. Statistics concerning the tens of thousands of women subjected to such procedures in Sweden, Finland, and Norway suggest a national policy aimed at ridding the Nordic states of its troublesome Indigenous population. An interview with Swedish scholar Gunnar Broberg provides context for seeing the hunt for Sámi skulls, the development of intelligence tests, and eugenic sterilizations as instances of a longstanding and dominant twentieth-century tendency to try to reduce human culture and diversity to easily handled formulas and numbers, a tendency that dehumanizes and disenfranchises Indigenous people.

The final segment of the documentary details the relatively swift about-face of University of Oslo officials when petitioned by the Sámi Parliament for the return of the skulls of Mons and Aslak. Where Mons's skull is recovered fairly easily and returned to the Somby family, Aslak's skull has gone missing and is eventually relocated in a collection in Denmark, where it ended up as the result of a collector's trading it for two Greendlandic Inuit skulls. The events are matter-of-factly described by a Danish official, adding a further touch of irony and absurdity to the film's long account of injustices. The funeral service at Kåfjord is depicted, along with Niillas standing outside the church in the cold, refusing to enter. Preparations for burial of the skulls are shown, with the implication that the place selected for their burial will soon be covered by a parking lot. The graves of Somby and Hætta can be seen today at Kåfjord, and although not covered by parking lot pavement, they nonetheless suggest the turbulent history of racism inherent in events from the time of the 1852 uprising to the present. The film closes with a reading of the 1854 Norwegian condemnation of the men, which calls attention to the barbarity of their act and the disrespect for authority that, the statement avers, represents a threat to all civilization.

Simma's film shares with the earlier *Ofelaš* a Sámi fondness for underdog protagonists. Niillas Somby is depicted as wounded yet perseverant, battling authorities that seemingly hold all the cards. But whereas the villainous Čuđit of the earlier film are remote and historicized, the persecutors in Simma's documentary are the present-day Nordic states and state functionaries. We are shown a state still firmly tied to the racist discourse of the past, through a colonial apparatus ready to deploy police whenever challenged by Sámi protestors. It is a state that maintains educational/scientific institutions that are still deeply invested in exoticizing, and depicting as inferior, the Sámi populace whose lands the state has appropriated. In an interview sequence conducted in English, Holck displays his institute's oldest skull, which, he asserts, is not Sámi but rather Norwegian. Anachronistically applying the term *Norwegian* to a skull dating to millennia before the existence of the Norwegian state, Holck demonstrates the specious logic of Norwegian colonialism that depicts Sámi as "other" and "foreign," while unproblematically imagining a Norwegian nation deeply rooted in the region's past. That this logic connects Nordic states with a Nazi past, and that Sámi petitions for redress are routinely brushed aside, lends a dark ominousness to the colonial present of modern Nordic states.

Nils Gaup's *Guovdageainnu stuimmit/Kautokeino opprøret* (2008)

The topic of the Guovdageaidnu uprising surfaced again in Nils Gaup's deeply sentimental *Guovdageainnu stuimmit/Kautokeino opprøret* of 2008. Appearing a decade after Simma's *Oaivveskaldjut* and fully two decades after Gaup's own groundbreaking *Ofelaš,* Gaup's film represented—particularly for a Sámi audience—an instance of a well-known filmmaker approaching a well-known topic. The film was well received, particularly in Norway, where it was nominated for six Amanda awards and won four, including one for best leading actress (Anni-Kristiina Juuso) and best score (Mari Boine). Yet despite the prominence of its topic and participants in a Sámi context, a broader Norwegian and international audience by and large greeted Gaup's portrayal of the events surrounding the rebels beheaded in 1854 as shocking and heretofore unknown revelations, characterizing the film as a revealing exposé of nineteenth-century Norwegian state hypocrisy and colonialism. Drawing on familiar international images of the complicity of state churches in colonial suppression of Indigenous cultures and the villainy of capitalist entrepreneurs in the disenfranchisement and abuse of Indigenous people, Gaup's film offered audiences tangible evidence of Norwegian participation in the colonial wrongs of the past. Grounded in the uprising's nineteenth-century context, the film seemed to speak less of present-day situations than does Simma's *Oaivveskaldjut*. Yet the film's closing scene, with its call to Sámi to keep hope alive despite all oppression, aims explicitly to link the historical narrative to the present-day experiences and decolonizing acts of modern Sámi, including the people involved in the film. As both Kari-Synnøve Morset (2009) and Cato Christensen (2012) have shown, the film *Guovdageainnu stuimmit* became an "event" in Norwegian society, provoking wide-ranging discussion concerning colonization, state culpability for past wrongs, and the importance of recognizing and reversing the disenfranchisement of Sámi people that led to the historical uprising and the ongoing frustrations of Sámi today.

Both Morset and Christensen discuss the role media coverage played in shaping public reception of the film. The premiere at the Tromsø International Film Festival in January 2008 was accompanied by an academic seminar on the topic of the uprising, featuring academics such as Nellejet Zorgdrager, whose authoritative dissertation analyzes the uprising in careful detail (1989), community members, descendants of the participants of the uprising, and actors and artists involved in the film. An online exhibit about the uprising was mounted by the Tromsø State Archives and Sámi Archives, and reviews and features appeared in most or all of the major Norwegian newspapers. Media attention concerning the film had started already years before, as Gaup worked to raise funds for the production, making the film's début a much-anticipated event. Gaup's status as a descendant of the strong-willed Elen Skum, a leader in the rebellion—something the filmmaker had not known until after completing his work on the film—added weight to the notion of the film as the Sámi side of a story that had only been described before from a Norwegian perspective. The confidence of the Sámi community in Gaup's ability to tell the story responsibly was attested to by leading Sámi intellectuals, including Ole Henrik Magga, also a descendant of those involved in the uprising. The Norwegian Minister of Culture and Church Affairs Trond Giske stated that "the film is more important than a hundred textbooks" (Christensen 2012: 67), underscoring the pedagogical value of the film. Christensen argues that journalist Anders Giæver's much-publicized dissenting view of the film as condoning terrorism and religious fundamentalism helped galvanize broader support among other journalists and public figures, who came to characterize the film not as a factual reporting of the historical events but as an ethnopolitical act of memorialization and decolonization.

The film opens to melancholic piano and orchestral music composed by Mari Boine, the opening interlude of her *Biegga Bárdni* (Son of the wind), the theme song that Boine composed especially for the film. Beneath a colorless overcast sky, a grassy hillside comes into view, over which Norwegian soldiers are marching, rifles held aloft. Two wagons emerge in the procession behind them, containing two condemned prisoners (Aslak Hætta and Mons Somby, played by Mikkel Gaup and Nils Pedar Isaksen Gaup), flanked by soldiers and community members walking. As Sámi women are heard conversing as they hurry toward the place of execution, a young boy in Sámi gákti is seen following the procession. Suddenly he is intercepted by a Sámi adult (Máhtte, played by Aslat Mahtte Gaup), also in gákti, who escorts him to a nearby cabin and instructs him to wait for him there. The boy asks if the soldiers have brought his mother and the man (his father) says no. The scene cuts to an outdoor stage, upon which a minister is waiting, then back to the boy, now looking out of one of the cabin's glassless windows. A narrator's voice is heard: a woman, tender and thoughtful, addressing the boy, sympathizing with his confusion and his missing of his mother—the narrator—who was not there, and regretting his seeing something that was not right for him to see. She notes the passage of seventeen years since they were together. The boy manages to wriggle out of the window and hurries to the seaside, where he sees the first of the men kneel before the executioner's chopping block. As the screen dwells on the confused face of the child among the assembled onlookers—some Sámi, some Norwegian—the narrator states that she will explain the events that happened, so her son can pass on the story after she is gone. The gray and windy scene fades to white as a flashback ensues, introducing the audience to the woman behind the voice, a shivering Elen Skum (played by Anni-Kristiina Juuso) standing watch over her family's reindeer herd in wintry weather.

Much as in the opening titles of *Ofelaš,* the film's opening scene frames the narrative as a quintessentially Sámi story passed on from generation to generation, a notion that is reinforced in the film's closing scene as well. But whereas the written titles at the opening of *Ofelaš* ascribe the narrative to an otherwise unspecified Sámi oral tradition, passed down for a thousand years, *Guovdageainnu stuimmit* uses a soft and melancholic narrator's voice, the voice of a woman and mother, to indicate that the story will be a personal one, tinged by all the personal details and perspectives that one would expect of a story told about a lived event, one that occurred in the past but that has deeply affected the narrator and her inscribed audience, her son. In the process, the filmic suspense that could have surrounded the narrative of the uprising is dispensed with: there is no doubt that the events will culminate in an execution, and that the two men we have seen in the wagons will lose their heads. Instead, however, a different set of questions is introduced: the identity of the boy and his mother, and their relation to the uprising that is billed as the main topic of the film. This shift announces to the viewer clearly that the film will not approach the events in the manner of a historical report or documentary, but rather from a quintessentially personal and human perspective.

As the flashback develops into the film's main narrative, Elen recalls the frequent absence of the boy's father due to the temptations of the "čahppes viessu" (black house), that is, den of iniquity. A conversation with an older woman sharing in the watch (Elen's mother, played by legendary joik artist Inga Juuso) makes it clear that Máhtte has a recurring drinking problem and that his drinking debts are being paid for by forfeiture of reindeer. The film's central conflict is introduced as we see the Sámi family struggling with the effects of addiction to a substance, that, as the narrative soon makes plain, is made available by unscrupulous members of the Norwegian majority, with the full support and backing of the Norwegian state. The boisterous and uncouth tavern run by local merchant Ruth (played by Swedish actor Mikael Persbrandt)—in the center of the village of Guovdageaidnu, nearly adjacent to the church—emerges as one of the key recurrent settings of the film. Here, we witness Máhtte's drunken behavior, his irrational attempt to take supplies for himself against Ruth's orders, Elen's refusal to pay for Máhtte's bar tab, Máhtte's outraged shoving of the Rev. Stockfleth after the latter has caned Máhtte's mother-in-law, Elen's accidental igniting of a table as she angrily pushes aside alcohol she is offered, the frustrations and machinations of the evil Ruth, the final killing of Ruth's henchman Bucht (played by Peter Andersson), and the burning of the building to the ground, not before it has caused the downfall of Aslak, Mons, and Elen. The "čahppes viessu" is revealed as a locus of evil in the film, a place that contrasts with the bright Sámi camps and sun-drenched mountainsides that the Sámi and their reindeer share—places of community, solidarity, and peace. Visually, Gaup erects contrasts of settings and lighting that mirror the villain/hero dichotomies characteristic of his narrator's storytelling style, and emphasizing Ellen's controlling point of view.

Within this narrative structure, and perhaps as a further delineation of Elen's views after years of unjust incarceration, Gaup makes the essentially colonial nature of the Guovdageaidnu situation abundantly clear in his film. Through their local monopoly on trade and aggressive marketing of alcohol, the rapacious merchant Ruth and his perpetually unhappy wife aim at extracting as much wealth as possible from the local Sámi, amassing ill-gotten riches to finance their planned grand return to Álaheadju (Alta) as prosperous leading citizens. The Norwegian characters' frequent references to "civilization" and to "respect for authority" employ a colonial discourse already familiar to audiences through representations of English and American colonization. While turning their backs on the state church and its nefarious representatives, the Guovdageaidnu rebels also form a buying cooperative that travels regularly to Gáresavvon (Karesuando) to purchase supplies, thereby breaking Ruth's monopoly. Sámi recourse to basic legal protections is depicted as constantly and systematically blocked by Norwegian authorities, who collude with Ruth in his efforts to disenfranchise and impoverish the Sámi in the interest of securing his own wealth. The Sámi characters' frequent reference to their herds as both their wealth and their basis of economic survival, as well as Aslak's noting that the buying collective can prove a profitable venture for the family, underscore the fact that the Sámi as depicted in Gaup's film are not opposed to capitalist enterprises or the operation of a market. Rather, they oppose discriminatory economic frameworks designed to rob and silence them.

Alongside but largely subordinated to this economic narrative, Gaup sets up the religious conflict that had previously been portrayed as the primary cause of the conflict between the Guovdageaidnu rebels and the shopkeeper Ruth in historical accounts of the uprising. Having decided to buy supplies in Gáresavvon, the family is shown arriving at the village as one of the Rev. Lars Levi Læstadius's church services commenced. Aslak and Elen enter the church to warm up and listen to the preacher, while Máhtte, clearly hungover and out-of-sorts, lingers outside. Eventually he, too, enters the church, in time to hear Læstadius's stirring words regarding the evils of drinking. Fainting in response to the preaching, Máhtte is shown from above lying unconscious in the middle of the church, attended by Læstadius, Elen, and Aslak. An instantaneous cut to a lone flying bird conveys the spiritual conversion of the moment, after which the scene depicts the congregation departing the church, as Elen asks Læstadius for help regarding the liquor sales back home in Guovdageaidnu. Læstadius gives her copies of his pamphlets and tells her that she must take matters into her own hands. She leaves, smiling obediently and, seemingly, with a sense of hope at last. The next scenes give evidence of the conversion suggested in the church scene. Máhtte is shown washing himself as an appreciative Elen looks on. He then does active work around the camp and interacts with his eager son. Elen and Máhtte together spearhead similar transformations for other addicts and begin to assume a leadership role in the community's spiritual life.

While certainly paying attention to the religious underpinnings of the Guovdageaidnu uprising, the film refrains from delving into Læstadian beliefs or practices to any extent. When the nascent Læstadian community is depicted back in Guovdageaidnu, they appear measured and academic, quietly reading the Bible and Læstadius's works aloud until they are accosted and attacked by the newly arrived Rev. Stockfleth. Gaup's film directs attention toward Læstadian Christianity as an anticolonial response rather than as a theological movement per se. This is similar to his handling of shamanism in *Ofelaš*: attention is focused on the communal, political function of the religious tradition for the good of the Sámi collective, while leaving the details of the tradition's worldview, doctrines, or practices–its soteriology and ritual, to use Fitzgerald's (2000) terms–suggested but not detailed. This move can be seen as a gesture of respect, but also avoids the potential of the film becoming viewed as a proselytizing tool for Læstadianism.

Where Læstadius is depicted warmly, the film's portrayals of the Norwegian clergy are on the whole much less glowing. Here the portrayals again reflect the point of view of Elen, as she describes each of the men in ways that relate directly to how they assist or resist her efforts to save and restore the troubled souls of the community. First there is the drunken and debauching Zetlitz, pictured drinking in the back room of the tavern, lasciviously grabbing the barmaid, and never uttering any lines during the film. Then there is the sly, authoritarian, and abusive Stockfleth (played by Bjørn Sundquist), the black-clad, raven-like, mean-tempered minister who couches his acts of oppression in honeyed and sanctimonious discourse. Things get worse and worse for Elen and her family as the minister sets his sights on breaking her will and forcing the wayward Sámi into conformity. Her angry characterization of Stockfleth as a priest of the devil is the main act leading to her initial one-and-a-half year prison term, later expanded to seventeen years after the killing of Ruth and Bucht. The visiting Bishop Juell (played by Nikolaj Coster-Waldau) clearly takes the Sámi's side against their local oppressors and is depicted as warm, forthright, and reasonable. Stockfleth's ill-fated successor F. W. Hvoslef (played by Hallvard Holmen) is depicted as clueless and wooden, despite his central role in the actual events of the uprising. In Elen's telling, he is a marginal figure at best, since he arrives after the situation has deteriorated to the point of utter desperation for Elen and her family. Hvoslef's chief role in the film is to offer the two condemned men absolution for their sins, which both men resolutely refuse, leaving the minister puzzled and tongue-tied. Viewers could–and in reviews following the début of the film did indeed–take issue with some of these portrayals, particularly of Stockfleth, Juell, and Hvoslef, as Christensen (2012) details in his analysis of the film's initial reception. Yet to do so misses the point of Gaup's narrator, who acts as a lens coloring all details of the narrative, and particularly those associated with Elen's family and her community's spiritual welfare. The film presents its story as openly and naturally partisan in this respect, underscoring in so doing the right of Sámi to have explicitly *Sámi* perceptions of their past.

The film's step-by-step presentation of the painful cat-and-mouse between Elen and her powerful Norwegian adversaries Ruth and Stockfleth shows the continual worsening of the family's economic and social position, as each act of resistance on the part of the Sámi leads to more draconian reprisals. The family loses its reindeer, its freedom, its status in the community, and even the lives of its members as a result of refusing to accept the unjust ultimatums of the local merchant, minister, and magistrates. Yet in the closing scene of the film, a serene Elen, now aged, tells her grown son that the family has retained its most valued possession: hope. Addressing the son as the two sit beside a campfire on a headland by a lakeside at the close of day, Elen describes hope as a spirit that jumps from heart to heart and generation to generation and that is like a spring breeze predicting a warm summer. As she urges her son, now a young man, to hold onto that hope, she speaks seemingly to all Sámi. The scene fades to black, after which captions inform the audience that the heads of Mons and Aslak were shipped to Oslo for study and not returned to their descendants for proper burial until 1997. The captions suggest the historicity of the film, further bolstered by the closing execution scene, which follows closely details of the event recounted in Norwegian newspapers of the time (Gripenstad 1990: 107)

Simma's *Oaivveskaldjut* locates its emancipatory potential in revealing unpleasant suppressed history and symbolically condemning it through the formal demand for the return of the skulls of the two men executed as a result of the Guovdageaidnu uprising. In contrast, Gaup's *Guovdageainnu stuimmit* seeks to bring into the open not a suppressed history so much as a covert counternarrative, the understandings of injustice and oppression that the descendants of the uprising's many participants harbored and passed down from generation to generation while the Norwegian state's version of the events went unchallenged. Where Simma's film argues for a de-objectification of Sámi—a rejection of a reduction of Sámi culture into racial categories and scientific characterizations—Gaup's film argues for allowing Sámi to be the *subjects* of their own history: interested, eloquent, and intentional. His portrayal of Elen is a portrait of a complex and imperfect woman who loses much in her struggle against more powerful adversaries. Yet her fervent strivings for her family, her community, and principles of justice shine clearly throughout the film, particularly in contrast with the hypocrisy and opportunism of her Norwegian opponents. And as such, she provides a hero at least as great, if not more so, than the clever budding noaidi Aigin in Gaup's earlier *Ofelaš*.

Mari Boine's *Bas riikkažan* (2009)

In 2009, director Hans Lukas Hansen and coproducers Ole Eliassen and Sindre Sæbø of Norway's TV2 invited Mari Boine to perform a rendition of Ole Paus's popular song "Mitt lille land" (Boine 2009; My little country). Paus had composed the light, country-style song in 1994 as part of a campaign to convince Norwegian voters to authorize Norway to join the EU. The song describes Norway's scenic landscapes and secure and positive social life, ending with an evocative but obscure verse:

> Mitt lille land
> Der høye fjell står plantet
> mellom hus og mennesker og ord
> Og der stillhet og drømmer gror
> Som et ekko i karrig jord
>
> My little country
> Where high mountains stand fixed
> between houses and people and words
> And where silence and dreams grow
> Like an echo on barren ground. (DuBois 2017: 600)

The TV2 series of performances invited popular musical artists of Norway's multicultural present to perform the song each in their own way. Filmed in the areas of Norway in which they made their homes, the artists reworked the song in terms of rhythm, backup music, tempo, and style to create their own distinctive versions. Film footage of the singers performing was intercut in the broadcasts with footage of

Norwegian landscape, images of warm social conviviality, and scenes of sorrow or pain—funerals, protests, people in hospitals, et cetera. The renditions were then aired as part of the series *Dokument,* an investigative journalistic news program that frequently focused on social and environmental issues. It was perhaps the thought-provoking intercutting of images inherent in the aired renditions that helped lead to the central role the song came to play later on, when its performance became centrally featured in public ceremonies marking the Oslo terrorist attacks of 2011 (DuBois 2017: 600–601).

Mari Boine's rendition is the only one to date to forego the song's Norwegian text. Instead, in recognition of the status of Sámi as a national language of Norway, Boine opted to sing a translated North Sámi rendering of the song composed by Rawdna Carita Eira. In a news release published August 29, 2009 (Søum 2009), Boine expresses her admiration for Ole Paus and her excitement about the impending performance. She also describes the work of translation and how it has "lagt vekt på at Norge er et hjem for flere kulturer. Særlig godt liker jeg linja Et hjem, du er et hjem for alle oss" (laid emphasis on the fact that Norway is a home for many cultures. I especially like the line "a home, you are a home for all of us"). Significantly, this line finds no counterpart in Paus's original, yet it is not further discussed in the brief news release. The song lyrics that Boine eventually performed are reproduced below, along with a translation that Rawdna Carita Eira generously provided for this study:

Bas riikkažan,
don jiehtanasaid jiellat
nástegovat du čiŋahit.

Bas riikkažan,
go stuora bárut máraidit,
du njávket litnasit.

Leat ruoktu min buohkaide.
Du sallii mii dorvvastat.

My little land,
you treasure of giants
adorned by constellations.

My little land,
as great waves thunder
they gently caress you.

You are home for us all.
In your embrace, we all seek comfort.

The song's first line "Bas riikkažan" closely and artfully reproduces the denotation and warm connotations of Paus's original "mitt lille land." Several other lines in the Sámi text also hearken back to images presented in the Norwegian text. But Paus's ambiguous image of silence and dreams—growing "like an echo on barren ground"—is replaced in the Sámi text with a much more concrete statement of the nation and its responsibilities: "You are home for us all. In your embrace, we all seek comfort." The verb at the close of the piece is used in contemporary Northern Sámi for acts of giving shelter and also for the granting of political asylum. As such, the lines have an overt political tone enmeshed and partially contrasting with the evocative image of the nation as a parent extending welcoming arms to its denizens, both human and animal. Boine chose to emphasize this ideal of an inclusive Norway in her Norwegian interview, alluding quietly to the rising tide of xenophobia and intolerance that was then plaguing Norway, as well as other Nordic countries. Yet the eventual broadcast of the song contained no subtitles, and its Sámi text was only comprehensible to audience members who speak Northern Sámi.

The song was first broadcast on Norwegian television in late August, 2009, and soon was uploaded on YouTube. A TV2 Facebook post of November 25, 2009 shares the YouTube address with readers. The broadcast version presents Boine singing her song to the accompaniment of a West African *kora*. Distance shots of Boine walking amid the rocks and waters of the rugged North Norwegian coast alternate with close-ups, in which the singer, pictured in partial profile, turns to look directly into the camera, singing in a serious and forceful manner. The topical intercuts of the piece begin with a man beholding a large statue of Jesus in a church, and include other images of shamanic and Indigenous religious ceremonies. Also included are images of mountains, a sports fisherman, reindeer, an explosion that may be connected with mining, an aerial shot of a tanker ship, ducks struggling in the aftermath of a massive oil spill as a salvage worker attempts to vacuum away oily sludge, the burning of what looks like a small flag on a terrace of a public building, with Norwegian news cameras trained on the act, and a woman amid a crowd of protesters in a prominent Oslo square covering her mouth in horror. Cuts of Boine show her disappearing and reappearing as she advances toward the camera, adding an aura of mystery that seems to play on majority images of Sámi and other Indigenous people as cryptic, somber, and magical. This superficial reading of Boine as a sort of Chief Seattle stand-in is upended, however, for anyone conversant in Sámi, who sees instead Boine's stare as insistent, serious, and direct.

The environmentalist message of the intercuts would have been easily comprehensible to a Norwegian audience member attuned to the program *Dokument*, and plays in ironizing ways off the lines of the Sámi translation. Where Paus's original text makes mention of a little country "Der havet stryker mildt og mykt" (Which the sea strokes mildly and softly), Boine describes a land where "stuora bárut máraidit, du njávket litnasit" (great waves thunder, they gently caress you). In the film piece, this line coincides with the intercut of an apparently stranded ship and subsequent images of a massive oil spill suggestive of the Full City oil spill that occurred in July of 2009, when an oil tanker ran aground off the island of Såstein, Norway, causing a massive oil slick that fatally injured thousands of sea birds and other wildlife. Much as in the Álttá protests, an easily comprehensible environmentalist message is overlaid upon a less obvious but nonetheless thoroughly engaged call for cultural pluralism and minority culture rights. This same meshing of environmental and Indigenous agendas recurs in works of later artists and activists.

Sofia Jannok's *Áhpi* (2013)

From the time of her initial début in the early 2000s, along with Anna Kärrstadt in the Aŋŋel nieiddat-inspired duo Sofia och Anna, through multiple Sámi Grand Prix and Swedish national Melodifestivalen entries, and eventually in a series of well-received solo albums (Čeaskat [2007; White], *Áššogáttis* [2008; By the embers], *Áhpi* [2013; Wide as oceans], *ORDA* [2016; This is my land]), Sofia Jannok has adopted a progressively more openly activist stance, using her music and celebrity status to speak out on issues of crucial importance to her—particularly Sámi and broader Indigenous rights, especially as related to a threatened environment. She notes with certain pride that this stance is a longstanding part of her familial and local identity: Paulus Utsi, the influential poet described in earlier chapters of this study, was Sofia's great uncle, and the Luokta-Mávas Sámeby in which she grew up has produced important cultural and political leaders for Sámi people, such as Israel Ruong and the contemporary Sámi politician Lars Anders Baer.

The development of a politically engaged stance, and Jannok's conscious and canny use of media to extend the reach and effects of her musical interventions are illustrated well in the YouTube video produced to accompany the title track of Jannok's third album *Áhpi* (Jannok 2013a; Wide as oceans). The video (Jannok 2013b) was directed by Sámi filmmaker Oskar Njajta Östergren of Bautafilm, the second chair of the Sámi Filbmabargiid Séarvi (Sámi Filmmakers' Association) and an accomplished filmmaker and documentarist in his own right. Uploaded to YouTube on October 15, 2013, the video had garnered more than fifty-eight thousand views at the time of this writing (2018).

The video begins with the low sound of blowing wind, accompanied by an image of tall meadow grass and the name Sofia Jannok. The song's use of unglossed recorded natural speech in Sámi—recurrent in a number of the album's tracks—conveys a sense of an ongoing Sámi discourse in which the present song is to be interpreted. In this case, audio of Jannok interviewing her parents about the meanings of the word áhpi is included at the outset of the track. A line drawing of a Sámi brooch appears over a gray snowscape of mountains and fields, identifying the video as part of a series produced to accompany the album, and gradually facilitating the audience's realization that the video will be entirely in black and white. As the song's insistent and beckoning instrumental sequence begins, the scene shifts to a dramatically silhouetted man skiing in the mountains, a bright sun appearing just over the horizon. Here the song's lyrics begin:

> Olmmoš gal lea áhpi.
> Ii leat geahčige.
> Muhtimat leat jeakkit.
> Muhtimat mearat.
>
> Son lei ábi viidodat.
> Ii lean geahčige.
> Álggus orui aktonas
> Loahpas agibeavvi áhpi.
>
> áhpi, go áhpi, áhpi.
>
> Son lei ábi čábbodat
> Gáddeguoras gilddii

Vahágis gáiddai fávlái
iige gáddái boahtán šat.

áhpi, go áhpi, áhpi.

Olmmoš gal lea áhpi.
Das ii geahči lea.

In the notes to the YouTube video, Jannok has provided a translation of the text:

People are like oceans.
There is no end.
Some are like the boglands.
Others like the sea.

He was wide as oceans
with no end in sight.
Appearing lonesome at first
Seemingly endless at last.

endless, seemingly endless, endless

She was the beauty of the ocean
Glimmering at the shore.
Happened to drift out to the deep
Never returned to the beach.

Endless, seemingly endless, endless
Endless, seemingly endless, endless

People are like oceans
They have no end.

The translated lyrics are prefaced by a note by the singer, which states:

> This is a song about suicide. I wrote it as a tribute to those who left and comfort to us they left behind, when brothers and sisters went across the ocean, the endless tundra, and never returned. The suicides among indigenous youth are far too many. The exploitation pushes people away. When earth cries, hearts die. This video reflects that with photos from exploitation areas in Sápmi (Alta and Gállok among others), and the struggle for existence and human rights that has been going on for hundreds of years. We are still here. Love and respect, Sofia. (Jannok 2013b)

The video proceeds to develop these points by intercutting footage of Jannok singing the song with six different sets of images: slow-motion footage of an increasingly perturbed man skiing, eventually abandoning his skis on a mountain top and marching away without them; slow-motion footage of an evidently distraught young woman running through the forest, coming to the seashore (revealed as the site of the opening image of blowing grass), resolutely removing her belt and other clothing and disappearing into the waves; Jannok wielding a can of spray paint as she intently writes something on a wall; historical images of the Álttá demonstrations; still images of current environmental degradation in the Nordic region; footage of the 2013 Gállok mine protests; and a single image of Sámi leader Elsa Laula seated alongside other Sámi women in a group photo from the early twentieth century. The video's black and white format makes the elision of these disparate elements more complete, as the video advances visually the argument put forward in Jannok's public statement, that is, that environmental degradation—illustrated by Álttá and Gállok—helps lead to feelings of sorrow and frustration that can lead to suicide among Indigenous youth: "When earth cries, hearts die."

The song's lyrics closely mirror the first two elements of this complex layering of images, while making no explicit mention of the environmental issues depicted so powerfully in the video. In the persona of the skiing man—described without gender ascription in the Sámi *son* (he/she: a third-person singular pronoun that refers to either a male or female human being) but designated as "he" in the provided English translation—we see a man alone and lonely, eventually trudging off toward the horizon with little likelihood of return. By abandoning his skis, he signals his abandonment of a life that has been rendered impossible by the processes of colonialism. The footage makes use of sharp black and white imagery: the man's dark clothes and often silhouetted profile contrast markedly with the stark whiteness of the winter mountain landscape. In the persona of the woman who enters the waves, we see the lyrics "son lei ábi čábbodat" translated in the provided gloss as "she was the beauty of the ocean." The filmic depiction of her actions are executed in more grayed and subdued tones than the footage devoted to the skier, creating a visual contrast between the two recurring storylines. At the same time, her action exactly parallels that of the man: she abandons the clothing and belt essential to her survival in response to an experience of an existence under colonialism that fails to provide what she needs for a meaningful or effective life. As the English version puts it, she "happened to drift out to the deep/never returned to the beach."

The visual unfolding of these impending suicides occurs piecemeal over the course of the song, in slow-motion scenes, with relatively long pauses in action and characters frozen in contemplation. In contrast, the predominantly still images of environmental degradation occur in swift staccato, shown in sync with the song's instrumental backup. In close succession, the video presents an onslaught of images—including open pit mines, a wind farm, a pool of mine tailings, a hydroelectric dam, masses of power lines, pine trees being timbered and hauled, and a dead reindeer—before returning to footage of a distressed Jannok, eyes closed, singing the second verse of her song. Here, iconic images of the Álttá protests are shown in succession, beginning with the famed shot of the demonstration slogan "Elva Skal Leve!" (Let the River Live!), written in black on a snow bank in front of protesters' tents and a lávvu. These historic images, again, are presented in rapid succession, moving from depictions of the protests at Álttá to those in Oslo, to a depiction of male and female police carrying away protesters. Here the flow of images is interrupted by the static image of Laula and other women, included with subtle panning (i.e., Ken Burns effect). Where the image of the women is vividly clear, the footage of Jannok singing is blurred, dark, and partly obscured by shadow, with her glinting jewelry standing out and incomplete depictions of the singer's head and torso in semiprofile. The video intercuts images of the skier flinging snow away and the swimmer removing and throwing aside her belt and shoes. From there, footage of police removal of Gállok protesters echoes the earlier Álttá images before the film returns to Jannok singing and a second set of historic Álttá protest images, intercut seamlessly with images from the Gállok protests. Given the swift succession of images and the overarching black and white format of the video, it becomes difficult for a viewer to separate Álttá and Gállok images, helping underscore a continuity of Sámi resistance to colonization that stretches back a century and that remains important today. The sequence then gives way to Jannok once again depicted spray-painting her as-yet-unrevealed text. The video presents the swimmer disappearing beneath crashing waves and the skier walking away from the camera, dwarfed by the mountain landscape, until the scene cuts to a depiction of his abandoned skis and poles, left lying on a mountaintop, with the sun again glinting at the horizon. As the song enters into its final quiet phase, the scene cuts to the seascape, with the woman's abandoned belt and the empty seascape, brightly glinting in the sunlight. As the song's instrumental coda comes to an end, the video cuts at last to a full view of the large graffiti artwork that Jannok has been contributing to throughout the video. As a dimly visible Jannok departs from the scene in slow motion, and the video's opening sounds of blowing wind return, the viewer is left to behold the declaration "Leat Dás Ain," eventually overlaid with the English gloss in bold white capital letters "We Are Still Here."

Amid this seemingly pessimistic theme, the video holds out three images of hope: the evident resolve and energy of the Álttá and Gállok protesters, the visionary calm of the fleeting image of Elsa Laula and her compatriots, and the video's final reveal of the spray-painted text.

Throughout the song, Jannok is figured as both a describer of these interlocking situations—the sorrow of Indigenous suicide, the degradation of the natural environment—and a powerful voice of resistance, pleading through her impassioned singing for a change of heart among the world's powerful that would turn away from the exploitative practices destroying the Indigenous world at present. Jannok's tearful expressions, captured through close-ups of her body and face, contrast with the calm resolve of Elsa Laula and the bold enunciation of Indigenous perseverance encapsulated in the video's final image. In many ways, the video's defiant final statement predicts the refrain of Jannok's 2016 song in English, "We Are Still Here."

While engaging the environmental theme evident in Mari Boine's *Bas riikkažan,* the *Áhpi* video makes a point of articulating the theme from a Sámi perspective, in which some of the technologies hailed as "green" are castigated for their adverse effects on Sámi livelihoods and nature. Hydroelectric power—popular among environmentalists of the 1960s and 1970s—had devastating effects on wild fish stocks and spawning and figured centrally in Sámi activist discourse and the poetry of people like Paulus Utsi, Jannok's great uncle. The Álttá protests were mounted against a proposed dam. Similarly, wind farming has been strongly criticized by Sámi reindeer herders, who have noted the equipment's negative effects on reindeer health and welfare. By placing images of these industries alongside those of open-pit mines, forestry, and a dead reindeer, the video suggests a societal approach to nature that is destructive, not only of the environment but of Sámi culture. The video's final image unites its disparate elements into a singular statement of presence, persistence, and resistance to the processes of destruction and alienation that beset individuals and the environment alike.

Jon Henrik Fjällgren's *Manne leam frijje* (2015)

The musical career of Jon Henrik Fjällgren illustrates both the complex ways in which celebrity can figure in modern media-driven stardom and the canny ways in which artists can harness fame for causes they care about. Fjällgren emerged abruptly on the Swedish national stage through his 2014 appearance on the Swedish equivalent of *American Idol*, *Talang Sverige*. Born in Colombia and adopted by a South Sámi family, he grew up as part of the Mittådalen reindeer husbandry siida. Although he had already released his first album at age sixteen, it was his *Talang Sverige* appearance at age twenty-six that propelled him to national prominence. In that performance he appeared in traditional Sámi dress, singing a vuolle he had composed about a deceased friend Daniel and playing a subdued piano keyboard accompaniment. Fjällgren's powerful voice and evident strong emotion captured the hearts of the studio audience and celebrity judge panel alike, and Fjällgren received a standing ovation for his prize-winning song. A YouTube video of the performance (Fjällgren 2014) has garnered nearly eleven-million views from the time of its 2014 appearance to the time of this writing (2018). Fjällgren released a subsequent album (*Goeksegh*; Fjällgren 2015a) and began a series of performances on prominent national stages.

In 2015, Fjällgren entered the Swedish Melodifestivalen, the national song contest that selects the Swedish contestant in the annual Eurovision Song Contest. Fjällgren came in second in the Swedish national competition, and returned to compete again in 2017. Fjällgren's 2015 "Manne leam frijje/Jag är fri" (2015b; I am free), one of only three songs in the competition's final twelve *not* composed and performed in English, represented a complex celebration of traditional joik, melded with modern dance rhythms, haunting lyrics, and an exuberant and memorable performance routine. Co-written by Fjällgren, Erik Holmberg, Tony Malm, and Josef Melin, the stage version video of "Manne leam frijje" begins with a full body view of a man and woman dressed in blue Sámi gákti and leather leggings and boots facing each other and holding hands. The music starts with a powerful percussive buildup as the camera cuts to a shadowy heap of gnarled branches resembling assembled firewood or discarded reindeer antlers. Behind it is pictured the white drumhead and one can see the drummer beating out the song's rhythm. A cut from above shows the Sámi man inviting the woman to dance with him, and the couple soon begin an energetic and affectionate couple's dance. In some performances of the song during the competition, flashing floor lights evoked the notion of a campfire, while in others, the dancing couple were accompanied by a real burning fire, along with artificial fog. The fire contributed to the scene's key effect: a Sámi couple in traditional dress engaged in a somewhat formal but thoroughly stylish romantic dance. Different eras and styles are artfully melded in the scene as the camera pulls back to locate Fjällgren on an adjacent, slightly higher stage, beginning his joik sequence of the song. Where the dancers are dressed in fairly predictable blue and red traditional dress, Fjällgren is arrayed in a full leather gákti that both recalls the lines and styles of traditional South Sámi dress yet looks strikingly contemporary. Behind him, one can see for the first time the three female chorus members of the ensemble, dressed in long flowing fabric outfits that are suspended in the air behind him. While Fjällgren joiks, looking directly at the camera, the chorus members provide softer backup chorus in Swedish:

> I det regn som faller
> Innan natten blivit dag
> Står vi före stormen
> Tillsammans bara du och jag
>
> I den vind som blåser
> Vilar våra andetag

In the falling rain
Before the night has turned to day
We stand before the storm
Together just you and I

In the blowing wind
Our breath rests

As Harald Gaski has suggested (personal communication), the mystical appearance and staging of the chorus, their outstretched arms and choreographed moves, combined with the chorus text's images of rain, wind, and daybreak, suggest the supernatural, perhaps an evocation of the three Áhkkát goddesses said to reside beneath the goahti or lávvu in traditional Sámi cosmology. The camera swings between images of the chorus, close-ups on Fjällgren, and occasional returns to the drummer and two dancers, still joyfully revolving on the thrust stage.

Two-thirds of the way through the carefully choreographed performance, Fjällgren drops to one knee and adopts a speaking voice, noting his status as a joiker and speaking the song's title "Manne leam frijje, frijje" (I am free, free). In the Melodifestivalen final performance, Fjällgren added a further statement in Swedish: "Sverige, den här joiken—den är er" (Sweden, this joik, it's yours), gifting the joik and its significance as a Eurovision song contest entry to the Swedish nation. The implication of the statement, greeted by cheers from the arena audience, was that Swedish viewers—song contest voters— could receive and acknowledge this gift by voting up the song. The performance ends with Fjällgren shouting "Tack så mycket" (Thank you so much) and leaving the stage. In the end, a majority of voters did not choose to acknowledge Fjällgren's gift in the hoped for manner, selecting instead a song in English. Yet the power and implications of Fjällgren's act far outdistanced the song contest itself, becoming a potentially affirmative and even healing enunciation of an acceptance of Sámi culture as a treasure for Sweden to embrace, celebrate, and sustain. Fjällgren's personal history as an adoptee, his performance's vibrant meshing of ancient, traditional, and modern elements, the combination of South Sámi and Swedish words, and the upbeat tempo and setting of the musical number, created a richly nuanced enunciation of Sámi as an integral part of modern Sweden and its engagement with the world, both international and Indigenous.

Jörgen Stenberg's *Vuortjis* (2013, 2015)

Jörgen Stenberg furnishes a fourth example of the canny uses of media for political purposes in Sámi popular music during the Sijvo era. Stenberg is a Forest Sámi reindeer herder and joiker from Malå, Sweden. Along with maintaining a career as an active herder, Stenberg performs both traditional joiks and modern adaptations at festivals, social events, and clubs, often delving into archival materials to develop his repertoire. Gifted with a powerful voice and sensitive performance style, he often combines joik performances with personal viewpoints concerning the different ways in which colonization continues to play a role in modern Swedish Sámi experiences.

On August 8, 2013, in anticipation of a forthcoming compact disc, Stenberg uploaded to YouTube a memorable rendition of the traditional joik, "Vuortjis/Kråkan" (Crow), performed along with modern instrumental backup. The performance combines a short traditional joik that imitates the cawing of a crow with a menacing hard rock backup with a catchy tune and virtuoso instrumental riffs. In the August 8, 2013 version (Stenberg 2013), the YouTube video features Britta Marakatt Labba's famed embroidered crow tapestry, which depicts a flock of crows transforming into policemen who converge on a Sámi community to harry and make demands. Labba, part of the Máze group, was central in the Álttá era use of art to depict and criticize Nordic institutionalized racism. The video contains a slow pan of Labba's long tapestry and ends with a statement from Stenberg, repeated in the notes section of the YouTube upload page:

Vuortjis (Kråkan)

Kråkan har alltid legat lätt i min mun, velat jojkas. För en tid
sedan
betraktade jag Britta Marakatt Labbas bild Kråkorna. Att se
hur kråkorna
sakta förvandlas till poliser som motar bort de kämpande för
Altaälvens
överlevnad berörde mig djupt och fick mig att förstå kråkans
underliggande betydelse—en symbol för överheten.

Alta, Biedjovággi, Gállok, Storliden.

Jag hoppas att jojken når ditt sinne, ligger lätt i din mun.
Överheten, de höga herrarna, ska jojkas.

Crow

The crow come easily to my lips as a subject to be joiked.
Some time ago I became acquainted with Britta Marakatt Labba's picture Crows. Seeing the crows slowly transform into policemen who oppose those fighting for the survival of the Alta river moved me deeply and led me to understand the crow's underlying meaning—a symbol of authority.

Alta, Biedjovággi, Gállok, Storliden.

I hope the joik reaches your consciousness and comes easily
to your lips.
The authorities, the men in power, must be joiked. (Stenberg,
2013)

On August 28, 2015, activist Tor Tuorda, in cooperation with Stenberg, uploaded a new version of the song (Stenberg 2015a), combining live footage of Stenberg and his band performing the piece with intercuts of crows, footage of the Gállok mine protests of 2013, and a sampling of the voice of attorney Hans Forsell, equivocating on the rights of Sámi people to make demands on the Swedish state on the basis of their status as an Indigenous nation. Forsell's arguments were made during a May 2015 court case in Jiellevárri (Gällivare) concerning the rights of the Girjas sameby reindeer herding community to limit hunting and fishing activities in the lands used by reindeer herders for calving. Forsell's arguments attracted international attention for their incorporation of race biological concepts and seeming disregard of Swedish recognition of Sámi Indigenous status, enshrined both in the Swedish constitution and in the Swedish ratification of the UN Declaration on the Rights of Indigenous Peoples.

In an August 28, 2015 Facebook post introducing the new version to fans, Stenberg writes: "Gállok och Alta. Rasforskning och småviltsjakt. Oavsett hur överheten talar sitt maktspråk är kulturen mitt vapen, jojken mitt spjut" (Stenberg 2015b; Gállok and Alta. Race biology and small game hunting. Regardless of the language of power employed by the government, my weapon is culture, and joik my spear).

In the YouTube upload information space for the new video, Tuorda writes,

> ny version, nu med mina bilder från Gállok 2013 och advokaten Hans Forsells torra stämma som blottar statens arrogans och okunskap. Vreden präglar Jörgen Stenbergs jojk Vuortjis–kråkan, samma figur som Britta Marakatt-Labba använt på sin odödliga bild från Altaupproret. Daniel Wikslunds brutalt drivna stråke kastar tusen iskalla knivar genom luften. En jojk som var Same-SM i Malås största behållning. Tack Jörgen Stenberg och ditt fantastiska band! Motståndet växer!

I rättegången där samebyn Girjas stämt den svenska staten kommer här ett belysande citat av statens advokat Hans Forsell, som också upprepas i musikvideon:

Statens "inställning är också, att samebyns påståenden om att samerna är ett ursprungsfolk, saknar betydelse i målet. Sverige har inte några internationella förpliktelser att erkänna särskilda rättigheter för samerna, vare sig dessa anses vara ett urfolk eller inte."

New version, now with my pictures from Gállok 2013 and the lawyer Hans Forsell's dry voice that reveals the state's arrogance and ignorance. Anger characterizes Jörgen Stenberg's joik Vuortjis—the crow, the same figure that Britta Marakatt-Labba used on her immortal image from the Alta Rebellion. Daniel Wikslund's brutally delivered fiddling casts thousands of ice-cold knives through the air. A joik that was the greatest asset of the Same-SM organization in Malås. Thanks Jörgen Stenberg and your fantastic band! The resistance grows!

In the trial in which the Girjas Sameby sued the Swedish state, the state attorney Hans Forsell delivered the illustrative words quoted in the video:

"The state's position is also that the Sameby's claims that the Sami are an Indigenous nation has no bearing on the question. Sweden has no international obligations to recognize special rights for the Sámi, regardless of whether or not they are considered Indigenous."

In the revised video, the scene opens with three hooded crows silhouetted against a backdrop of white snow. The crows jostle with each other for position and their cawing can be heard. The screen then turns black, introducing the text in white, "Jörgen Stenberg med band" (Jörgen Stenberg and band), followed by the text "joijkar Vuortjis, kråkan, en symbol för överheten" (joiks Vuortjis, the crow, a symbol for authority). Signaling the edited nature of the video, the video then cuts to a contact sheet, filled with black and white images of lone crows, with a single color image of the Gállok mine protests, in which the bright yellow-green flak jackets of five pictured policemen stand out. As the camera zooms in on this colored image, we see the police move in slow motion, as the ominous violin backup of the musical performance begins. The sound of a crow cawing is heard continually in the background. The silent slow-motion depiction of walking policemen gives way to footage of the police removing protesters from the Gállok encampment in late July 2013. This footage is accompanied by the sounds of the protests: people talking and shouting and other sounds of activity. As the music mounts, the video presents a swift succession of images of Swedish state authority, including the flag, and views of statues, soldiers and inscriptions at the royal palace in Stockholm, before cutting back to more footage of the Gállok protests. A brief return of the image of crows in snow fades into footage of Stenberg and band on stage as the vocal part of the piece begins. Stenberg is dressed in Western clothes as he sways slowly while performing the traditional joik in conjunction with the driving rhythm and intensity of the instrumental backup. As the vocal rendition closes, the video cuts back to slow-motion images of policemen walking at Gállok and crows walking in snow. An overlay of crows tussling on the ground and the band playing is then overlaid with the polished and authoritative voice of Forsell making the statements quoted in the YouTube text. The footage cuts to crows harrying an eagle on the ground, and the band is pictured in a lull in the performance, as if listening intently to the attorney's outrageous characterizations. As the sampling of the attorney closes, the video cuts back to Gállok images, beginning with a piece of spray-painted protest art by the artist Anders Sunna showing a Sámi man giving the finger as a seeming response to Forsell's ungrounded assertions. Footage of various protesters of different backgrounds and nationalities are intercut with an image of Stenberg, dressed in gákti, singing at the protests, his arm raised in a fist that combines both a symbol of protest and a typical gesture of Sámi joikers during performance. The music again features the instrumental buildup and the joik as the footage cuts back to images of Stenberg on stage in Western clothing, intercut with footage of Sámi protesters, people painting protest signs, and people applauding a speaker at the Gállok encampment while a police helicopter hovers menacingly overhead. Closing footage shows the band completing the piece on stage, with audience applause, as the video fades back to the earlier image of the crows and the eagle. The camera zooms in on a single cawing crow as the screen fades to black, introducing in white letters Forsell's quoted statement with a background recording of a cawing crow. The words then disappear and the names of the band members appear. The final frame of the video credits the photos to Tor Lundberg Tuorda (with the URL, www.kvikkjokk.nu).

Stenberg's listing of protests and controversies, "Alta, Biedjovággi, Gállok, Storliden," in his first 2013 upload of the YouTube video clearly suggests an overarching pattern of colonization against which the Sámi must struggle. In introducing the new version of the video edited by Tuorda, Stenberg repeats the notion that the "state must be joiked," and notions that culture is his weapon, joik his spear. While the ways Stenberg uses these weapons in his performance are distinctively his own, they are shared with other Sámi artists and activists. Sámi joik becomes a spear, but wielded in a way that, Stenberg's statements suggest, tie back to the *vaššeluohti* ("hate joiks") of the past, demonstrated by Krister Stoor on track 9 of his *To Yoik Is to Live* album (Stoor 2003a), and recalling Johan Turi's famous words from his *Muitalus sámiid birra* of 1910:

> Juoigamuš lea dakkár go lea rievttes čeahkes juoigi, de lea nu hávski gullat, goase čirrosat bohtet guldaleddjiide. Muhto go dakkár juoigit leat, guđet garrudit ja bániid gasket ja uhkidit goddit bohccuid ja velá isida nai, ja de dat leat ahkidat gullat. (2010: 183)

> Joiking is such that if it is really artful, it is very pleasant to listen to: tears nearly come to one's eyes while listening. But if it is that kind of joiking that includes swearing and gnashing of teeth and threatens to kill reindeer or even their owners, then it is terrible to hear. (2012: 199)

By reminding his audience that joik can be used as a means of social censure, and then deploying it as such to criticize the enduring racism of state lawyers, Stenberg weaponizes joik in his performance, creating a hard-hitting and confrontational performance of Sámi music as a tool for fighting against state disregard of Sámi rights.

Katja Gauriloff's *Kuun metsän Kaisa* (2016)

As this chapter opened with a discussion of filmmaking and the remarkable infrastructure and creative momentum that today surrounds Sámi film, it is fitting to close the chapter with a discussion of two notable films, each of which contribute to Sámi image making in the Sijvo era in dynamic and innovative ways. Where Paul-Anders Simma's *Oaivveskaldjut* (1999) demonstrates the power of the documentary genre to spotlight injustice and uncover suppressed history, Katja Gauriloff's *Kuun metsän Kaisa* (2016; Kaisa's enchanted forest) uses the genre to present a more open-ended and melancholic look at the destruction of Skolt Sámi culture in the era of World War II, and the unique friendship of a Skolt matriarch and storyteller and a Swiss tuberculosis convalescent and writer who met and became fast friends in the midst of this time of phenomenal change. And if Nils Gaup's *Guovdageainnu stuimmit* (2008; Kautokeino uprising) harnesses the potential of the period film genre to decolonize Sámi and broaden public memories of an important event in Sámi colonial history, Amanda Kernell's *Sameblod* (2016; Sami blood) uses the genre to tell the broader story of the horrors of the 1930s boarding-school era of Swedish Sámi education, the racial investigations of state-funded academics during the era, and the psychic toll of such colonial institutions on Sámi youth, both those who chose to remain within the Sámi culture and those who abandoned their culture for a hoped-for life of acceptance and "normalcy" within the Swedish majority society. Neither Gauriloff nor Kernell offer as clear-cut a dichotomy between heroes and villains as is portrayed in the films of Simma and Gaup, and neither provides as straightforward and unambiguous a way forward for Sámi in the aftermath of the events described. Yet both contribute vitally to the ongoing filmic contemplation of the Sámi experience, particularly as it unfolds in relation to colonization. And both films seek to speak to Sámi and majority cultures regarding the importance of maintaining and *recovering* Sámi culture in the here and now.

Katja Gauriloff's *Kuun metsän Kaisa* premiered at the Sodankylä film festival in June 2016. The fourth film of Gauriloff's career, it followed her earlier short *Huuto tuuleen* (2007; Shout into the wind), which also focused on Skolt culture, an internationally focused *Säilöttyjä unelmia* (2012; Canned dreams), which looks at the hands and people involved in the transnational production of a can of pork, and *Voimanlähde* (2013; Source of strength; co-produced with Joonas Berghäll), which presents the stories of four women battling breast cancer. Produced by Oktober, the film company that Gauriloff helped found, *Kuun metsän Kaisa* was nominated for two Jussi awards, one for best documentary, which it won, and the other for best sound design. On the international film circuit, it also received the 2017 Murmansk Northern Character festival's Grand Prix award and an award for best animated documentary at the Leipzig DOK festival. It was featured at the Toronto Hot Docs festival as well as the program of the 2017 Berlinale NATIVe—A Journey into Indigenous Cinema. Gauriloff was named Skolt Sámi of the year by Finland's Skolt Sámi organizations in 2016 (Porsanger 2017: 30).

The film opens with the grainy sound of a gramophone record, suggesting antiquated recording equipment and/or the sounds of early talkie films. As eerie music rises in the background, a woman's voice is heard in Skolt Sámi stating that she will not serve coffee. An image comes into sight of Kaisa Gauriloff—the subject of the documentary—posing amid her work of spinning yarn. She sits facing the viewer, a distaff to her left loaded with wool, a spindle held deftly in her right hand while she stretches the yarn she is producing with a confident smile. Animated effects make it look like the spindle and yarn are moving, as the narrator's voice says she will serve a different sort of drink, prepared from the blood of the earth, that gives life to all things, though not life in this world; blood from the veins of the earth, where life and death flow side by side. The image fades to a pen-and-ink cartoon of gnarled trees in front of a starry sky, with an animated moon proceeding across the sky. The film's title appears. This early introduction of cartoon images foreshadows the extensive use of animation and cartooning in the film, used whenever Kaisa's folktales are being recounted. It also establishes Skolt Sámi as the film's first language, although, as noted below, the Skolt narration will mingle with narration in French, as well as occasional narrated speech in German and English. Much of the factual information provided in the film is conveyed through titles on black screens, mimicking old cinematic newsreels or early ethnographic films. These titles are in English.

Throughout the film, Gauriloff uses black and white footage, static text screens, and vintage recordings to give the look and feel of early cinema, a styling that works well with the abundant newsreel footage of World War II Finland and London incorporated into the film. The choice of look also foregrounds the documentary as "found art," an examination drawn from preexisting elements combined in creative and novel ways. Gauriloff seeks to recover and celebrate the unique friendship and collaboration of her great grandmother Kaisa Gauriloff (1885–1980) and the Swiss writer Robert Crottet (1908–87). Dennis Harvey (2016) characterizes the film's technique as "a collage documentary, composed of various archival materials plus some discreetly slipped-in reenactment bits." Although Gauriloff had long hoped to produce a film about her great grandmother, the notion of telling the story through the eyes of Robert Crottet emerged only after getting in contact with Crottet's surviving partner, Enrique Méndez. In an interview with E. Nina Rothe at the 2017 Berlinale, Gauriloff notes the importance of the materials that Méndez had preserved for the shape and substance of the film: "Then I got a hint in Spain. We sent a postcard to Enrique Méndez and he sent a postcard to us and it was signed 'Enrique Méndez'. He invited me, he was already nearly ninety years old and I didn't even know that he was alive anymore. I went there in 2013 and he said, 'I have all the material here,' all the films, hundreds of photos, all the written material, everything that was left from Robert" (Rothe 2017). Black-and-white and color footage of Robert's travels, his own documentation of his 1938 experiences in Suenjel, and his eventual postwar visits to Kaisa in her resettled home in Mustola, Finland, create a vivid and touching through-line in the film, as the narrative makes sometimes abrupt and circuitous turns following the fortunes of Kaisa and Robert in a war-torn Europe of World War II.

Gauriloff's film resists all conventions of documentary detachment, as it presents a touching story of the remarkable friendship and collaboration of Kaisa and Robert, two lively intellects and lovers of story who came into contact during the final year of the intact existence of the Suenjel siida. Robert, born in Russia and raised in Switzerland, comes to the community in search of rest and healing after prolonged suffering with tuberculosis. Kaisa, proficient in Russian from her girlhood work as a servant for the Petsamo monastery, befriends and cares for the visitor like an adopted son. When the opening of the Winter War forces Robert to leave, he returns to Switzerland and then travels to London, where he becomes stranded during the war. In the meantime, Kaisa's son is killed in the war, while her community is evacuated to western Finland, losing their homes, reindeer, fishing equipment, and cultural context. Robert manages to raise money to help the Skolt community resettle after the war and returns repeatedly to Finland to visit Kaisa and the community in the decades that follow. Robert becomes part of Kaisa's extended family, one that includes Katja Gauriloff, Kaisa's great granddaughter. Katja's relation to Kaisa is clearly enunciated late in the film, where a photo dated to 1973 shows a beaming Kaisa holding Katja as a toddler.

Central to the narrated relationship of Kaisa and Robert, and artfully incorporated into the documentary, are Kaisa's repertoire of traditional folktales and legends. According to narration presented as the words of Robert early in the film, and drawn from the introduction to his book *Forêts de la lune* (Crottet 1949a, 1949b; The enchanted forest), Robert's request that Kaisa tell him a story was initially brushed aside by his hostess, who protested that she did not know any stories and had little knowledge. When, however, Robert came into affectionate contact with Kaisa's jet-black reindeer Musta, Kaisa took it as a sign that Robert was worthy of hearing her stories and she began to dictate them to him systematically. Robert admired her old-fashioned Russian, and carefully wrote down her stories, which he reworked and published in French and English at the end of World War II.

One of the stories was Kaisa's account of the origin of the northern lights. Gauriloff notes that although her mother knew the story and feared both the northern lights and the full moon, Katja, raised in Rovaniemi in the aftermath of the postwar destruction of Skolt cultural continuity, came to know the story only through Crottet's books and archival recordings of Skolt folktales. Recovering the story as part of her film, Gauriloff deploys it in three parts, distributed over the course of the documentary and accompanied by the striking cartoons and line animation of St. Petersburg artist Veronika Bessedina (Elokuvasaatio 2017). It is a grim story of cannibalism, transformation, and perseverance, in which a young girl honors the wishes of her murdered and devoured mother, is captured and sewn into a seal skin by her ill-willed step-sisters, becomes the lover of the Son of the Sun, is forced to marry one of the three violent men who nightly fight with knives (producing the lights and colors of the northern lights), and is eventually rescued from her predicament by her solar lover. Bo Lundmark

(1982: 147–48) and Jelena Porsanger (2017: 32) discuss the tale's meaning in Skolt tradition, where the northern lights stand as the grim afterlife destination of those who die by iron or are killed in war. Gauriloff's use of the story in the film creates resonances between its traditional content, the life experiences of Kaisa and Robert (both of whom lost their mothers early in life), and the harsh realities of World War II. The full political potential of the story becomes evident only late in the film, where Kaisa uses it to criticize the policies of Stalin. Referring to the two books of stories Crottet published as a result of his time with Kaisa, the film's title states, "the collection of Skolt legends, The Enchanted Forest, was published in 1949 in France, Germany and Britain. It was translated into Finnish in 1954. Maouno de Finlande (Mauno the Reindeer) was published in 1941, but it wasn't translated into Finnish until 2003. Robert Crottet donated the proceeds from the book to the Skolt Sámi people."

Crottet's interest in Skolt folktales related to his romantic conceptualization of the Skolt Sámi, as Gauriloff makes clear early on in the film when she quotes Robert regarding all Skolt Sámi as perpetual children. Gauriloff makes evident her irritation at such statements in an interview with E. Nina Rothe (2017) in which she states, "There is a lot of romantic stuff that he was writing and I was very critical about it." The fact that Robert operated in the mindset of the 1930s—the same period critiqued so powerfully in Simma's *Oaivveskaldjut* (Give us our skeletons)—becomes evident as we hear him employ racial categories to describe the Skolt and ultimately to plea for funds to help them recover their lives after World War II. Jelena Porsanger (2017: 28) suggests that Robert's prophetic dream of small people with bright eyes who would heal him of his tuberculosis, may have stemmed from traditions of the Skolt as healers and workers of magic, narratives Crottet may have become aware of through the Russian folktales and legends of his childhood. In any case, the seeming fancifulness of Kaisa's stories, furthered in the film by the cartoon depictions suggestive of a classic fairytale collection, plays against yet somehow reinforces the real-life trials of Kaisa, Robert, and the broader Skolt community as they experience very real occasions of loss, sorrow, and violence.

The film underscores Kaisa's penchant for using metaphor to describe aspects of her life, a tendency that captivated her Swiss collaborator. The tendency continued to the very end of her life, as the film repeatedly demonstrates through narration of Kaisa's words, reported in French by Robert. The tendency also suggests ways in which her great granddaughter's film uses stories to reflect metaphorically on Sámi situations today. This implication is made evident by the film's very deliberate use of the northern lights story to parallel developments in the life and times of the Skolt community. The story's three parts are narrated in Skolt Sámi by Sirkka Sanila. The fact that Kaisa dictated her stories to Robert in Russian, and that Robert produced his written adaptations of them in French, is underscored throughout the film, making the fictiveness of this seeming recording of Kaisa telling her story evident to the viewer. It is a filmic recovery of her storytelling, but one overtly tied to the broader narrative agenda of the film in telling the story of the Skolt community's harrowing experience of World War II, period of evacuation, and postwar resettlement and struggle to remain intact as a culture and community. Katja Gauriloff perhaps draws attention to the metaphorical nature of her film through her quotation of Robert, featured toward the end of the film and repeated in its international trailers. Responding to Kaisa's reference to the books they created together–Kaisa dictating, Robert writing–as "lies," he states: "Kaisa ce n'est pas vrai. Nous n' avons pas menti dans ces livres. C'est ne pas de notre faute si l'histoire de ton pays et de ton peuple ressemblent autant à une conte" (Kaisa, it is not true. We did not lie in those books. It is not our fault if the history of your country and your people resemble a fairytale so much). The viewer is invited to see the film as a strategic story, one brilliantly aware of the capacity of metaphor and tale to express the pain and tragedy of human existence and to call for a happy ending for people whose lives are shattered by the hardships of war, displacement, and forced acculturation.

In certain respects, Gauriloff's film seems at first to break with broader patterns of Sámi ethnopolitical filmmaking. For one thing, the film avoids a pan-Sámi perspective, instead focusing attention on the specificities of the Skolt Sámi situation. Already in Karl Nickul's study of the Suenjel siida (1948) the community's way of life was described as the most "primitive"—and therefore original—Sámi way of life, making the community stand for Sámi culture more generally in its complex relations with forests, fishing resources, and reindeer. Yet Gauriloff undermines this notion of Sámi universality by emphasizing the orthodox religiosity of the Skolt community and of Kaisa in particular. She also features the story of the northern lights that, although prominent in Skolt and other eastern Sámi cultures, is absent from the traditions of Sámi in Sweden or Norway. While reindeer are depicted in the film and play a role as draft animals in many of its scenes, Gauriloff pays particular attention to freshwater lake fishing and to sheep husbandry, with the production of wool, processing of yarn, and knitting of mittens recurrent and prominent elements throughout the film. The heroine in the folktale hides herself by transforming into a spindle, and from the outset of the film Kaisa is shown carding, spinning, and knitting wool. When quoting foreign descriptions of the Skolt Sámi, the film enunciates repeatedly the distinctiveness of the Skolt and their seeming uniqueness in Scandinavia.

Where this distinctiveness is certainly foregrounded in the film, it is also possible to see the Skolt Sámi as representatives of broader Sámi experiences. Porsanger (2017: 28) points out that the film's bringing together of Skolt Sámi and French narration was a powerful ethnopolitical act in itself, as it united one of Europe's least numerous languages with one the continent's most widely spoken and most prestigious. The survival of Skolt Sámi can stand for the survival of the other Sámi languages, regardless of their relative numbers. The cross-border travails of the Skolt Sámi—the fragmentation of their homelands between Norway, Finland, and the Soviet Union/Russia—parallels the cross-border travails of Sámi in Norway, Finland, and Sweden, so powerfully discussed by North and Lule Sámi writers and activists. The loss of an age-old Skolt seminomadic way of life, following relocation to Če′vetjäu′rr (Sevettijärvi) and wider dispersal across Finland, parallels the loss of traditions of migration and seasonal movement familiar to Sámi from other regions. The forced acculturation that Skolt Sámi faced after the war, wryly described in the film's English titling as "Finlandization," employs the terms of political science to emphasize the nationhood of Skolt, and by implication all, Sámi: their situation in relation to the Finns is discursively made to parallel the postwar experience of Finland in relation to the Soviet Union. Crucially, Gauriloff's film makes a place for the Skolt story within the broader narrative of Sámi colonial history, just as its thoughtful use of Skolt *leu'dd*, including sound recordings of Kaisa herself singing *Kotkan leu'dd*, make a place for Skolt music within the broader use of joik in Sámi image making. Perhaps most powerfully, in its abundant and effective use of newsreel, ethnographic film recordings, recorded folktales, and preserved personal movie footage, Gauriloff's documentary continues the process of recovering and repurposing the products of past colonial encounters, echoing the powerful work of Nils-Aslak Valkeapää in *Beaivi, áhčážan*.

Amanda Kernell's *Sameblod* (2016)

"Everyone says there are three rules for your debut film: You shouldn't do a historical film, no children, and no animals. I did all of that on a small budget" (Buder 2017). So states Amanda Kernell in one of the numerous interviews she gave in connection with her immensely successful feature film *Sameblod* (Sami blood; figure 4.1). Kernell won the Youth Jury Award at the 2017 Luxembourg City Film Festival, a prize for the best young director at the 2017 Venice Days (Giornate degli autori), and an award for best director at the 2017 Riviera International Film Festival. The film garnered awards at the 2016 Thessaloniki Film Festival and Tokyo International Film Festival, as well as the 2017

4.1. Poster for Amanda Kernell's *Sami Blood* (2016). Pictured is Lene Cecilia Sparrok playing the film's lead character. Used by permission, Nordisk Film Production Sverige AB.

Trondheim International Film Festival, Newport Beach Film Festival, Santa Barbara Film Festival, Santa Fe Independent Film Festival, and Seattle International Film Festival, among others. It was named the Best European film of 2016 by the Europa Cinema Label, and at the 2017 Göteborg Film Festival it received the Best Nordic Film Prize. At the 2018 Guldbaggegalan–the Swedish equivalent of the American Academy Awards–it received eight nominations and four awards: winning for best manuscript (going to Amanda Kernell), best female leading role (Lene Cecilia Sparrok), best editing (Anders Skov), and the public choice prize for best film. Kernell received the 2018 Culture Prize awarded by the Swedish national newspaper *Dagens Nyheter,* and a prize for her contributions to human rights through the film, awarded by Svenska FN-förbund. Seldom has a Nordic film garnered so many international accolades, made all the more impressive by the fact that the film in question was a debut work. Amanda Kernell became established overnight as a major new voice in Sápmi's ever-expanding media world.

As noted above, what Katja Gauriloff does for the documentary genre in her 2016 *Kuun metsän Kaisa*, Swedish Sámi filmmaker Amanda Kernell, originally from Ubmeje (Umeå), accomplishes for the historical period movie genre. Where Gaup's *Guovdageainnu stuimmit* (2008) lets a single painful moment in a specific community's history stand for a broader Sámi colonial experience, Kernell's 2016 film presents a pair of South Sámi everyman characters to embody the painful history of boarding school education and racial investigations in the "*Lapp ska vara lapp*" (Sámi must be Sámi) era of Swedish Sámi history, when Swedish law prescribed the clothing, housing, and foods that Sámi were permitted to use without relinquishing their status as Sámi (Lundmark 1998: 97–104; Lantto 2012). As in Gaup's film, *Sameblod* opens up an often unspoken history. It revolves around the estrangement of Sámi family members and friends who left their communities and identities behind in order to try to blend in to a broader Swedish majority. They did so in an era in which Sámi were regarded as racially inferior and were blocked from access to a wide range of educational and occupational opportunities. These opportunities became available only to those people who embraced and attempted to enact the Swedish majority culture. As the film presents the contrasting decisions of the film's main character Elle-Marja/Christina (played by Lene Cecilia Sparrok) and her younger sister Njenna (played by Mia Erika Sparrok), it surveys the range of frequent, nearly inevitable, responses of young Indigenous people to the personal and structural racism they experience(d) in school and in broader society. The film does so in a way that underscores the particularities of the Swedish Sámi colonization: its legal insistence that Sámi not be exposed to elements of Swedish culture, like eating with forks or consuming non-Sámi food unless the individual chose to abandon Sámi culture (and attendant rights to reindeer husbandry) through assimilation into the Swedish majority. Yet the film tells its story of estrangement and identity change in a way that reaches audiences of every kind in an era in which forced or voluntary migration, and the shaping of one's cultural and physical identity, have become prevalent as never before. As Kernell notes in an interview with Emily Buder (2017): "People have really recognized themselves in the movie. We've been showing it in Japan and Canada. So many people have said, 'Oh, this film is really about me.' And I hadn't even thought about it before making it, but it rings true for a lot of people with a migration background. Of course, people can relate even more if they're from minorities or oppressed groups." Where Katja Gauriloff studied filmmaking at Tampereen ammattikorkeakoulu, Kernell received her training in Copenhagen at Den Danske Filmskole. Her first films were shorts, including her breakthrough *Stoerre Vaerie* (Northern Great Mountain), which premiered at the 2015 Sundance Film Festival and won an award at the Göteborg International Film Festival that same year (Vivarelli 2017). With accomplished Sámi actress Maj-Doris Rimpi playing an elderly Christina Lajler, a Sámi woman who has willfully left her Sámi identity behind until she is confronted by her past at the funeral of her sister, the short created the framing beginning and end sequence for Kernell's first feature-length film. Its success also leveraged the funding Kernell needed for her new undertaking.

The opening of *Sameblod* reuses material from *Stoerre Vaerie.* Opening to the voice of Christina's grown son as he knocks on her door, apparently urging his mother to prepare for the long drive ahead of them. Christina, dressed in black, stares out a window, smoking a cigarette. The scene cuts to Christina looking out of the window in the passenger seat of her son's car, as modern joik music plays on the car's music system. The son tells her that the music comes from where she is from, but Christina shows little interest, dismissing the music as shrill and ugly, while she attributes a range of negative attributes to "dom" (they), meaning, apparently, Sámi people. After a clearly strained and unpleasant ride, Christina and her son and granddaughter arrive at the church, where the dialogue reveals that they have come to attend the funeral of Christina's sister. After some coaxing, Christina consents to go inside the church, so long as they do not stay long.

As the family enters, the minister is preaching in South Sámi. Heads in the congregation turn with surprise and perhaps some displeasure to see Christina, who takes a seat far in the back. The minister mentions the estrangement between the deceased and her sister, and notes that Christina's sister loved joik as a way to find strength. After a rendition of joik (performed by Jörgen Stenberg), the church service ends. As people stream out, Christina remains seated, clearly uncomfortable and seeking to hide her face. Yet she is inevitably eventually recognized by an old man, one of her childhood associates, who addresses her as "Elle-Marja" and asks her in South Sámi why she never returned. Christina/Elle-Marja pretends not to understand his words, as he endeavors to tell her that her sister persisted in marking her reindeer calves for her all these years since her departure. (Maintaining a reindeer herd preserved one's status as a reindeer herder in Swedish law, so this act has literally preserved Christina's status as a herder during her apparently long absence.) At coffee time after the service, Christina sits alone, while her son and granddaughter eagerly begin to become acquainted with the relatives they apparently have never before met. When the granddaughter receives the gift of a gákti, Christina rises to inform her son that they must leave. The embarrassing moment worsens when the son refuses to acquiesce to her order, instead stating that they will spend the night with Christina's sister's family and attend a calf marking in the morning before driving home. Christina refuses, taking her suitcase and announcing she will stay at the local hotel. "Jag klarar mig själv" (I can take care of myself), she comments matter-of-factly, enunciating a life choice which in fact characterizes her life experience since leaving her Sámi community behind.

Alone in her dark and drab hotel room, Christina's silent and unhappy life becomes evident. She washes her face vigorously and carefully arranges the hair over her ear before descending to the hotel's main lobby, where she blends in with the other Swedish guests as an elderly schoolteacher from Småland. There she hears her "fellow Swedes" complain about the nuisance of reindeer-herding Sámi in the national park and how their activities and use of motorized vehicles disturb and inconvenience other people. Christina listens in silence, outwardly indicating agreement, although her discomfort at the conversation is clear. After a silent and lonely night, her son tries again to convince her to join them in the calf marking, pleading with her through the hotel door to help him as they prepare to take a helicopter to the site. He plaintively recites through the door the smattering of South Sámi words he has learned, possibly from Christina, including words for mother, love, some basic verbs, and a few numbers. Christina listens, but makes no response, and the son and granddaughter depart. After returning to the lobby to see the other hotel guests dancing, Christina looks out the hotel window, where she sees her son and granddaughter board the helicopter and leave.

The opening of Kernell's film depicts the familiar experience of "undercommunication" explored by Andrea Amft in her study *Sápmi i förändringens tid* (Amft 2000: 175–78). Christina's acquired and convincing alter-identity as a school teacher from Småland lets her hear the unpleasant racist remarks that her fellow Swedes frequently share when confronted by the cultural differences and activities of Sámi. As Amft notes, Sámi are often painfully familiar with a majority-culture perspective that only recognizes Sámi as Sámi when they are clothed in traditional dress or engaged in stereotypical Sámi activities (e.g., reindeer husbandry). When Sámi who dress in majority-member clothes or are employed in careers shared by majority-culture counterparts, their identity as Sámi often becomes invisible to their coworkers, clients, and even friends. When they speak of their Sámi identities in such contexts, they can often face dismissal as not "real" Sámi, that is, failing to conform to the dominant culture's stereotypes of Sámi "authenticity," the very ones encoded in Swedish policy during the *Lapp ska vara lapp* era. As Kernell notes in the interview with Emily Buder (2017): "The friends I grew up with would say they haven't met a Sámi person except me and my father. I am sure they have; they just don't know it because people don't know what to look for. Some people think, 'Oh, they live in the mountains somewhere, or maybe in a teepee.' But we're everywhere." The film's main character disproves her era's assertions of Sámi intellectual inferiority and racial alterity by performing her acquired Swedishness flawlessly. Yet rather than use her achievement to disprove the prevalent stereotypes, Christina herself repeats the stereotypes she has internalized about her people, characterizing them as whining, dishonest, and backwards.

In *Sameblod*, an expanded new version of Kernell's earlier short, this opening frame story cuts abruptly to the film's main (extended flashback) portion. As Christina watches the departing helicopter disappear on its way toward the mountains, her alter ego, a talented and intelligent adolescent Elle-Marja, takes the stage. In early scenes, she is shown skillfully marking the ear of a reindeer calf held by her sister and preparing for her departure to boarding school. We learn that she is the oldest daughter of a widowed mother and is expected to gain an education at the regional Sámi nomadskola (boarding school for reindeer herding) and return to the siida to help her mother in the work of maintaining the family's reindeer herd. She is also expected to help her younger sister Njenna adjust to life at the school, since this will be her first year there.

With her father's ear-marking knife as a keepsake and a tearful little sister in tow, Elle-Marja begins her journey to the school, crossing lakes, fields, and forests, and passing by the homes of suspicious, sometimes openly hostile, Swedish farmers. At a key point in the journey, Elle-Marja performs a vuolle to cheer her sister up, reminding her that she can bring back memories of the local mountain by joiking it. At the same time, she warns her sister not to joik at school, where vocal performances and conversations in Sámi language are strictly forbidden.

While eschewing the historical exposition of a documentary in preparing the materials for her film, Kernell employed ethnographic methods to approach the question of the motivations and experiences of people who eventually rejected their Sámi roots, such as her character Elle-Marja/Christina. She notes: "I interviewed people who left and now live in Stockholm and haven't taught their children Sámi and don't want them to wear the Sámi clothes. Some of them have completely changed identity and can't talk about it. But those that did want to talk, I asked them what they missed. How it felt sitting there when the reindeer stand around you, all calm, and it's quiet, and you feel at peace. Also, what hurt the most in school" (Buder 2017).

Kernell's film depicts Sámi schooling of the day in all its oddity and inconsistency: while aiming to preserve "Sámi as Sámi" by restricting the students' access to non-Sámi clothes, non-Sámi foods, and certain subjects and activities (like swimming and gymnastics), it nonetheless mandates exclusive use of Swedish and requires Sámi to learn poems and hymns in praise of a Swedish nation. The children are punished for speaking to each other in Sámi and, in general, are treated with little warmth by the school's staff. When they are marched through the countryside on school outings, they endure the hostile stares and jeering taunts of a surrounding farmer population.

Despite this daunting environment, Elle-Marja's young and charming teacher Christina Lajler (played by Hanna Alström), encourages the talented Elle-Marja by inviting her into her home one evening for coffee. There Elle-Marja sees the racial biology books that are her teacher's evening reading, but otherwise is charmed and delighted by her visit, in which she imitates her teacher's genteel manner of holding her coffee cup and learns about the things necessary for being a good teacher. Christina introduces her to Swedish poetry (including the famous 1925 poem by Edith Södergran, "Jag längtar efter landet som icke är" (I long for a land that is not there). Afterwards, Elle-Marja is shown in possession of a book about Uppsala–apparently the book her teacher gave her–which she avidly reads at night, seeking to comfort her homesick sister by reading to her about the wonders of the distant metropolis. A fantastic world of technological and cultural marvels seems to lie in wait outside the cramped world of the Sámi, with Swedish language and education the keys to accessing and enjoying it. In the manner of "worlding," Elle-Marja comes to long for a land that is not there, one that is the purported center of the world and that renders Sápmi a shabby and irrelevant colonial periphery (Ashcroft et al. 2000: 225; Storfjell 2017). Later in the film, she will follow her dreams, or illusions, to Uppsala and find it every bit as grand and wondrous as the book described, but thoroughly a place in which Sámi do not belong, except as racial specimens and ciphers. Filmed on location in Hemavan, Kernell's film avoids direct naming of its sites apart from one mention of the village of Udden in Tärnaby, heightening the contrast between a seeming Sámi "nowhere" and a purported Uppsala "center."

A key element of Kernell's film is its depiction of the cooperation between the boarding school institution and race biology. As noted above, the topic of Nordic scientists' racial investigations of Sámi people had already been explored in detail by Valkeapää in his *Beaivi, áhčážan* (1989) and by Simma in his *Oaivveskaldjut* (1999). Simma's film includes the first-person reminiscences of an elderly Skolt woman recalling the visit of Finnish racial investigators during her childhood and the humiliation and embarrassment of being forced to stand for nude photographs. Valkeapää includes in his *Beaivi, áhčážan*'s images 410 and 411 on pages from a 1926 publication produced by the Swedish State Institute for Race Biology (headquartered, significantly for Kernell's film, in Uppsala), contrasting the physiques of individuals purportedly belonging to three different "races"—"Nordic," "East Baltic," and "Lapp." Captions under the images of the three photographed women underscore the social and cultural assumptions tied to their physical appearances: the "Nordic" woman is described as a "Daughter of an overseer," while her shorter and stockier "East Baltic" counterpart is described as a "Farmer's daughter from Norrbotten." The photograph of an even shorter "Lapp" woman is depicted holding what looks like a spear shaft and is labeled "Nomad woman from Jämtland (Undersåker)." In 2015, Maja Hagerman's fascinating and disturbing biography of Herman Lundborg was published (2015), stirring up considerable public discussion, as it presented the development of Lundborg's Uppsala institute and its aims at maintaining the "purity" of the Swedish race through investigating, and stigmatizing, intercultural marriage. Racial investigators were aided in their studies by both Swedish church and school institutions, who gave investigators unfettered access to Sámi children and, in the case of nomadskolor, were in turn influenced by the assertions/conclusions investigators made regarding Sámi intellectual capacities and appropriate occupational horizons. In 2011, Sámi activists had called for a special commission of clergy and academics to study the historical relations of the Swedish church and Sámi people over the course of history, and in 2016, after a series of well-publicized conferences, a massive two-volume anthology of articles appeared, some of which addressed the church's complicity in twentieth-century racial investigations directly (Oscarsson 2016; Hagerman 2016).

Kernell's film portrays this toxic collusion of various state institutions in reifying and thereby disenfranchising Sámi as racial inferiors. Throughout the early scenes of the film, we see the teacher Christina Lajler busily preparing the children for the momentous visit of a delegation from Uppsala. Because of her excellent Swedish, Elle-Marja is given the task of welcoming the guests, and she is shown assiduously practicing her lines of welcome during her free time in the children's dormitory. When the Uppsala scientists arrive, however, they show little enthusiasm for the Sámi's traditional crafts or Elle-Marja's carefully rehearsed speech, although Ms. Nordström, the Uppsala team's female member, eagerly inspects the clothing and hair textures of the assembled children and finds the two sisters Elle-Marja and Njenna particularly captivating. The children are taken inside, where Elle-Marja is instructed by her teacher to set a good example for the rest of the children by dutifully allowing her head and nose to be measured and then stripping nude to be photographed. Elle-Marja's repeated questions are summarily ignored by the cold, sometimes violent male scientist, who forces her to submit to a series of photographs. The horror of the situation is conveyed visually by the jarringly loud and bright flash of the photographer's camera apparatus. Elle-Marja's nakedness is observed by leering Swedish boys peering in at the window, adding to the voyeurism and humiliation of the moment. Soon after, Elle-Marja is enraged when she hears the boys describe her, and other Sámi, as occupying a lower rung on the evolutionary ladder. Explaining her inclusion of these details in her film, Kernell states, "it's not an educational film. It's about healing. I wanted to explore shame and the colonisation of your mind, not explain how this and that works. I also wondered more and more, where does the shame come from? And the anger. [It comes from] knowing that you are considered a person at a lower step in evolution. That also defines rules and regulations and what the state does with people whom it thinks are not able to take care of themselves" (Vivarelli 2017).

The essential dismissal of Sámi humanity inherent in such acts becomes brutally clear in a following scene, in which Elle-Marja is wrestled to the ground by Swedish boys and ear marked like a reindeer. Kernell notes that she drew this scene from the testimony of one of her interviewees: "One of the Sámis told me he got his ear cut by a schoolboy, like how you mark a calf. So I put that in the film" (Buder 2017). Equally violent, though more insidious, is the teacher's rigid refusal to assist Elle-Marja in gaining further education. Despite her cleverness, Elle-Marja is informed, neither her schooling nor her racial characteristics suit her for further education or possible life in a city. Elle-Marja is made to see herself trapped in a racially inferior body, unable to explore any other future than the static, bestialized status the state has defined for Sámi in its Lapp ska vara lapp policies. The perceived danger of miscegenation is depicted in the film through Elle-Marja's short-lived relationship with a tall and wealthy Niklas Wikander of Uppsala (Julius Fleischanderl), who welcomes sexual intimacy with her only until he is informed by his concerned parents that she is likely Sámi.

While the state's essentializing discourse of Sáminess separates Sámi and Swedes into rigid, mutually exclusive categories, the film portrays the relative ease with which Elle-Marja is eventually able to create a Swedish persona for herself as a new iteration of Christina Lajler. By donning a flowery or black dress, learning how to dance and swim and eat with a fork, and gradually building up a credible background story for herself as a native of Småland, Elle-Marja is able to assume a completely non-Sámi identity and build a successful career as a teacher. Characters in the film certainly show suspicions: Niklas's parents easily see through her initial claims to Småland ancestry when she cannot name the place in Småland where her relatives purportedly live, and the gymnastics teacher at her new school in Uppsala clearly doubts her claims to being unfamiliar with gymnastics routines because she has been living in Germany. But passing as a Swede seems the most logical and least radical solution to the quandary of what to do with a Sámi girl who wants to become a teacher, and by and large, Christina's Swedish counterparts accept her assertions. The full psychic toll of this fabrication becomes apparent to Christina only at the end of the film, when the scene shifts back to the frame story. There we see a distraught Christina finally coming to terms with what she has lost through her life of impersonating a Swede. Filled with guilt and sudden resolve, she apologizes to her sister's corpse and then scrambles up a mountainside in her fancy shoes and black dress to join her son, granddaughter, and extended family at their calf marking.

In contrast to interludes of romantic love in films by Gaup—where Sámi characters are shown forming warm love relationships as part of the films' overarching narratives—Elle-Marja/Christina's love life and interpersonal relations show few joys. In the main flashback sequence of the film, a desperate Elle-Marja throws herself at Niklas at the first dance she attends, seeking to gain access to Swedish culture and a life in Uppsala through him. Niklas welcomes her openness to sexual intimacy only until he realizes that she is Sámi. In the frame story, an aging Christina Lajla has one son but apparently no living or present husband. And although the son and granddaughter are aware of their Sámi heritage, they receive no support from Christina in exploring the culture by coming into closer contact with Christina's natal family. Love and affection are hardly in evidence in the strained relation between Elle-Marja and her frustrated and depressed mother, and the only real tenderness in the film consists of scenes in which Elle-Marja and Njenna interact privately. Elle-Marja endeavors to cheer up her homesick sister, carries her on her back, and, later, introduces her to swimming. It is Njenna's rejection of Elle-Marja's ambition to become Swedish that seems to injure Elle-Marja the most. Both in its frame story and its main-feature flashback, Kernell's film is about sisterly relations and the pain that ensues when sisters make diverging life choices. Kernell cast real-life sisters in the roles of Elle-Marja and Njenna to help portray the complexities of this relationship on screen.

Where Sámi image making since Álttá has used Sámi cultural items as emblems of Sámi identity and cultural worth, Kernell makes careful and canny use of them in her film. Self-consciously Sámi images recur throughout in the film, creating resonances or echoes within the narrative and tying the frame story to the flashback. One example is joik. In the opening frame story we see Christina's hapless son trying to interest his mother in her Sámi background by buying her a modern CD of Sámi joik. At the funeral, a joiker performs by Njenna's coffin, as the pastor notes the deceased's love of joik. In the flashback, when the sisters are first on their way to the boarding school, Elle-Marja joiks to cheer up her sister, telling her that singing the vuolle of the local mountain will help her get through the loneliness of life at school. At the same time, she warns her sister not to joik at school, noting implicitly the disapproval of Sámi culture that the institution evinces. Njenna does indeed joik at school, however, using the genre to tease her sister in the time of the class's preparation for the momentous visit by the Uppsala delegation, as Elle-Marja nervously rehearses her Swedish speech. When Elle-Marja reaches Uppsala, she is urged to joik by two of Niklas's Swedish friends at the birthday party she goes to (uninvited). They have learned about joik in an anthropology course and are anxious to hear an example of the genre in person. Elle-Marja/Christina's sorrow and embarrassment at becoming once again an exotic attraction for majority culture members is combined with their lack of comprehension or appreciation for the short and simple vuolle. Like Elle-Marja in her boyfriend's imposing house, her vuolle is like a fish out of water. The complex layering of these various instances of joiking underscores the pain and estrangement that tears Elle-Marja from her natal community and transforms Sámi culture for her into a source of stigma and embarrassment.

Similarly, the film builds a repeated series of images of reindeer ear-marking, beginning with an initial flashback scene in which Elle-Marja competently marks a calf with her sister's mark, to the brutal moment in which Elle-Marja herself is ear-marked by violent and racist Swedish boys, to the moment in which her disfigurement is noticed and questioned by Niklas, to the repeated images of the frame story in which an aged Christina endeavors to hide her damaged ear beneath locks of graying hair. At the funeral, Elle-Marja/Christina is informed that Njenna has faithfully continued to mark Elle-Marja's reindeer for her in all the years since her leaving, and it is at a calf-marking the following day that Elle-Marja and her son and granddaughter eventually reconnect with their Sámi identity. Closely related to these potent images are scenes involving Elle-Marja's knife, a tool she has received from her deceased father by way of her grandfather, and a symbol of her expected return to the family to take up herding. The audience is shown Elle-Marja wielding the knife artfully in the calf-marking scene, and then brandishing it menacingly as she threatens the taunting Swedish boys. Her knife is discovered by her new-found friend at the Uppsala academy, who questions her about why she would own such an object, an indication that the older girl suspects Christina's hidden Sámi identity. In a poignant scene of frustration, Elle-Marja uses the knife to kill a reindeer on a mountainside near her family's home when her mother initially refuses to give her her father's valuable belt to sell so that she can afford her tuition at her new Uppsala school. Employing emblematic, stereotypical symbols of Sámi culture—reindeer earmarking, knife use—the film deploys the images both to signal Elle-Marja's connection to her natal culture, and Christina's embarrassed alienation from it. The simultaneously valued and stigmatized nature of Sámi culture—to young Sámi raised in a society that in many ways continues to regard the culture as backward, antiquated, or violent—can be recognized by Sámi adults as well as Sámi youths watching the film. In interviews, Kernell herself notes that when going to South Sámi class as a girl, she told her friends she was going to music lessons, and recalls the frequent discomfort she experienced wearing Sámi traditional dress in many public venues, despite her conscious pride in her Sámi identity (Buder 2017).

Within the broader project of Sámi image making, Kernell's film makes a space for the South Sámi experience both linguistically and historically. Like Gauriloff's use of Skolt in her film, Kernell inserts South Sámi into the filmic soundscape of Nordic film, to stand alongside the now relatively familiar North Sámi of previous feature films and documentaries. A lack of specificity regarding the locations of the school, church, and siida allow the narrative to take on a generalized character, making the Swedish South Sámi experience emblematic of the colonial experiences of Sámi communities more generally. Where Gaup's *Guovdageainnu stuimmit* is set in the village that is today the linguistic heartland of modern North Sámi life, Kernell's film makes a claim for Sámi experiences in other, less well-known locales.

At the same time as she gives filmic voice to South Sámi, Kernell also depicts Sámi characters who cannot speak any Sámi language (like Christina's son and granddaughter) or those, like Christina, who choose to abandon their language altogether. Her film explores narratively the ways in which some Sámi participate in the erasure of Sámi culture through their daily choices of undercommunication or through long-term choices of cultural abandonment, bringing such processes out into the open not necessarily for castigation or condemnation, but for acknowledgement. Elle-Marja/Christina has made choices in her life, but these have been necessitated largely by a colonial system that mandates and maintains a dichotomy between Indigenous identity and mainstream social integration. Forced to choose between the two, Elle-Marja chooses life "as a Swede." But, the film suggests, in so doing she is not so much a villain as a victim: a byproduct of a rigidly binary system that refuses to imagine an existence that would include elements of traditional Sámi life as well as access to prestige and career success in a dominant-culture context. In comparison with earlier films surveyed here, Kernell's *Sameblod* displays a greater degree of comfort in depicting its characters as flawed and imperfect, reflecting in so doing the ambiguities and ambivalences of modern Sámi identity negotiation. As in Gauriloff's documentary, there is no easy way forward for Kernell's characters at the end of the film: the disjunctions created by colonization render the recovery of real competence in Sámi culture difficult if not impossible for Christina's son and granddaughter, even if they now have access to their once estranged extended family. Sámi decolonization, the films of both Gauriloff and Kernell suggest, is no easy matter regardless of the attitudes of the present generation. It will take long and concerted efforts, and broader community support, to achieve the recovery of Sámi culture and traditions so optimistically suggested by the films, poetry, and music of Tjïekere era. And while contributing to this ongoing project through creating greater visibility and continued decolonizing acts, the artistic works of the Sijvo era recognize and acknowledge these undeniable hurdles.

The selection of Sámi films, music performances, and YouTube videos surveyed here are by no means comprehensive. Sámi artists abound in the Sijvo era, and many prominent performers and genres have been ignored. One might note the vigorous development of Sámi rap, beginning with the Aanaar Sámi Amoc (Mikkal Morottoja) and including the North Sámi Slincraze, as well as the prodigious array of musical artists who combine Sámi musical traditions or lyrics with eclectic musical styles, including Frode Fjellheim, Ánde Somby, Ingor Ántte Áilu Gaup, Sara Marielle Gaup Beaska, the late Inga Juuso, Elin Kåven, Wimme Saari, Tiina Sanila (president of the Finnish Sámi parliament at the time of this study, 2018), Maxida Märak, Krister Stoor, and groups like Adjágas, Ulda, Ára, Moivi, Vajas, Fri Flytt, Fádnu, and many others (Jones-Bamman 1993; Moore 2004; Hilder 2015; Nordström 2017).

In comparison with the artists and works featured earlier—when Sámi musical works and films were generally considered alluring or intriguing novelties—the artists and works of the Sijvo era can address a well-established market niche of fans and consumers. For many consumers, Sámi and non-Sámi alike, Sámi culture is today a known and valued commodity. To be sure, Sáminess is still typically marked by emblems of Sámi cultural distinctiveness in the products surveyed here—language, joiking, reindeer husbandry, Indigenous reverence for nature. Yet, as we have seen, artists recurrently play upon, expand, and adapt these emblems so as to deepen their meanings and widen their range to cover the diversity and complexity of modern Sámi life.

And as visible as Sámi become, they still face erasure in Nordic states where the provision of Sámi language services, inclusion of Sámi perspectives, and respect for Sámi self-determination remain more asserted goals than attained achievements. It is still unusual for non-Sámi Nordic citizens to learn to speak a Sámi language, and a Nordic vacationer is probably more likely to visit Spain or Thailand than Sodankylä or Tana. The onus to preserve, maintain, and further develop Sámi languages and cultures—although identified as priorities in ratified documents like the UNDRIP or the European Charter for Regional and Minority Languages—remains mostly on the Sámi or the Sámi parliaments, who must often advocate vociferously in order to receive financial support or institutional encouragement for their efforts (Pietikäinen 2008). Yet this majority-polity disregard can also become a source of affirmation and strength, as Sámi themselves rise to the challenges they face as a community and produce works that answer the needs and extend the dreams of their people. And in this collective labor—as the coming chapters will demonstrate—social media represents both a great resource and a powerful tool. It allows individual Sámi to participate in and advance the goals of Sámi self-determination in ways that echo and answer the works of produced media presented above.

5

Rahte

Contextualizing Sámi Uses of Digital Media

JÅHKÅMÅHKKE, FEBRUARY 6, 2016. THE STREETS OF THIS TOWN in northern Sweden are packed with people looking at the stalls of food, handicrafts, souvenirs, and warm socks. Greetings can be heard from the throng, cheerful voices from people meeting and catching up. For a few days each year, about forty-thousand visitors occupy the small town that usually counts less than three-thousand inhabitants. They come for the winter market, a yearly event of major significance in Sápmi. The market is an occasion to meet, gather, and maybe make new acquaintances. It is a meeting place that has been a central event in Sápmi ever since 1605, that is, even before the town existed. Jåhkåmåhkke was one of the permanent marketplaces established in Sápmi by the Swedish King Karl (Charles) IX (1550–1611). At that time, the market was organized as an occasion for trading and also as an opportunity for the authorities to collect taxes, spread and inculcate Christianity, and bring under control the Indigenous population of the north. It has since developed into a yearly meeting place for people in Sápmi. Today, the market includes other activities beyond trading, and invites a broader range of visitors and participants from throughout the world.

Nowadays, the Jåhkåmåhkke Winter Market is also a festival, with cultural events, exhibitions, conferences, and concerts. Students of duodji from the Sámij Åhpadusguovdásj—the Sámi education center—display their creations at the Swedish Mountain and Sámi Museum, *Ájtte*. Artists and artisans present and sell their works at the market. February 6 is also the Sámi national day, celebrated this year with, among other things, a concert with singer/song writer Katarina Barruk, one of the few artists singing in the Ume Sámi language. Other scheduled events include activities that reflect the ideological and political engagements of cultural workers, such as demonstrations against mining in the area, and the release of the fanzine *Sápmi 2.0*, a product of a decolonizing art and language project.

The multiplicity of activities illustrates the fact that the winter market is not about offering a picturesque, souvenir-filled experience for tourists. Nor is it solely about socializing and gathering: it is also a political arena. A year earlier, the Swedish Minister of Culture and Democracy Alice Bah Kuhnke, while visiting the market, was met by activists who read a manifesto for Sápmi, calling for a protection of the land against exploitation and demanding better support for Sámi culture (Holmberg and Laiti 2015). In a symbolic act, a female activist allowed one of the other protesters to cut off her hair while she read the manifesto—symbolizing her personal and tangible grief over what has been done to her land and her people. The proximity to Gállok, a reindeer herding area under consideration for excavation as an iron mine, has led to protests and demonstrations against mining that have become recurring elements at the market for the last few years. Nowadays, not only the traditional ride with reindeer and sleds go through the market, but also protest marches and other actions. In 2014, *Tjáhppis rájddo* (the black ride) took place as a demonstration against the mining industry, performed by activists wearing black plastic bags instead of the colorful Sámi gákti, with white painted faces and a reindeer skeleton in a sled.

5.1. Jokkmokk market. Photograph by Thomas DuBois.

These events were not only part of the locally situated market, nor were they geographically restricted: they were highly mediatized. The political actions were covered, posted, and shared by social media, thereby circulating in Indigenous networks both nationally and internationally. Jåhkåmåhkke is anything but a remote town in Sápmi; it is the center of attention at the time of the yearly winter market, but also for many Sámi a node for education (through the Sámi education center), for handcrafters (through the Sámi Duodji handicraft foundation and the Ájtte museum), et cetera. Perhaps it is not by pure coincidence that SameNet, the first Sámi digital social networking service (discussed in chapter 6), was operated from this very place.

In Sápmi, a large area that spans over four countries, marketplaces—such as the winter market of Jåhkåmåhkke and other meeting places such as the church village of Faepmie (Fatmomakke), or the midsummer celebrations in Åanghkerenjeeruve (Ankarede)—are examples of places, occasions, and events for gathering, sites for meetings between relatives and friends from far and near, and for making new acquaintances. These occasions—and, consequently, these places—play a significant role in a context where the traditional land, Sápmi, and kinship, are strong markers of identity. Reindeer herders, a minority of the Sámi population but considered important bearers of tradition, make use of large areas for their livelihoods.

Strategies for managing and mastering distances have always existed in Sápmi. In response, technology has long played a significant role in building and maintaining Sámi culture and identity: trade routes, roads, railways, snowmobiles, helicopters, mobile telephony, internet—all have shaped and responded to Sámi culture. The Sámi population has used the available technologies not only in order to further their livelihoods and embrace social and cultural changes in society, but also, as we will discuss later, to maintain, in sometimes new guises, traditional modes of communication with relatives, friends, representatives, and others.

The title of this chapter symbolizes the path created by previous media uses and its continuity with different means and users. *Rahte*, a path in the snow resulting from where people have walked, hiked, or transported goods, is an important concept in traditional and modern Sámi life. The snowmobile may replace the sled, and digital media may replace or complete the marketplace, but communication goes on along and through that path, a path established in past by path breakers but maintained and extended through the actions of people using the path in the here and now.

Contextualizing Sámi uses of social media in relation to the ways these media are employed in other Indigenous communities, we present findings from interviews conducted with Sámi regarding their uses of these tools. In the digital age, a Sámi sense of community, fellowship, and belonging is also maintained and constituted online through digital media, allowing us to talk about "digital places" within Sámi culture. At the same time, social media is used in the Sámi context mainly as a supplement and enhancement of already existing offline communities rather than as a place for the creation of entirely new virtual communities. This fact reflects the sense of current social media use as displaying continuity with past forms and uses of communication media, ones that, as Nils-Aslak Valkeapää suggests in his 1989 *Beaivi, áhčážan*, extend all the way back to prehistoric petroglyphs.

In presenting these findings, we draw on concepts arising in the field of Indigenous methodologies, particularly the work of Linda Tuhiwai Smith (2012), to explore networked global media in a Sámi context, highlighting in particular the notions of connectedness, networking, and sharing. We furnish examples of how these ideas become manifested in Sámi participatory media, as well as in that of other Indigenous communities. Attention is focused particularly on two Sámi protest actions—the *Gulahallat eatnamiin* YouTube video (October 2015), and the *Sami manifesto 15* (February 2015)—which combined the concrete here-and-now with the more globalized virtual. These examples demonstrate how produced media of the type discussed earlier take on new dimensions and significance when circulated on social media, both within Sámi networks and in broader pan-Indigenous international contexts.

As discussed previously, Sámi groups did not wait for the internet 2.0 to find a way to make their voices heard. The continuity of cultural expressions and the ways in which people have adapted media have been examined in previous research, both regarding traditional mass media such as newspapers, magazines, radio, or television (e.g., Dégh 1994) and in connection with digital media (e.g., Blank and Howard 2013). As we argue here, the potentials of these media are not inherent in the media themselves, but rather are made possible by the social and political climate that operates within Indigenous communities.

Mass media—usually dominated by the majority population, and in a global context, dominated by world centers of media production like the United States or England—have repeatedly been criticized for their lack of attention to minority issues (Council of Europe 2016, 2017). Misrepresentations can become vehicles for disempowering and exoticizing stereotypes (Meadows 1994: 64; Tremlett 2017). This is also the case when it comes to online media, as discussed by Iseke-Barnes and Danard (Dyson et al. 2007), and similarities can easily be found in the Nordic context in relation to the Sámi population (Johansson Lönn 2014; Ledman 2012; Omma 2013). The so-called "new media," such as participatory online media, have therefore been seen as a chance for minorities and Indigenous groups to make their voices heard, use their languages, and bring to the fore issues central to their communities. They offer possibilities to exert influence over information, representations, and knowledge to a far greater extent than is possible in traditional media, and suggest a potential to become a tool for questioning and challenging structural and power relations (Bruns 2008; Fuchs 2010; Rainie et al. 2012; Morozov 2011). The speed, mobility, and sharing possibilities of these "many-to-many" media create new prerequisites for users, compared to older forms of media. The web 2.0–characterized by user-generated content–supports and incites interactivity and collaboration, thereby encouraging discourses of empowerment and democratization, discourses that previous research examines in detail (Dean 2003; Fuchs 2010; Dijck 2013; Jenkins 2006; Lovink 2005). Participatory media are part of larger social and cultural contexts, which effect both how the media are shaped and how they are used, their contents and their impacts (O'Neil 2014; Sassen 2004).

In the Nordic countries, where the internet has been considered an important service provided to all people (including minorities and Indigenous communities), the new media have opened possibilities for greater cooperation between the nation-states that claim control over Sápmi, and offer increased possibilities of access for Sámi audiences. Mass media such as radio and television, and to some extent, newspapers, publish news and reports online in addition to offering them through more traditional channels (see, e.g., Sameradion).[1] And, of course, social media channels are widely used for many purposes, such as personal initiatives or organized campaigns to share and circulate news articles, resources, or personal messages, conveying in these ways political and ideological messages.

Sámi Views of Social Media: Interview Data

How social media are perceived and used, and the role they are accorded as sources for receiving and sharing information or for knowledge production, vary greatly between generations and cultural groups. The issue of identifying culturally accepted and appropriate modes of communication, in a heterogeneous Sápmi, was a point of discussion in a pre-study conducted by the Swedish Sámi Parliament to survey the status of the Sámi languages in Sweden (Saami Parliament 2015a). As documented in this report, consultants, who participated in the pre-study, note that family members (father, mother, siblings, uncles, aunts, cousins, and other close relatives) often are their first sources of information about Sámi issues or events occurring in Sápmi. Other important channels of information are acquaintances or friends within the Sámi community. One of the consultants in the pre-study suggests it is important to be able to refer to someone he/she knows personally when discussing a Sámi topic. Social media is regarded as a good source of information when it comes to more general questions and updates, but it supplements rather than replaces closer interpersonal communication channels (2015: 34–35).

Views and approaches to social media were discussed and corroborated in interviews conducted in connection with the present study (2016–17). Nine interviews, resulting in about twelve hours of recorded data, were conducted with social media users and, in some cases, with people having a specific role in a project or a campaign. In respect for the anonymity and confidentiality of the participants, name, age, or location of consultants were withheld—apart from cases when the consultants had a specific position, for instance as a project leader and interviewed as such. In most cases, the interviews, conducted by author Coppélie Cocq, took place as face-to-face conversations, recorded (sound) and transcribed. Three interviews took place over Skype and one via email. The conversations were held in Swedish, which is the mother tongue, or one of the mother tongues, of the consultants. The consultants were given the opportunity to read and comment on the draft chapters of the manuscript. As a qualitative study, the data does not constitute a basis for significant findings statistically. Instead, the interviews are illustrative anecdotally of previous experiences through our own social media interactions and observations with Sámi groups and users.

When asked about the potential role of social media as a source of information, one consultant recounted that social media is good for sharing experiences and advice, for example, if someone wonders how one's child can get Sámi language education:

> Eller nån som sa "jag ska ha barn snart, jag vill att mina barn ska lära sig samiska, hur ska jag göra?" Då kom det en massa tips, och reaktioner "vad fint att du har tagit steget" . . . Så där är det . . . det är fantastiskt. (Interview 1)[2]

> Or like someone said [on Facebook] "I am going to have a child soon, I want my child to learn Sámi, how should I do that?" Then she received lots of pieces of advice, and reactions "so nice that you are taking this step." So it is . . . it is fantastic.

For the Sámi generation that has not had the opportunity to learn the language, providing a Sámi speaking environment and conditions for a child to have access to the heritage language can be difficult. The lack of places and situations where Sámi languages are naturally spoken, and the scarcity or, in some municipalities, absence of resources when it comes to language education, means that parents need networks and knowledge exchanges in order to find solutions. As the quotation above illustrates, social media (here, Facebook) facilitates this information gathering, and, at the same time, can serve as a platform for support and encouragement.

The importance and benefits of social media for communication are also related to a need for contact, particularly in relation to the dispersal of family members and friends across large geographic areas. As one of the consultants puts it:

> Vi använder sociala medier för att hålla kontakt med familj och släkt som inte bor på orten. Och det är viktigt för barnen, att hålla kontakt med släkten i Sápmi [. . .]. Det är lättare att hålla kontakt med sociala medier, vi behöver inte uppdatera oss varje gång vi träffas. (Interview 1)

> We use social media to keep in touch with family members who don't live in the same city/village. And it is important for the children, to keep in touch with their relatives in Sápmi [. . .]. With social media, it is easier to keep up; we don't need to catch up on things every time we meet.

The role of such contacts and relationships is more than just about socializing, however, as another consultant elaborates:

> Kontaktnätet i Sápmi, eller . . . det känns fel att säga kontaktnät, men de där människorna, det är min koppling till mitt land och mitt ursprung [. . .]. Vi måste jobba med kontaktnät i Sápmi, och det är därför barnen konfirmerar sig. Och sociala medier har också den typen [av funktion] . . . Det är viktigt att mina barn har ett samiskt kontaktnät. (Interview 2)[3]

> This network of contacts in Sápmi, or . . . it feels wrong to say "network," rather: these people, it is the connection to my country and my origins [. . .]. We need to work on our network of contacts

> in Sápmi, and this is why the children have the confirmation.[4] And social media also plays that kind [of role]. . . . It is important for my kids to have a Sámi network.

The consultant stresses the importance of developing and maintaining contacts and relationships in Sápmi—not only with friends and relatives, but also with an origin, a place, and a sense of belonging. The notion of a network creates a sense of unity and interaction that can compensate for a lack of face-to-face contact on a daily basis.

Although all the interviews confirmed the central role of social media in the lives of the consultants, people also emphasized that social media was only a complement to more ordinary forms of communication:

> Man har träffats på Jokkmokksmarknad och Allahelgonacupen [. . .] Men de har inte ersatts, sociala medier har inte ersatt dessa naturliga mötesplatser. De har bara förstärkts. Det blir oftare [att man har kontakt]. Det är mycket finare att träffas öga mot öga, man kan ha djupare samtal, men man kan hålla igång, skicka bilder [på sociala medier]. (Interview 1)

> We used to meet at occasions like the Jokkmokk Winter Market or the tournament of All Saints' Day.[5] But these occasions have not been replaced, social media has not replaced the natural occasions for meeting. They have been reinforced. We have more contact [. . .] It is much nicer to meet in person, we can have deeper discussions, but [with social media] we can keep the discussion going, share pictures.

The need for direct communication is also emphasized when it comes to language learning: "Att sitta med en app eller så det är . . . det räcker inte, för mig blir det ganska ointressant, och för mig att lära mig, det handlar om att jag måste vara med" (Interview 2; Apps and such, it is not enough, for me it is not interesting and in order to learn, for me, it is about participating). The extensive use of social media and the advantages of digital communication do not undermine the value of "real life" contacts. On the contrary, the importance of offline communication is underscored as a contrast to what is sometimes experienced as a more superficial and less safe form of communication.

A further issue to address when approaching new media as a means of cultural communication is to investigate to what extent social media can support communication based on social structures appropriate to the Sámi community—for instance, intergenerational relationships, central in Sámi society. The question arises as to how new media might or might not replicate such relationships in the new media environment. Consultants emphasized the inclusion of elders in Sámi networks, in contrast with what they observed in Swedish (majority-language) networks:

> I samiska sammanhang, det är alla generationer. Men inte i de svenska. Det är märkligt egentligen, jag vet inte. . . . Nej, i det svenska eller i majoritetssamhället, där blir det jämnåriga. (Interview 1)

> In my Sámi networks, all generations are present. But not in my Swedish networks. This is odd, I don't know why. . . . In the Swedish [networks] or in majority society, we are of the same age group.

> Samer i Umeå har en grupp, och där är alla med, de äldre och så. Och jag tror att det har att göra med hur vi behandlar äldre personer, i det samiska, det är inte som i Sverige. Inom det samiska är de äldre viktiga, och man behandlar dem med värdighet, man hälsar, man har ett intresse för vad de äldre har att säga—som man inte har i det svenska samhället, i alla fall inte i samma utsträckning. (Interview 4)[6]

> We have the [Facebook] group "Sámi in Umeå," for instance, and everyone is there, elderly too. I think it has to do with how we consider our elders; it is not like in Sweden. In the Sámi society, the elders are important, we treat them with dignity, we say hello, we are interested in what they have to say–in a different way than in the Swedish society, or at least to a different extent.

These observations are supplemented by another consultant, who observes how social media is influenced by the social logic of majority society:

> Det tänker jag att det är skillnad i umgängestrukturer, det skiljer sig på sociala medier och "traditionellt". Om jag tar Jokkmokksmarknad som ett exempel, det har alltid varit jag och min farbror, och en äldre kusin, vi har alltid gått tillsammans på Samedans. Det är så naturligt att vi umgås, och inte bara i skogen eller så. Men på sociala medier det är mer en västerländsk struktur. Sen är jag "kompis" med alla möjliga kompisars barn etc, men . . . [vi har inte så mycket kontakt] (Interview 2)

> I think there is a difference in the structures of social relations–it differs between the social media and the traditional. If I take the Jokkmokk winter market as an example: I used to go to dancing [to the Sámi dancing party of the winter market] with my uncle and an older cousin. It was natural to do things together, and not only when going out in the forest or such. But on social media, there is more of a western structure for social relations. I am "friend" with friends' kids etc, but . . . [we don't have much contact].

In many ways, when studying digital practices in a Sámi context, we are clearly dealing with cultural and social practices strongly anchored in the relations, practices, and modes of communication that take place, which are shaped, performed, and maintained offline.

Although early analysis of digital communication tended to overemphasize online networking as a means for strangers to connect based on shared interests (e.g., Rheingold 1994), perceptions of online communities as distinct from the offline world have received valuable qualification in later research. As Kirshenblatt-Gimblett states: "the online and in-the-flesh worlds can and do converge, and online communication is being used increasingly to further offline concerns. Some electronic lists are extensions of prior face-to-face relationships, while others organize occasions for the listers to actually meet. It is not uncommon for particular online communities to have an IRL geographic center" (1996: 29). This aspect is especially relevant when it comes to geographically localized groups. What digital media does, however, is to create a virtual bridge between localities and global issues.

Social Media in Indigenous Contexts

One example of Indigenous media use, where social media came to play a central role, is the Idle No More movement, often referred to as #idlenomore due to the extensive use of the hashtag on Twitter and other social networking services for spreading news or expressing solidarity. This massive movement began in Canada in November 2012, calling for peaceful protests, manifestations, blockades—and overall for an increasing awareness of the rights and conditions of the First Nations of Canada. The core issue of the movement was protesting against the legislation that limits Indigenous rights and the lack of consultation of Indigenous people in decisions that concern them and their land. Idle No More is an example of Indigenous social media mobilization that received attention internationally. On the listing of www.indigenoustweets.com (see Arvi, Introduction), the hashtag #idlenomore was at the beginning of 2013 still the number one trending topic among tweets in Indigenous languages, for example, in North Sámi.

Twitter, as the venue for the spreading of information and as a channel for support and sympathy, illustrates how Indigenous people the world over engaged with an issue that might appear at first local and specific to a community (the Attawapiskat First Nation), and a country (Canada), but that is in fact an issue of concern for many Indigenous groups—the right to participate in decision-making through consultation and consent, concerning rights to the land, and contemporary relationships between the colonizer and the colonized. The hashtag #idlenomore demonstrates how digital technology offers the possibility for solidarity to emerge in a manner that can hardly be accomplished through traditional and mainstream media. It is also a means for giving and receiving support beyond the epicenter of the movement. Several years later, the hashtag and the symbols associated with the movement, for instance the flag used by the movement, circulate online in various Indigenous contexts.

Such was also the case during the Gállok protest movement in Sápmi in 2013, when reindeer herders, locals, artists, and environmental activists protested against the mining boom in Sweden in general and the plan for an iron mine in the reindeer herding area of Gállok in particular. A British prospecting mining company (Jokkmokk Iron Mines AB, JIMAB, a subsidiary company of the British Beowulf Mining) had been granted permission to complete exploratory drillings for iron ore. Since July 2013, Gállok, a reindeer grazing area located outside the city of Jåhkåmåhkke, has become a symbol for a growing environmental movement for Indigenous rights, tightly connected to similar protest movements elsewhere and linking back to other Indigenous movements—for instance the Álttá dam protest. The prospecting process raises concerns: Gállok is situated in Sámi land and reindeer herders have used the area since time immemorial. If an iron mine were to be built, it could jeopardize the ability of people living in the area to carry out traditional reindeer herding and other livelihoods. There is also a risk for pollution in the Lule River and the ecosystem of the valley. At the same time, the possibility of a mine gives hope to people of this rural area for employment, economic growth, and a positive effect for the development of municipalities suffering population decline. At the core of this struggle we find a heated debate about the exploitation of natural resources in a Swedish context in general, and in Sámi land in particular.

Gállok is one of many sites where mining companies have received prospecting rights: the Swedish Mineral Act is generous and advantageous for foreign companies to prospect and exploit the land for minerals, and locals have a very limited power of influence. JIMAB initiated exploration in the summer of 2013 and protests on the site reached new levels when the blasting for further prospecting was about to begin. From July 1 to mid-September, a group of environmental activists, rapidly joined by locals and supported by a portion of the area's population, established a camp in Gállok in order to delay the mining company's drilling and blasting. A series of confrontations with the police occurred that were documented and spread rapidly on the social media platforms YouTube, Facebook, and Twitter. Activity on social media increased in parallel with the events on the geographical site. People at Camp Gállok received support from the local population, who brought food and supplies on a daily basis. People from other parts of the country also visited the site and donations were collected. In this struggle, cultural workers play(ed) a significant role. Performances and concerts took place every week during that summer and artists from the Jåhkåmåhkke area contributed through the production of paintings and art installations.

In the case of Gállok, as in Álttá, the conflict brings to the fore the question of the legitimacy of political decisions that violate Indigenous rights. Further, it underscores the insufficiency and inadequacy of contemporary minority politics and the need to revise existing environmental legislation. The growing attention that the Gállok movement received—where social media play a significant role for sharing information, building networks, and giving support–shows parallels with the Idle No More movement. We find similarities in the use of social media and digital technology for contestation: grass-roots initiatives for the protection of Indigenous rights, and how something considered a local issue grows into a global issue of concern on an international level. Also, the role of cultural workers illustrates the power of culture as a vehicle for the communication of values.

The coverage of the Gállok encampment, from everyday life to political actions, has spread through social media: on Twitter with the hashtags #Gállok #Kallak, on Facebook groups, on YouTube, blogs, et cetera. The echoes of the mining boom in Swedish Sápmi reached an international audience at the end of August 2013, when the *Washington Post* published an article on the topic, and the news spread rapidly on the internet and through international newspapers. By then, the debate about the mining projects in Sámi lands had been ongoing for several years, and the site-specific manifestations had taken place for almost two months. But prior to that time, the debate, information, and reports were covered and circulated almost entirely through social media. Gállok and the environmental debate related to Indigenous land rights is therefore illustrative of the role of social media in social and cultural movements.

The use of social media in the struggle has implied that a local concern has been framed on a global arena. The issue of a possible mine in Gállok relates to a global debate about Indigenous rights and exploitations around the world. Social media usage–mainly Facebook, but also Twitter–has strengthened the voice of several communities by underscoring the scope of the problem. Also, the media have increased the degree of interplay between online and offline networks and initiatives by facilitating the organization of demonstrations and information exchange.

YouTube was used for publishing videos and updates during the struggle on the site of Gállok in 2013, not least during interventions and confrontations with the police. Also, short clips were produced

5.2. Screenshot of a YouTube video linked to the website www.whatlocalpeople.se. The site and the video were produced in response to the executive for Beowulf Mining Saintclair-Poulton's rhetorical question when asked by investors whether local people in and around Gállok would be in favor of the proposed mine. The answer, in the form of the video and website, displays the faces of local people who would be affected by a mine.

and published on YouTube as contributions to the environmental debate. Videos on YouTube were published via the account "whatlocalpeople," a reference to a question asked by president of the British mining company at a presentation of one of its mining projects. When asked about possible objections from the local population to a mining project, he asked, "What local people?" His remark reflected his view of the area as unpopulated, and showed a lack of awareness of land-use activities like herding, that rely on the land but minimally alter it. The question–rhetorical or simply ignorant–was viewed as a provocation by the groups that live in the area: it doubted their existence, dismissing the considerations of any local and Indigenous populations. A reaction was published as a website using the very phrase "whatlocalpeople" as the domain name,[7] displaying a series of photographs of people who live and work in the area, with the words "We are the locals!"

The last action on site took place on September 3, 2013, and Camp Gállok was then packed up. But the resistance movement and the debate continue—not least on Facebook, Twitter, and other digital media sites. For the protesters of the mining project, the debate in its initial phase was located on social media and websites, and continues there now, enhanced by demonstrations and occasionally, art exhibitions. But the issue of exploitation of natural resources and the Swedish mineral law is now, at last, also discussed nationally via traditional media (radio, newspapers, and television), who took their cue from social media and eventually followed up with investigations and journalism of their own. Traditional media had been slow to respond to the call for attention of the Sámi at the beginning of the events of summer 2013. The first updates about the events took place on Facebook, Twitter, and YouTube, thanks to the initiative of locals involved in the struggle. Some local media published short reports after international media started writing about the situation. Ironically, Swedish media on a national level were among the last to publish articles on what was going on in Gállok.

Coverage of the summer 2013 events on social media took advantage of the affordances of web 2.0. The ease of producing and uploading self-produced media material, and the quick diffusion of videos and reports, enabled activists and locals to share news and receive support. Interestingly, a number of posts on Twitter used the #idlenomore hashtag along with #gállok—as a means for connecting to other Indigenous movements and calling attention internationally to Indigenous issues, and thereby reaching global networks, and parallel protest movements, such the North American "NoDAPL." This form of connectedness, networking, and sharing can be interpreted as part of an Indigenous framework, as illustrated below.

Online Indigenous Communities and Indigenous Communities Online

As the findings presented above suggest, the concept of "online community" needs to be qualified in a Sámi context, bearing in mind the geographically defined area, the relatively small number of members, and the importance of family, relatives, friends, and acquaintances in immediate social networks. An "online" community, in a Sámi context, does not mean a community that emerges online, where members meet around a specific issue or interests. From this perspective, social media in Sápmi is to a great extent a mode of maintaining, strengthening, and extending offline communities. Groups on Facebook, for instance, are often used to discuss and keep contact with acquaintances, and are seldomly used to recruit new members or share information with people outside the Sámi (offline) community.

Discussions and debates within the rising field of Indigenous methodologies (e.g., Tuhiwai Smith 2012; Porsanger 2004; Louis 2007; Kovach 2009; Chilisa 2012) provide relevant points of departure for approaching networked global media in a Sámi context, not least in relation to the concepts of *connectedness*, *networking*, and *sharing*. As a field of study, Indigenous methodologies examines epistemologies, methods, and questions with a focus on Indigenous matters from the perspective of Indigenous people, and for their own purposes (Tuhiwai Smith 1999: 39). Such an approach emphasizes the importance of dialogue, dissemination, restitution, and questions of whom the research is for, and how it can benefit the communities in which it is conducted. From this angle, Indigenous methodologies have much in common with principles enunciated in community-based research and participatory action research (e.g., Chevalier and Buckles 2013; People's Knowledge Editorial Collective 2016).

Linda Tuhiwai Smith (2012) writes about twenty-five Indigenous projects that reflect an emergent agenda for Indigenous research. Her list defines ambitions and intentions in Indigenous decolonizing research, based on values, needs, and interests within Indigenous communities. One of these projects is *connectedness*. Tuhiwai Smith describes what it means from an Indigenous perspective: "Connectedness positions individuals in sets of relationships with other people and with the environment. Many indigenous creation stories link people through genealogy to the land, to stars and other places in the universe, to birds and fish, animals, insects and plants. To be connected is to be whole" (2012: 149). Her description gives another dimension to connectedness, discussed earlier in relation to new technologies. The words may be specific to the Māori perspective that she represents, but the perception of wholeness, holism, and connection with genealogy and the environment has also been expressed in Sámi contexts, as illustrated by the lyrics of Mari Boine quoted in chapter 3: "Gula máttut dál du čurvot . . . Gula máttaráhkuid jiena" (Listen, as the forefathers call to you . . . Listen to the voice of goddesses).

This perception of connectedness, both within Sápmi and globally, has been more recently articulated in the *Gulahallat eatnamiin* ("we speak Earth" or "we communicate with the Earth") message and joik mounted on YouTube by Sámi environmental activists. *Gulahallat eatnamiin* posits a common language between humans, the planet, and the environment; a language that the Sámi and Indigenous people speak and understand. The joik, performed by Sara Marielle Gaup Beaska, was first shared on YouTube in October 2015, with an explicit invitation to viewers to join in the singing by posting their own renditions of the joik on social media in preparation for the coming Paris Climate Conference COP21 of December 2015.[8] In the video, in North Sámi with English subtitles, Sara Marielle Gaup Beaska tells how global warming and climate change already have created many challenges, not least in Sápmi, where the temperature has risen by 1.5 degrees. She warns that we are all done for if climate change is not halted and notes that she and many others are planning to go to Paris in December 2015 to try to convince the world's leaders to take needed measures while there is still time. While thinking about these issues, she states, a joik came to her, *Gulahallat Eatnamiin.* While she performs the joik, the camera cuts to a woman dressed in gákti walking in the woods and eventually finding and fetching a white stone from a river. At the end of the joik the film cuts back to Gaup Beaska, who states, "Mun ávžžuhan dii buohkat filmihit iežadet go juoigabehtet dan luođi ja bidjat filmmaid nehttii," translated in the YouTube captions as: "I urge you all to film yourselves joiking Gulahallat Eatnamiin and to share those films on the internet and social media." Noting how fun it would be if we could all perform this joik together in Paris, she repeats the dates of the COP21 climate conference and expresses her hope that we will see each other there. As the joik returns to the audio track, the film cuts to still images of Sámi landscape with exhortations in English: "Let's build pressure towards the politicians negotiating our future–here are two things you can do: Go to Paris and join the mass action on December 12th: dl2.paris, film yourself performing this joik and share it widely." As the video fades to black, a quotation from Nils-Aslak Valkeapää appears in white letters, in English:

> "Take a stone in your hand and close your fist around it
> until it starts to beat, live, speak and move."
> Áillohaš
> Nils Aslak Valkeapää

With these words, the video references one of the artistic leaders of the Sámi revival and reminds a knowing audience of the Álttá dam protests. The white stone in the video further links to another action in relation to the COP21 climate conference, that is, the *Run for Your Life* relay race that started in Giron (Kiruna), as environmental activist and artist Jenni Laiti, a white stone in her hand and quoting Valkeapää, began a run that ended in Paris at the time of the climate conference (Sandström 2017).

With its well-crafted combination of North Sámi monologue and English subtitles, allusion to past Sámi environmental protests, and generous invitation to others to join in learning and performing the joik, the *Gulahallat eatnamiin* message spread rapidly on Facebook, Twitter, and other social media platforms with the hashtag #gulahallateatnamiin. The joik was performed by professional artists such as Sofia Jannok, Elin Kåven, and Max Mackhé, who followed Gaup

5.3. Video (on YouTube) with Sara Marielle Gaup Beaska presenting the Gulahallat Eatnamiin-joik—the importance of engaging in debates about climate change—and inviting everyone to join in Paris performing the jojk (October 2015; https://www.youtube.com/watch?v=H2LhBAi-Q8I&t=18s).

Beaska's instructions and uploaded on YouTube videos of themselves performing the joik. They were rapidly joined by diverse amateur groups and others who chose to take part in this "environmental joik," as it was called in the media.

Joik, a strong symbol of Sáminess and usually considered exclusive to the Sámi, creates and illustrates here a connectedness between groups of people and between human beings and nature. All are invited to learn and perform the joik, thereby sharing in a Sámi Indigenous sense of unity with the environment, and also acknowledging Sámi possession of such a sense in contrast with a majority-culture polity. Well after the Paris conference, Gaup Beaska's joik remains popular among Sámi, particularly when introducing joik to non-Sámi audiences or associates.

Yet another example of such asserted connection is illustrated by the *Sami manifesto 15*, a statement written and performed by a group of Sámi artists at the Jåhkåmåhkke Winter Market in 2015 and then shared on social media. It enumerates the background, motives, and values behind the Sámi rights movement in nine items, starting with "We live and work for this." The second item illustrates directly the value and principle of connectedness:

> 2. Because everything begins and ends with Eanan, mother, land. Eanan is the base for everything. Eanan is the question and the answer. Nothing defines us better than her. Our survival depends on her. It is our responsibility to protect, respect and take care of our mother, so that we, and all the generations to come can live as one with her. Reconnected.

The Saami Manifesto 15: Reconnecting through resistance, by Niillas Holmberg and Jenni Laiti, was published in its totality on March 23, 2015 on www.idlenomore.ca, the website of the Idle No More movement that started in Canada and spread to Indigenous groups around the world. The English-language version of the text begins with the powerful statement: "Sápmi, our homeland, has been colonized and exploited. We, the Saami people, have been dislocated and disconnected from the land and from each other. We are struggling to hold on to the remains of our self-determination, our territorial and cultural rights. Without having the rights to exist and determine our future, we are unable to live as a distinct society." Illustrations and links accompany the text: a photo of the hair that was cut during the protest in front of the Swedish minister of culture and democracy at the winter market, a video link of the same action, and photos from the protest. The text summarizes the action: "This is the story of our non-violent direct action called The Saami Manifesto 15. It shows how peaceful resistance can be powerful, healing and encouraging." The manifesto in itself, with the nine items, appears after the text. At the bottom, a list of names tells us more about the group of artists and activists behind the manifesto. In addition to Niillas Holmberg, poet and musician, and Jenni Laiti, artivist, we find Anders Sunna, known for his large paintings representing conflicts between the state and the reindeer herders,

Max Mackhé, singer/song writer of Swedish origin dedicated to the movement for Sámi rights, and the siblings Maxida and Mimic/Timimie Märak, central in the Gállok protests through their music and spoken word performances. The reconnection is here between human beings and Earth, relying on mutual responsibility, respect, and care—principles identified as central in Indigenous epistemologies (Louis 2007). Images and accounts of the protest online went viral, reaching, according to the protesters, some half-million viewers, gaining marked exposure and attention for the protesters' concerns.

Tuhiwai Smith also brings attention to concepts and practices of *networking* in Indigenous contexts: "Networking has become an efficient medium for stimulating information flows, educating people quickly about issues and creating extensive international talking circles. Building networks is about building knowledge and databases which are based on the principles of relationships and connections" (2012: 157–58). Networking is identified by Tuhiwai Smith as an Indigenous project, that is, one of the twenty-five themes she sets on the agenda for Indigenous research. Networking is based on trust and on the value of individual contacts to include new members; it underscores the importance of gathering. As illustrated in our interviews with Sámi consultants, direct communication is considered essential in Sámi contexts, and contacts developed on occasions of gathering are central, while social media functions mainly as a mode of maintaining and sustaining these contacts.

Networking is also "a form of resistance," as Tuhiwai Smith explains. Networking implies taking a stand, as expressed in activist movements. This has been illustrated and confirmed, for instance, by the Gállok protest movement in 2013, bringing together locals, reindeer herders, environmentalists, artists, and politicians to oppose the plan of building a mine on land long used for reindeer grazing. The cross-references between the movements #IdleNoMore, #Gállok, and later #NoDAPL (the Dakota Access Pipeline protests led by the Standing Rock Sioux and allies that culminated November 2017), illustrate

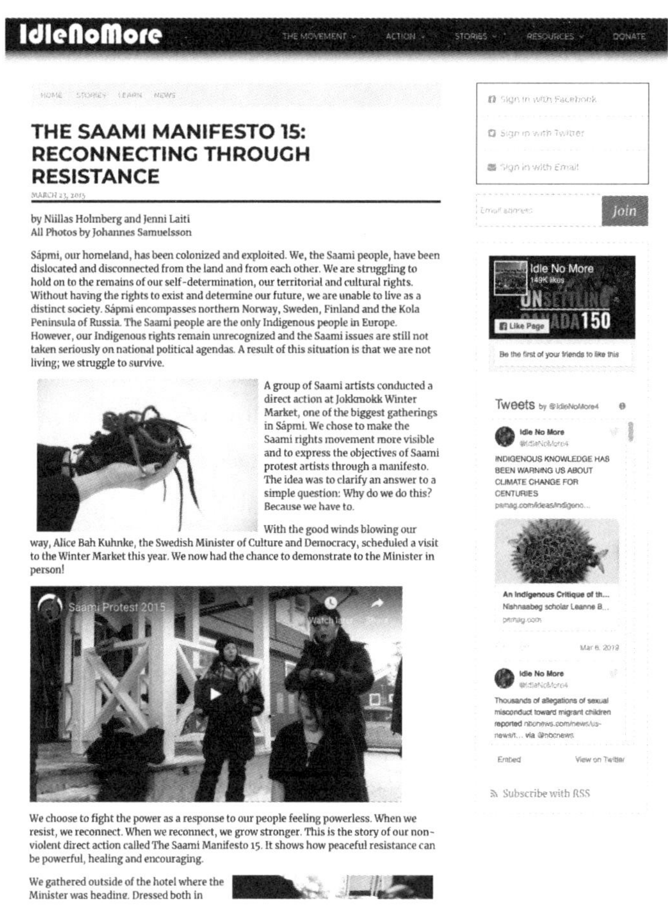

IdleNoMore THE MOVEMENT ACTION STORIES RESOURCES DONATE

THE SAAMI MANIFESTO 15: RECONNECTING THROUGH RESISTANCE

MARCH 23, 2015

by Niillas Holmberg and Jenni Laiti
All Photos by Johannes Samuelsson

Sápmi, our homeland, has been colonized and exploited. We, the Saami people, have been dislocated and disconnected from the land and from each other. We are struggling to hold on to the remains of our self-determination, our territorial and cultural rights. Without having the rights to exist and determine our future, we are unable to live as a distinct society. Sápmi encompasses northern Norway, Sweden, Finland and the Kola Peninsula of Russia. The Saami people are the only Indigenous people in Europe. However, our Indigenous rights remain unrecognized and the Saami issues are still not taken seriously on national political agendas. A result of this situation is that we are not living; we struggle to survive.

A group of Saami artists conducted a direct action at Jokkmokk Winter Market, one of the biggest gatherings in Sápmi. We chose to make the Saami rights movement more visible and to express the objectives of Saami protest artists through a manifesto. The idea was to clarify an answer to a simple question: Why do we do this? Because we have to.

With the good winds blowing our way, Alice Bah Kuhnke, the Swedish Minister of Culture and Democracy, scheduled a visit to the Winter Market this year. We now had the chance to demonstrate to the Minister in person!

Saami Protest 2015

We choose to fight the power as a response to our people feeling powerless. When we resist, we reconnect. When we reconnect, we grow stronger. This is the story of our non-violent direct action called The Saami Manifesto 15. It shows how peaceful resistance can be powerful, healing and encouraging.

We gathered outside of the hotel where the Minister was heading. Dressed both in

Idle No More
149K likes
UNSETTLING CANADA150
Like Page
Be the first of your friends to like this

Tweets by @IdleNoMore4

Idle No More
INDIGENOUS KNOWLEDGE HAS BEEN WARNING US ABOUT CLIMATE CHANGE FOR CENTURIES

An Indigenous Critique of th...
Nishnaabeg scholar Leanne B...

Idle No More
Thousands of allegations of sexual misconduct toward migrant children reported

Embed View on Twitter

Subscribe with RSS

5.4. Screenshot of the Sámi Manifesto, a statement written and performed by a group of Sámi artists at the Jåhkåmåhkke Winter Market in 2015, shared on social media and here published on the site for the Indigenous movement (Idle No More).

how networking– this time on a global Indigenous level–is a means for resistance.

The value of networking between "marginalized communities" (Tuhiwai Smith 2012: 158) is obvious, and although Tuhiwai Smith underscores the essential role of face-to-face encounters, digitally mediated communication has taken on a central role for facilitating networking today, at local as well as global levels. In terms of networking as a form of resistance, digital media have played, and continue to play, a significant role in bringing together groups and allies across the world.

Sharing is yet another Indigenous project that contextualizes Sámi media uses: "Sharing is a process that is responsive to the marginalized contexts in which indigenous communities exist [. . .]. Sharing is also related to the failure of education systems to educate indigenous people adequately and appropriately" (Tuhiwai Smith 2012: 162). The failure of mainstream media to include Indigenous perspectives and cover Indigenous issues, as well as the failure of education systems to offer culturally sensitive and appropriate teaching (Nutti 2012; Owens et al. 2012; Keskitalo et al. 2014), naturally leads people to look for alternative ways of sharing information. The accessibility and ease of use of digital media have come to play an important role in this process. Tuhiwai Smith comments that "the face-to-face nature of sharing is supplemented with local newspapers focusing on indigenous issues and local radio stations specializing in indigenous news and music" (2012: 162). In our contemporary context, we can add social media as yet another source that supplements modes of sharing. Mediated communication through digital media has increased and been applied to several Indigenous movements–as mentioned above in the case of land rights or environmental movements–where such media can allow for the sharing of knowledge and information between Indigenous peoples.

The emergence of digital tools for sharing knowledge about the Sámi languages illustrates this type of Indigenous project. When formal education does not meet the needs for language learning, groups, associations, educational prime movers, and enthusiasts find alternative means for sharing knowledge. Language activism and efforts for revitalizing Sámi languages illustrate how sharing through social media comes as a response to an identified need for an improvement of educational systems. It reflects increasing entwinement of vernacular and institutional efforts in the development of resources for language teaching and learning (Outakoski et al. 2018). Sharing, not least, is addressed in Indigenous methodologies as a "responsibility in research" (Tuhiwai Smith 1999: 161; compare Chilisa 2012).

Connectedness, networking, and sharing are not novel practices emerging in a digital context; nor are they new uses of media. The importance of these practices as "Indigenous projects," as Tuhiwai Smith classifies them, is enacted both online and offline. Researchers must be aware of and critically engage with these values to ensure that research connects in positive ways with those involved in the research. These notions also illustrate the close–and increasingly entwined–relations between global and local. On the one hand, Indigenous groups are strongly cohesive within their communities, connected through strong offline bonds. On the other hand, they are linked to other Indigenous groups as parts of increasingly important international digital networks. Rahte, as the path that was wandered in the Tjïekere and the Sijvo eras, goes through the geographical and the digital places of Sápmi, and strengthens ties between people and places–from #IdleNoMore in Canada to #Sápmi, and from #Gállok to #StandingRock.

6

Sállat

New Tracks

THERE ARE NUMEROUS EXAMPLES SOCIAL MEDIA USES BY SÁMI groups and communities. Groups on Facebook, public or closed, gather people around a broad range of issues, from handicraft to language development, political groups, cultural events programs, and other areas of interest. Twitter and Instagram are used by Sámi authorities for campaigns, as well as by individuals, to engage in the public debate, comment, and discuss media reports and articles. YouTube channels are yet another tool for reaching out, for instance in environmental movements, as illustrated in the preceding chapter in relation to the Gállok events. Social media facilitates network building, such as support networks for parents or for sharing of resources for various purposes, from language learning to genealogical research.

Social media has been around for a while. For many, the web 2.0 and the mobile internet are often integrated in everyday life. But as discussed in the introductory chapter Arvi, media build on each other and the notion of social media as somehow novel should therefore be revised. In order to better understand contemporary media uses and user practices, a look at early examples of participatory media in Sápmi gives us a useful background. The place for departure in this chapter is therefore the internet, more specifically SameNet—the first major Sámi tracks in the digital landscape. We have chosen the digital as one of the places to highlight since this chapter also provides examples and discusses how, when, where, and if the internet can contain and support Sámi places or safe spaces for Sámi individuals and groups.

Sállat

SameNet is a point of reference in Sámi digital media and an early form of social networking service. Contemporary social media platforms such as Facebook are often discussed in comparison with SameNet in Sámi contexts. It is therefore valuable from a historical and intellectual point of view to examine this milestone in the history of Sámi media. In many ways, this early form of service for digital communication was about sállat—putting down new tracks where no one has traveled yet.

SameNet was created as a Sámi network in the Nordic countries, with the ambition to develop a technology that was easily accessible to many, taking into account the lack of infrastructure in the mountain areas and the limitations it implies when it comes to the installation of antennas, poles, and power sources. It all began in 1997—a few years after the Sámi parliaments were established, that is, a favorable ideological context—at the initiative of the Sámiid Riikkasearvi (National Union of the Sami People in Sweden) as a platform supporting online learning, with a group of nineteen women in the county of Västerbotten in Sweden. They were all enrolled in a course about entrepreneurship for women, and the Sámiid Riikkasearvi was looking for a solution for distance learning in this specific context and with this specific target group in mind. The challenge was to find an efficient solution for distance learning adequate for women who wished to complete their education by taking courses, but, for family or other reasons, could not move to bigger cities (where most educational institutions are located).

SameNet was a low-tech solution based on a FirstClass server and web browser. Users also obtained an email address with the domain name @same.net, a mark of affiliation and visibility for a Sámi presence on the internet. It played an important role in this and other educational contexts, responding to a need for distance learning that would allow people with families to combine educational experiences with geographically bound activities in their home locales, thereby maintaining their way of living in rural areas where few universities or other educational institutions exist. From this modest start, SameNet was rapidly adopted not only by organizations and members of the administrative reindeer herding units—as its designers had anticipated—but also by a host of other individuals and institutions in Sápmi. SameNet soon became a digital meeting place, much like the Jåhkåmåhkke Winter Market, but now operating on a dispersed, virtual plane.

SameNet was funded through a combination of different sources: the European Union Interreg programs, the Swedish Sámi parliament, the county administrative boards of Sweden, and some dedicated funds from Norway and Finland. The Sámiid Riikkasearvi and the Sámij Åhpadusguovdásj in Jåhkåmåhkke were the main operators. At its height, it had about seven-thousand users (Sameradion & SVT Sápmi 2011) and some three thousand were still active on the site when it was finally shut down in 2011.

SameNet started with a number of "conferences," that is, groups in which users could meet around a specific topic or point of information or interest. Schools and organizations could have such a "conference," but also groups with a shared interest in a Sámi language, handicraft, social activities, or other issues. Rapidly, the amount of users increased and the *Sámij Åhpadusguovdásj* took over as project leader in order to develop SameNet and prepare for a larger number of users. As project collaborator at the Sámiid Riikkasearvi and main contributor Britt-Marie Barruk explains:

> Vi försökte tänka igenom vilka behov som fanns. Och det vi såg var: att man kunde kommunicera med varann, att man kunde skicka mejl utan att ha mejladresser, att man kunde skriva namn så kom det upp automatiskt. Och sen att vi kunde skapa konferenser för olika organisationer, så de kunde sprida sin information, så man skulle lätt kunna hitta information om olika saker. Och sen satsade vi mycket på språket. Att det skulle vara möjligt att skriva och chatta på alla samiska språk. (Interview 3)[1]

> We tried to think about what needs there were. And we could see that there was a need to communicate with each other, to be able to send a message to someone without email addresses, to be able to find each other "automatically" by entering a name. And also, that we could create places for different organizations to share and circulate information, and to make it easy for people to find information about different things. And then, we invested a lot in the language. That it would be possible to write and chat in all Sámi languages.

Thus, these three main identified needs—direct communication, sharing information, and language use—provided the basis for SameNet. The technical possibility for using the Sámi languages on computers was in its very infancy at that time. The Sámi orthographies include specific graphemes in addition to the letters in a Latin alphabet,[2] and therefore require a keyboard or adapted software that supports the use of Sámi characters. SameNet then became a place where one could use the Sámi language and meet other Sámi speakers. It was available in North, Lule, and South Sámi in addition to the Nordic national languages (Finnish, Norwegian, Swedish). It thereby offered something that was missing from other sites and services, for example, email clients.

According to Britt-Marie Barruk, direct communication was one of the principal uses of SameNet:

> Det var mycket med att chatta, att man kom i kontakt med andra. Man kunde ha chattgrupper och komma i kontakt med varann socialt, umgås med andra [. . .]. Och jag tyckte det vara jätteroligt för att man kunde gå in och kolla vilka som var uppkopplade, och man kunde skicka meddelanden till nån. Bara börja prata och sånt. Alltså samer emellan. För det är klart att man kan gå ut på nätet och så, chatta med vem som helst. Men här hade vi någonting gemensamt. Vi var tillsammans. (Interview 3)
>
> A lot was about chatting, getting in touch with each other. We could have chat groups and socialize, spend time together [. . .]. I really liked that I could see who was connected, and could send a message to someone [who was online at the same time]. It was a way to make new friends. To start talking to each other–I mean, between Sámi. Because of course, you can log in on the internet and chat and such, with anyone. But here, we had something in common. We were together.

The role of SameNet as a facilitator of communication between Sámi is also mentioned by another consultant:

> Det var en som skrev en e-post till mig "Hej. Jag är släkt med dig. Vi har aldrig setts och jag bor i Norge." Min farmor och hennes pappa var syskon. Vi hade aldrig setts! Och jag var så lycklig och glad. Jag gick upp i det blå nästan. Det där betyder så mycket att hon tog kontakt med mig. Än idag har vi kontakt. (Interview 1)
>
> Someone wrote an email to me once: "Hi, I'm your relative. We've never met; I live in Norway." My grandmother and her father were siblings. We had never met! And I was so happy; I was like walking on air. It meant so much that she contacted me. Still today, we keep in touch with each other.

The SameNet networking service included different forums for discussion and exchange of information, not solely for private users. Swedish authorities and organizations also had a presence, such as the county administrative boards. These had somewhat limited access, however: they could share information but had no accessibility to other groups. Although some functions of SameNet were available for authorities and for non-Sámi, SameNet played the role of a Sámi meeting place, as a form of intranet within Sápmi. Britt-Marie Barruk calls it a "citizen network," emphasizing that this aspect of a community grounded platform was crucial.

But SameNet was not only a social media service. It was also a project with the ambition to computerize Sápmi in reindeer herding areas in Sweden in the late 1990s, as Britt-Marie explains:

> Vi gjorde en inventering och det var bara en renskötare som hade en dator i hemmet. Och sen var det några som hade tillgång till dator via sitt jobb. Så vi datoriserade Sápmi. Vi delade ut 400 datorer och utbildade . . . ja, 1000 säkert, i datoranvändandet. (Interview 3)

> We made an inventory that showed that only one reindeer herder had a computer at home. A few had access to a computer at work. So we "computerized" Sápmi. We distributed 400 computers and trained . . . probably at least 1,000 users about how to use a computer.[3]

This initiative was funded by the county administrative boards (the boards of the regions of Västerbotten and Jämtland), and by the minister for communications (Kommunikationsdepartementet). The reindeer herding administrative units (*samebyar*) were key actors in the development of the system that developed gradually into a broader network. There is no doubt that this had a great impact on media use in Sápmi, both in the short and long term.

In an early project description, we can read how one goal of SameNet was "to provide a collaborative social networking environment that supports the already existing cultural interaction and democratic structures of the Sámi people."[4] Britt-Marie Barruk elaborates:

> Det var väldigt vanligt att informationen kom uppifrån. Men här byggde SameNet på något sätt på behovet som kom nerifrån, det människorna ville. Och alla var ju lika på SameNet på nå't vis. Det fanns ingen status eller så. Alla hade möjlighet att skriva, skriva det man själv ville, kände och tyckte, kunde uttrycka, i olika konferenser och så där. Det var inte nån som bestämde vad som skulle stå. (Interview 3)

> A very common way for distributing information was top-down. But SameNet was built in such a way that it corresponded to the need that was defined at a grassroots level, based on what people wanted. Everyone was on the same level on SameNet, in some way. People had no specific status. And everyone could write about whatever they wanted, whatever they felt or wanted to express, in different groups. There was no one who decided what should or shouldn't be posted.

This description of the ideology behind SameNet, free of hierarchical structures and open for users to contribute and collaborate, corresponds to what would a few years later be called the "web 2.0" (DiNucci 1999). This follows some of the expectations from the early development of the internet, that is, the ambition to provide access to information to anyone, anywhere (Howard and Cocq 2017; Turner 2006).

SameNet was developed as a grassroots, citizens' network. It illustrates the possibilities and ambitions of the World Wide Web. But it was also dependent on larger structures, as became clear as the needs and costs for maintenance and development increased. The costs for the FirstClass server were becoming prohibitive, pointing to the necessity of developing a new, web-based system, which would have required new funding sources. The project leaders had the ambition and a dedicated desire to develop SameNet further into a user-friendly and easily accessible platform. The success of the initial project and the solid base of users it attracted were good prerequisites for developing SameNet into a system that would fully embrace the possibilities of the web 2.0. Despite efforts and a number of applications for funding, however, the Sámiid Riikkasearvi and Sámij Åhpadusguovdásj recognized the lack of resources they faced and gave up on their plans. Rapidly, technological development–such as new social networking services and cheaper or open-access platforms for distance learning–contributed to making SameNet obsolete. After a period of uncertain financial support, SameNet was eventually closed in 2011.

For project collaborator Britt-Marie Barruk, the lack of financial support had larger implications: shutting down SameNet meant the loss of a cultural-specific network and channel for communication. Other media services, addressing a global audience, do not respond to the needs of the Sámi community in the same way or with the same degree of success. To the question about what she misses most, she answers: "Det där sociala. Att man alltid hade nån att prata med. Å att man bara kunde . . . öppna en ruta och prata med nån. Där kunde man prata med dem man inte kände. För att vi var samer" (The social aspect. That you always had someone to talk to. You could just . . . open a chat window and talk with someone. There, you could talk to someone you didn't know. Because we were all Sámi). The significance of a "Sámi space" on the internet is, for Britt-Marie Barruk, essential because of the specific situation in which Sámi groups live, that is, as members of a minority group in a majority context that lacks knowledge and awareness of Sámi issues. She states:

> Jag tycker att vi som ett urfolk har faktiskt rätt att ha ett eget kommunikationsnät. Och det där behovet, det finns fortfarande även om man tänker 'det finns Facebook' och det finns grupper

> uppe där, olika samiska grupper eller så. Men det är inte samma sak, för det där var bara för samiska ändamål. (Interview 3)
>
> I think that we, as Indigenous people, have the right to our own network for communication. And this need is still there, even if one can think "there is Facebook," and there are groups there, also Sámi groups. But it is not the same, because there it was only for Sámi purposes.

The need identified here is the one of a dedicated and owned space—designed, conceptualized, and controlled by the community. Britt-Marie underscores that it is about the right "to own and to communicate about our issues, about what is important to us." The social logic here, one shaped by the uneven power relations of minority group and majority population, carries over into social media and mirrors what is found in other forms of communication in the Nordic Sámi context.

Indigenizing Global Media

The difficulty for global media to replace SameNet is also discussed by another consultant I interviewed, a cultural worker and active user of social media:

> Facebook är fantastiskt bra, men det jag saknar med Facebook: man vet inte vad man riktar sig till. Man har vänner, men. . . . Man får begränsa, för vissa kan det bli "för mycket samiskt". Och att man kanske måste vara tydligare och förklara: det där är nåt samiskt, lite speciellt; istället för att inte behöva förklara nånting som det var på SameNet. Då kunde man gå till kärnan direkt. (Interview 5)[5]
>
> Facebook is fantastic, but what I miss, it is that you never really know whom you are addressing. You have friends, but. . . . One

> has to limit oneself, because for some it can be "too much Sámi stuff." So then you have to clarify and explain: "this is particular, it is a Sámi thing." Instead, you did not have to explain anything when it was on SameNet. You could go directly to the essence of the matter.

A shared cultural understanding is here identified as key for communicating without having to explain and justify oneself. Facebook offers occasions to share information and discuss everything from details of everyday life to serious personal, political, or global problems. But when it comes to specific topics, in this case issues of relevance in Sámi contexts, the heterogeneity of the "friends" in the network provokes frictions in communication.

The potential for Facebook to provide an equivalent to SameNet seems limited, as another consultant elaborates:

> Vissa saker är bra, att sprida info på Facebook är bra. Även att, umgås . . . men det där med språket tycker jag inte är så utbrett. Man ser ibland att någon skriver på samiska, det är liksom. . . . Man kan starta en grupp, men. Det var enklare på SameNet. Det var greppbart. Det är vi, och vi ser vilka som är med, är uppkopplade. Och det kändes säkert också. "Det är inte hela världen som läser det där som jag skriver nu. Utan det är vi som är här, det är ett sätt för oss att kommunicera." (Interview 4)

> Some things are good, like sharing information, Facebook is good for that. Also to socialize. But as for the language, it is not so used. You can see that someone writes in Sámi once in a while but. . . . Or you can start a group. But it was easier on SameNet. It was graspable, it was us, we knew who was there, who was online. And it felt safe too. "It is not like if all the world can see what I am writing now. It is us who are there, it is a way for us to communicate."

As illustrated here, having a graspable audience was one component that played a key role in the ease and accessibility of SameNet. For this consultant, it is not only the heterogeneity of the audience that complicates communication but also the fact that users do not have control of what they share. The risks for an unknown, unwelcome reader to access information that is shared within the network causes suspicion and a feeling of insecurity.

One of the consultants observes the different degree of personal contact on Facebook in comparison to SameNet:

> Får du ett meddelande på SameNet, det är mer riktat. Du måste ta hand om det. Medan man kan få inbjudningar [på Facebook], om jag ser jag har 70 inbjudningar kan vara till premiärer, jag *måste* inte gå in där. Jag kollar om jag är nyfiken. (Interview 5)

> When you received a message on SameNet, it was directly addressed to you. You had to take care of it. On Facebook, you can receive invitations. If I see that I have 70 invitations to openings and gallery nights, I don't *have to* even look at it. I can check if I am curious about it.

Facebook supports collective or group communication and enables people to share and circulate information broadly, easily, and to multiple audiences at the same time. The benefits of this service for recruiting, marketing, and for massive campaigns leave no doubt. The downside is the lack of personal contact, for example, when invitations to events are impersonal, shared information rather than personalized invitations addressed to a specific recipient.

Facebook, in its structure and affordances, corresponds to some extent to what SameNet was. Both platforms share the possibility for users to build groups, circulate information, and chat. In this way, it was not a big step for SameNet users to adopt Facebook. The main difference between the two platforms lies in the community of users: on the one hand, a specific community with a great degree of shared cultural knowledge and understanding, and, on the other hand, a broad global community of users for whom the only common denominator might be an account on Facebook.

A strain of nostalgia can be noted when SameNet is described, throwing a merely positive light on how it is narrated today. But despite the void left after SameNet was shut down, new forms of community networks emerge, illustrating how the needs remain, as Britt-Marie Barruk observes: "We have to create our own spaces now. And that is what people do. On Facebook, or Instagram, like many youngsters do" (Interview 3). But Britt-Marie, along with other Sámi users, is convinced that Facebook has not and cannot replace SameNet. What we can find are traces of it, in the form of groups that were once conference groups on SameNet, and that are now reconstituted as Facebook groups. One example is Samiska Posten ("the Sámi post office"), a digital ride-board group that used to be a popular "conference" on SameNet and that is now a Facebook group where people announce to each other their needs for a ride or for sending a package on the one hand, and their planned travels in Sápmi on the other hand. The purpose of such posts is to match and coordinate the transport of goods and people and to facilitate ride sharing.

The Facebook group with the same name counts 3,379 members as of March 2018. The group description reads, "Träffpunkt för resande, passagerare eller gods i behov av varandra. Här sätts reseinformation ut om man vill ha sällskap av en människa eller påse på sin resa" (A meeting place for travelers, passengers or goods in need of each other. Here, travel information is shared if you want the company of a person or a parcel along on your travels).[6] Posts are mostly short messages asking, for instance, if anyone will be driving from Giron to Jåhkåmåhkke in the coming days, or informing others that there is room in a car going from Gárasavvon to Guovdageaidnu later the same day.

6.1. Screenshot of the Facebook-group Samiska Posten (https://www.facebook.com/groups/214215213713).

Samiska Posten re-creates to some extent the safe zone that SameNet used to provide, as one consultant comments:

> Det är det som är tryggheten med *Samiska posten*, jag kan lätt ta reda på vem personen är, jag behöver inte söka . . . jag hör av mig till folk som känner nån som känner nån [. . .].
>
> Den där känslan att "jag behöver inte tänka", jag tror att det är det positiva, det är det som är [varifrån jag kommer]. Som den där gruppen [Samiska Posten]. Jag tänker inte att det är samer där.

Och det är det som är det positiva, att det är en samisk grupp. Det är våran . . . Ja, det är något väldigt positivt. (Interview 2)

This is why I can feel safe with *Samiska posten*, I can easily find out who people are, I don't have to search. . . . I contact people who know someone who knows someone [. . .].

This feeling that "I don't need to think," I think it is the positive thing with it, it is like [where I come from]. Like this group [the Sámi post office]. I don't think about the fact that we are all Sámi there. And that is what is positive about it, that it is a Sámi group. It is ours . . . Yes, it is something very positive.

The role of this group is emphasized by another consultant, who underscores the importance of keeping in touch with others throughout the large area of Sápmi and the importance of social media in facilitating such communication: "Som med *Samiska posten*, att kunna skicka ett paket till Stockholm. 'Är det nån som kan . . . Jag är på väg dit . . .' Och det kanske är en bekants bekant . . . nån man känner för att det är ens kusins barnbarns barn"; Interview 1 (With Samiska Posten, [it is easy] to send a package to Stockholm. "Is there anyone who can. . . . I'm on my way there. . . ." And maybe it is a friend of a friend . . . someone you recognize because it is the great grandchild of a cousin). The story behind SameNet makes clear that it was much more than an early form of social media. The ideology behind SameNet and the embrace it received in Sápmi confirms the needs identified by its founders. The impact it had on media use in Sápmi can hardly be questioned. First, SameNet was a catalyst for the implementation of computer use in Sápmi. Reindeer herders were given access to computers and to information in a way and at a speed that was not possible before, and the platform facilitated education by offering distance-learning courses. Second, SameNet succeeded in reaching a broad range of users, in term of generations, geographical locations, and professional groups. It was a door opener for implementing and developing the use of computers, internet, and, later, social media. Finally, SameNet as a project identified specific needs in the community. It pointed at the potential and possibilities of digital communication for Sámi groups to use their language, influence the flow of information, and create and strengthen networks.

(Re)creating Place

Practices and activities on the internet contribute to creating places—a form of geography—where people can meet, share experiences, and give support to one other. One of the consultants I interviewed, an active user of social media, expresses more explicitly the role of the internet (more specifically, Facebook in this case) in this context: "To me, Facebook is like Sápmi, it is my Sápmi, where I have access to all these people [. . .]. If you don't have Sápmi outside your door, then you can find it in there" (Interview 5).

The area of Sápmi is not a defined territory with geographical borders within which all Sámi people live. People live in different countries, move over time from rural areas of Sápmi to cities in the south or on the coast, and circulate in other ways over time and space. Sápmi has thereby a diffuse status, which opens it for negotiation, controversy, and disputing claims. Legal proceedings about grazing lands or about hunting and fishing rights in courts are examples of this dispersed situation. Sápmi has been colonized, populated by various other groups, and subjected to a variety of industries (forestry, mining, hydropower, tourism) on top of earlier traditional activities (herding, fishing, hunting). Today, many actors share the land of Sápmi, co-existing and negotiating with one other, but also entering into at times bitter disputes about rights associated with land and water. The reactions to the introduction of signboards with place-names in Sámi—greatly welcomed by some, defaced by others—are yet another example of the tensions taking place between groups in

Sápmi. These tensions become more palpable the more visible the Sámi become in given locales or in Nordic societies at large. Despite its lack of formal administrative and legal boundaries, Sápmi is a strong identifier for Sámi people. For some, it might be a place of belonging; for others a place of origin, and for others still, a place of heritage. It is, however, not only associated with ancestors or traditions of the past and inherited cultural knowledge. Sápmi is also a point of reference and a meeting place in the present, a site for engagement, activism, and innovation.

Relationships to physical places can strongly come to expression through digital place making, such as for instance in the case of diasporic communities (Srinivasan 2006), creating new places and venues for gathering and socializing (Bernal 2005; Ritter 2017). Also, the role of the internet for "space deprived" groups has been discussed in previous research (e.g. Hillier and Harrison 2007) and underscores the value of digital places for maintaining community values and building identity. In the case of Sápmi, the lack of acknowledged formal belonging to the land, for instance as citizens, in combination with a strong sense of belonging to the ancestral land, generates a need for defining a space in the sense of a social and cultural environment where one can feel "at home." Place making online can thus contribute to creating a form of social geography with the physical land as a referent and the digital place as its expression.

As one of the consultants puts it, Sámi groups lack a "homeland" (Interview 2). In this sense, place-making processes are less about the accessibility to the land and more about the recognition of the status of Sápmi as a land. Place making, then, is also about making Sápmi visible within the nation-states that claim it (Norway, Sweden, Finland, and Russia). These processes take place offline and online, and digital media can be seen as one means (among many) for articulating a sense of Sápmi. Social media facilitates communication, making it easier to keep in touch and stay up-to-date. The importance of this form of social interaction was underscored as one of the goals of SameNet, and as one of the main roles played by more recent social media platforms.

Social Media as a Public Space

The increased online presence of Sámi also brings with it a visibility that is not solely positive. The tensions, disputes, and contestations that take place offline emerge—not surprisingly—online as well. The internet and social media are public domains where perspectives, opinions, and conflicts are enacted; something that was mentioned by several of the consultants. As one of them puts it: "[Social media] can bring awful things. It is a disadvantage with social media. That people can be mean . . ." (Interview 1). The consultant gives examples of such a situation, connected with the hashtag campaign, #árgarasismamuvuostásápmelažžan (in North Sámi) and #vardagsrasismotmigsomsame (in Swedish)[7] (everyday racism against me as a Sámi), in which people were invited to describe instances of "everyday racism," that is, racist practice, meaning racism as common societal behavior (Essed 1991, 2004), they had faced in the Nordic countries. The campaign had been intended as an awareness-builing process, helping majority members understand the myriad ways in which Sámi can be made to feel excluded, exoticized, dismissed, or diminished in their daily interactions with majority-culture friends, coworkers, or neighbors. Posts were open to comments, however, and several received hostile and openly aggressive comments. The consultant explains:

> Jag tänkte på det där som Sameradion hade om vardagsrasism, kampanjen, och vilket gensvar det fick, och även otäcka saker. För jag skrev själv i den, under hastaggen, det kom massa folk som hade ett massa tyckande, som inte hade med saken att göra, och som lyfte sig själva till sån dager. . . . Shit! Och jag känner vissa personer [. . .] som uttrycker sig väldigt kritiskt mot samiskt . . .

> det blir bara "shit! Hur ska jag ta det där?" Det kom till ytan på nåt sätt . . . (Interview 1)

> I was thinking about the campaign about everyday racism. . . . This campaign, and the response it got, and even nasty things. Because I posted under the hashtag, and there were lots of people who had lots of opinions but had nothing to do with the matter. And they show themselves in such a light. . . . Shit! And I know some of these people [. . .] who express themselves very critically against Sámi . . . and I was like "Shit! How should I take that?" It brought things to the surface in a way . . .

The topic of conversation created by the hashtag opened a discussion in which "anyone" could participate: personal stories became public posts in a larger context. Visibility creates conditions of disclosure. On social media (Facebook in the specific case of the consultant quoted above), multiple voices compete for the chance of being heard.

The specific topic of the everyday racism hashtag campaign challenges in itself the idea of a protective, safe space. As Tobias Poggats, one of the journalists involved in the campaign, puts it, the aim was to create a place where "Sámi people could talk to each other, where Sámi stories were available, and people told us stories about a topic we had chosen (racism)" (Interview 7). As a "side-effect" or a secondary aim, the campaign would increase awareness about the fact that racism against the Sámi exists, and about its extent, as journalist and project leader Katarina Hällgren emphasizes:

> Från ett journalistiskt perspektiv: jag ville lyfta de berättelserna. Jag blev själv förvånad. Det är så normaliserat. Det blir en stor klyfta mot majoritetssamhället. Vi vet att det finns, men det är som "vaddå, vet inte ni att det finns?" [. . .] Det blev också en kampanj för att stärka det samiska, upptäckte jag. Det betyder nåt att inte vara ensam.[8] (Interview 6)

From a journalistic perspective, I wanted to throw light on the stories. I was surprised myself! It is so normalized. There is such a big gap compared to the majority society. We [Sámi] know it [racism] is there, but it is like "What?! Don't you know that it exists?!" [. . .] Also, I realized that it became a campaign that strengthened Sáminess. It means something, to know that you are not alone.

The lack of knowledge about the contemporary situation for the Sámi in Sweden—one of the motivations for the campaign—also helps explain everyday racism, that is, that it is not expressed in extreme situations, but through patterns of action in everyday life, for instance based on stereotypes (Skielta et al. 2014), that are not necessarily consciously held or engaged (Hällgren 2017). The two-fold aim of the campaign implies that there is an intended participatory audience—those who want to contribute and share their stories—and an (intended) passive audience, those who get to see, read about, and become more aware of everyday racism. The participatory nature of social media, however, made it possible for "unintended" participants to attempt to join the campaign. As Tobias Poggats explains: "På Twitter är det öppet. Det kom några 'ägghuvud,' vita nationalister, som försökte kapa hastaggen [. . .]. Men sen Instagram och Facebook var lättare. Det var att vara med och samtala och fråga" (Interview 7; On Twitter it's open. There were some eggheads, white nationalists, trying to hijack the hashtag [. . .]. But on Instagram and Facebook it was easier. It was more about joining the discussion and answering questions).[9] Despite these difficulties, the journalists behind the campaign viewed the inappropriate, misplaced, or offensive comments as limited. Also, Katarina Hällgren underscored how the fact that "trolls spoke up and tried to undermine the campaign only gave the hashtag even more power. It confirmed that it [racism] exists" (Interview 6).

Although such conflicts were viewed as distressing, another consultant also explains how racism on social media can be turned into something positive:

> Och det är ju väldigt bra också, att nättrollen kommer fram, så man kan peka och visa att de där åsikterna finns. Det är ingenting som du hittar på. Så på så sätt är det fantastiskt bra. Att det inte är något som någon sa när ingen annan hörde . . . svårt att bevisa annars. Nu är det skrivet. (Interview 2)

> And it is very good also that the trolls come out, so you can point at them and show that those opinions exist; that it is not something you make up. That way, it's surprisingly positive. It is not something that someone said when no one else listens, which is hard to prove. Now it is written.

In this sense, social media is a public space rather than a closed room. Its openness and accessibility might facilitate unpleasant and unwanted comments, but also ensure that any exchange is not limited to a transmitter and a receiver. The seeming heterogeneity and multiplicity of audiences entailed in such media may be particularly characteristic of participatory media, although, as we will discuss below, simultaneous communication to multiple audiences is by no means a new phenomenon, particularly in the Sámi context.

Narrative Strategies Online

Audiences on social media are rarely well-defined or clearly identified groups of users. Disparate audiences meet in one and the same network, and become to a great extent integrated into a single group of participants. This phenomenon has been described as the flattening of multiple audiences, sometimes termed a "context collapse" (Vitak 2012: 541; Marwick and Boyd 2011; Papacharissi 2010), but earlier formulations of the notion have been refined when studying specific forms of social action and online communication (Blommaert and Szabla 2017). In the case of SameNet, the context of communication was clearly defined and delimited. The form of community that unified the users is illustrated by the phrasing of consultant 4: "it was us." The groups shaped on the platform as "conferences" were administered and accessible to specific users. In comparison, in the case of Facebook, the platform aims at supporting the creation of networks, encouraging people to make new "friends" and connections. Bringing together audiences into a network is what is facilitated in this case. On this basis, SameNet and Facebook aim at opposite modes of networking: one striving for the strengthening of existing communities and groups, the other one striving for developing ways of reaching out and building new networks. The social network service Facebook offers the possibility of regulating how public a group or a post can be. The content of closed and secret groups is only accessible to members, who have to be approved by an administrator. But although Facebook can be used in various ways, the question of audience—who is present, who the potential reader is et cetera—was brought up by several of the consultants in the interviews conducted. The heterogeneity of the apparent audience adds a feeling of uncertainty and insecurity in communication through social media, as illustrated by this consultant's comment: "One has to limit oneself, because for some it can be too much Sámi stuff. So then you have to clarify and explain: 'this is particular, it is a Sámi thing'" (Interview 5).

Another aspect to be taken into account when discussing the impact of, and the adaptation to, the audience on social media is the discrepancy between what one user might have in mind when publishing or sharing a post, and the way in which the actual recipient of the post interprets or experiences it. In cases when the assumed reader includes a variety of people from different networks, messages carrying cultural-specific information may be avoided. The risk for misunderstanding or the reluctance to have to explain or justify oneself can thus result in self-censorship, the strategic selection of what can be communicated in a particular online setting.

The heterogeneity of likely audience requires an adaptation of the message, or at times even censorship, as one consultant explains:

> Det vi pratat om hemma när det gäller samiska frågor så får man alltid veta att "det där säger vi inte någon annanstans" [. . .].
>
> Det känns obehagligt när jag blir för personlig. Det känns som att jag förråder mitt folk. För att jag berättar om mitt folk. (Interview 2)

> What we talk about at home, about Sámi topics, we have always been told "we don't talk about this anywhere else" [. . .].
>
> I feel uncomfortable because I'm getting too personal [if I say too much outside a Sámi context]. It feels like betraying my people, because I tell about my people.

In online contexts, the knowledge of the presence of a broad, unidentified audience might lead one to choose not to share certain things. This form of audience accommodation can be a conscious strategy as well as a learned and acquired way of communicating. But it is not only possible context collapse and a mixed audience that complicate communication on social media. Also, potential readers (of a post, a status update, a tweet, etc.) can be part of an ominously invisible, inscrutable audience (Cocq 2015; Marwick and Boyd 2011). Being able to identify other members in the online platform or the forum, that is, to communicate to a known, defined audience, contributes to the sense of safety online. "Feeling safe" is also articulated by the consultants we interviewed as the opposite of being suspicious; for example, wondering or worrying about who might read a given post. Issues of surveillance and reliability are mentioned in the case of Facebook. The uncertainty of any guarantee of privacy and ownership in connection with posts, photos, et cetera causes problems when seeking a place to communicate freely, as one of the consultant comments:

> Man litar inte riktigt på sociala medier. Man vet inte, om det [man skriver] hamnar det nånstans, i nåt moln, där andra kan se . . . Det har jag också uppfattat från andra, andra säger så [. . .].

> "Det där tar vi via telefon": vi pratar i telefon när det är privat istället för att ta det på sociala medier. (Interview 1)
>
> You can't really trust social media. You don't know if [what you write] ends up in a cloud somewhere, if others can see. That's also what I have understood, what other people say [. . .]. "Let's take it on the phone." We talk on the phone when it gets personal, instead of social media.

Another active user of social media recounts that she is careful whenever writing something on Facebook: "You know that if it is on Facebook, it is on the internet, everywhere" (Interview 4). This view is shared by another consultant, who always thinks about "who can read this? Who can get access to this and read this?" when writing something on the internet (Interview 2). She underscores the importance of trust and safety in communication. This is not only in relation to the technological obscurity of the internet; it is also a matter of audience and addressee: "It is important to know who is part of the group [a Facebook-group or a network]."

The question of trust is directly related to the issue of privacy, that is, how skepticism toward the internet causes a concern for privacy and for what might happen with what is expressed online. The question of what is perceived and intended as private or public is a central point of discussion in internet research, and a key issue for many active internet users. For a digital space to function as a safe space, the thin line between public and private communication needs to respond to the expectations and values of the users. Even though what we write, post, and publish on social media forums, blogs, and other online sources becomes potentially public, the notion of perceived privacy is central in order to understand the intentions of users. As pertinently underscored by Markham and Buchanan, perceptions and definitions of privacy vary individually and culturally. Privacy, they state, "is a concept that must include a consideration of expectations and consensus. Social, academic, or regulatory delineations of public and private as a clearly recognizable binary no longer holds in everyday practice" (2012: 6). A channel for communication might be public; a topic of discussion or the theme of a post might not be identified as particularly personal. Still, the author might write with a specific addressee or limited audience in mind and with no intention to share his or her thoughts or opinions with others.

Here, perceptions on selfhood and identities may also come into play (Ess and Sudweeks 2001; Ho 1995). The importance of kinship and social relations in Sámi culture, for instance, means that questions of relational identities are central in discourses and strategies about privacy. This is in contrast with a predominant Western perception of privacy, which focuses on individual identities that can be defined independently of a wider group (Marwick and Boyd 2018; Rennie et al. 2018). A relational understanding of privacy is illustrated, for instance, in Interview 2 (quoted above): being "too personal" might result in the feeling of "betraying." The central role of the collective as well as the individual in Sámi contexts is also articulated in relation to right of self-determination and ethical guidelines, where collective consent has been identified and suggested as a key criterion for the feasibility of research projects about health or the use of biological data (Kvernmo et al. 2018).

In the context of social media use, this perception of privacy is articulated as a need for a space "of our own," "as Indigenous people" (Interview 3) and as a prerequisite for feeling confident about communicating via digital media. Perceptions of privacy and relational identities that do not match global, Western views and practices are here pitted against the technological affordances of the social media platform. A lack of privacy as experienced by social media users does not solely create a risk of self-censorship, as expressed in Interview 2 quoted above. Other communicative strategies and considerations may also come into play. Double communication, for instance, has been identified in Sámi contexts as a strategy to enable users to manage multiple audiences or "context collapse." This ability to adjust communication and the consciousness of what it implies has been described in previous research in the case of Sámi joik (Gaski 2000b), storytelling (Cocq 2008), art (Sandström, forthcoming). Harald Gaski has observed the secretive aspects of performances and texts in joik: "A subtle use of double meaning in the yoik poetry made it possible to communicate on two levels at the same time, so that one type of message was conveyed to a Sami audience and quite a different one to outsiders" (2000b: 196).

In a similar manner, narrative strategies indicate that "folklore can function at many different levels in the community" (Mathisen 1993: 40; see also Cocq 2008; DuBois 1996) and carry meaning, associations, and nuances that an audience outside the community might not perceive. Thus, messages can be embedded in a song or a story, and function as vehicles for a specific meaning for community members, making sense in a different manner to an outsider audience. The awareness of multiple audiences and the need to adapt to their varied expectations is not specific to the contemporary digital context of Sápmi, as consultant 5 notes: "Facebook . . . I think Sápmi knows about this form of communication. We are used to have to relate to many, different kind of people" (Interview 5). In this consultant's view, strategies in digital communication in terms of audience management are something well established in Sápmi, existing long before web 2.0 and outside of online contexts.

Filter Bubbles?

Participatory media—through which users can contribute with their own content, with a possibility of exerting influence over information, representations, and knowledge to a greater extent than in traditional media—hold the potential to become a means of questioning and challenging structures and power relations (Rainie et al. 2012; Fuchs 2010; Bruns 2008; Morozov 2011). However, participatory media are part of larger social and cultural contexts that affect both how they are shaped and used, that is, their contents and impacts (compare Sassen 2004; O'Neil 2014). One limitation that arises is the difficulty of reaching out (Lindgren and Cocq 2017) and extending one's audience beyond a cohort of like-minded users, or creating a space of dialogue and exchange for those on opposite sides of a debate, for instance, in environmental activism (Cocq 2016).

But, as we have noted, technological affordances and communicative practices on social media enable users to develop strategies in order to address multiple audiences simultaneously. For instance, tweets in Sámi can circulate in groups where Sámi is not understood by a portion of the potential audience. The reach of messages in Swedish can be enhanced by adding hashtags in English. Such practices can become a strategy for tweeters to connect to several groups, increasing the potential reach to new audiences. For geographically localized marginalized communities, social media enables communication with distant groups and places. But it is also, foremost, a means of making visible common (local) interests and goals on a global scale (Lindgren and Cocq 2017).

Such media use has the potential to empower community members by allowing them to take control over representations and information available through other communicative channels (e.g., government statements, news accounts, stated opinions of non-Sámi). Other empowering dimensions can be achieved by reaching out: for example, the use and application of media as tools and communicative channels can address the need to reach out to new audiences and burst the so-called "filter bubbles" that often enfold internet readers. Such acts can foster greater democratization of media and media content. Filter bubbles describe metaphorically the homogenized flow of information that results from the selection of information that algorithms (from search engines, social network services, etc.) compile for users based on their previous actions and behaviors and identified preferences. Consequently, internet users become separated from information that differs from their own cultural, ideological, or political views and interests. Filter bubbles may then result in ideological segregation, a concern that has been raised in several studies (Pariser 2011; Sunstein 2009; Pentina and Tarafdar 2014). The existence of such bubbles has, however, been revised in other studies, which also question the extent or effects and consequences of the filtering of information for internet users. Bearing in mind the multiplicity of existing sources, social media flows may become constricted, but they are not the only sources of input and information, and they are far from the only or even the primary mode of communication for users of social media. Moreover, even when the exposure to diverse ideological perspectives is limited, such limiting of viewpoints is not unique or restricted to online contexts; filter bubbles are longstanding parts of human societies (Barberá et al. 2015; Weinberger 2008). Researchers also point to the positive effects, or the need for, bubbles for group formation, collective identities, and for building relationships and political movements (Weinberger 2008; O'Hara 2014).

To some extent, SameNet can be described as having been such a space. It was designed for and aimed at increasing contacts and relations between Sámi community members, based on shared interests. It intentionally limited the degree of interaction with other actors. This was the result of the identification of a need for such a "bubble" in the broader Sámi community, and it correlates with the positive effects observed, for instance, by Weinberger (2008) in other contexts regarding the strengthening and building of groups, as well as the formation and maintenance of identities and relationships. Communicative strategies illustrate nonetheless that Sámi groups have embraced the possibilities for outreach communication on social media, making use of networks through links and hashtags and regulating the degree of openness or accessibility of groups. The importance of inreach communication, and of a need to control who has access to what statements, also leads to other strategies such as self-censorship and double-communication, both longstanding characteristics of Sámi communication in a longstanding colonial context.

Embodied Communities Online

SameNet was perceived as a safe space, specifically for the Sámi community. It was partly about creating a space apart from hegemonic structures, where one did not need to consider these structures when communicating. What consultants identify as "safe" and as a "need"—or even as a "right"—is a place where one does not have to accommodate modes and contents of communication in response to an audience outside the community, a place where one's statements, in a word, cannot be "overheard."

The feeling of safety, and the contrasting feeling of being at risk of speaking to a larger public than the one intended, recur as topics in many of the interviews conducted. The need for a "safe zone" for communication appears of central importance to many Sámi community members and may be strongly connected with the traditional importance of intimate interpersonal contacts within Sámi culture—with family, relatives, and friends.

A safe space implies feeling safe in a social sense, where community members can express themselves freely: free from fear and anxiety, away from stereotypes, and away from a general lack of knowledge that affects the ways in which Sámi are perceived by the majority population—or, at the very least, the way many often feel they are perceived. Such a space needs to be regulated by the group itself, which requires and presupposes specific efforts in the case of underrepresented minorities, who often have little direct access to leadership and decision-making in the wider society. Access to safe spaces affords minority groups another essential benefit: it can prove a crucial prerequisite for mounting resistance to discrimination and marginalization (Scott 1990).

In Nordic mainstream societies today, there is a general lack of knowledge about Sámi people, languages, livelihoods, or culture. As a consequence, Sámi community members who are active social media users often encounter situations in which they must explain, represent, or endorse various Sámi actions or issues, acting in other words, as ambassadors for their people and culture. Racism, discrimination, or simply a persistent lack of understanding regarding the contemporary situations of Sámi today mean that public debates and discussions on social media can turn into unpleasant, threatening, or aggressive encounters. The need for a platform or arena in which one does not need to deal with or can prevent these forms of encounters—a safe space—is legitimate.

Consequently, Sámi uses of social media for communication do not primarily aim at reaching out to a global audience or at extending networks. Instead, inreach communication—based on a shared cultural understanding and the strengthening of contacts within the Sámi community—is what Sámi users identify as most important aspect or purpose of social media in the interviews conducted. If outwardly directed communication intended for a global audience may offer valuable opportunities for increased visibility, a diffuse and partly unidentified readership engenders a risk for censorship, or at least for unease in communication.

The need for internet spaces that are safe and liberating, and the construction of such spaces by specific groups, are topics that have been identified in other online contexts. Studies by Kitchin (1998) and Sharf (1997) illustrate how the internet and social media can constitute a place where users who are marginalized or stigmatized within majority contexts can build networks and spaces for interaction in which they are protected from overt or seemingly unintentional aggression. Users can choose to engage in discussions and networks on social media platforms anonymously or through fictive identities. In situations where the social context may render it more difficult for people to express opinions and identities, such platforms can facilitate communication in a frame that feels safe to users. They make it possible for users to shape the norms and values of the specific (online) communities they choose to participate in, no matter how different they are from those of the mainstream context.

Communities that emerge online as the result of networks of users seeking platforms distinct from offline contexts are to some extent "disembodied," as described in previous research (Sharf 1997). Often, they are composed of participants who may have few offline interactions with each other. The Sámi contexts examined here differ to a great extent from what such past research has described. A "safe space" in a Sámi context is here described as a place where one is able to identify who one is talking to, and where there is a strong connection to the offline Sámi community and networks. Relations and knowledge about a network contribute to trust and confidence. Anonymity and connections distinct from offline life, on the contrary, create feelings of anxiety and threat. In this sense, the creation of Sámi online communication is not about a disembodied community. It is, rather, about a community whose online activity is (experienced as) safe and successful to the extent that it corresponds to existing offline networks and structures within Sámi groups, that is, as clearly linked to embodied networks. These various forms of community building—embodied or disembodied—and the ways they make different people or communities feel safe or threatened, correspond to specific social and cultural needs, perceptions, and contexts. Here, the need for maintaining and strengthening culturally specific forms of communication appears to be better achieved through online communities that are embodied. Still, one can feel safe in a specific online environment when discussing certain issues but prefer another forum for other topics or forms of communication. Rather than identifying one safe space, what we can observe in this Sámi context—as perhaps in situations among other minority or Indigenous communities—are differing practices and opportunities for creating a safe zone in different ways. Technologies, platforms, and communicative channels differ in the degree of control they afford to users. Whereas the algorithms and workings of modern search engines and social media services are often described through the metaphor of a "black box," SameNet featured a transparent structure and was managed by Sámi community members in direct relation with the users. The line and flow of production, use, and consumption of communications on SameNet were grounded in the community and controlled by a project leader and a collaborator with a physical presence in the community. From this perspective, Facebook–as well as other global social media services–differs drastically from the SameNet it came to replace, with obvious implications for the users' experiences in terms of privacy, ownership, and trust, both perceived and in fact.

7

Ruövddietjarvva

Beyond the World Wide Web

WITH DIGITAL MEDIA, NEW VOICES, INSTITUTIONS, AND narratives develop. We look at how this is taking place, and how institutional and vernacular authorities meet and increasingly interact. More particularly, we focus on efforts toward language revitalization and on digital activism. While Sámi language use and the situation of the Sámi languages has been touched on in earlier chapters, a closer look at language maintenance and revitalization efforts is necessary because it is one of the central issues debated in politics, schools, and homes of Sámi struggling to maintain, learn, or pass on their heritage languages. The use and role of digital media for activism has also been touched on as well, for instance, in relation to the Gállok protests of 2015. The focus here turns to the use of imagery in obtaining image sovereignty.

In our contemporary media context, Sámi initiatives benefit from the *ruövddietjarvva* that has developed. The conditions for digital media to support contemporary efforts by diverse Sámi groups can be compared to the specific snow conditions required for building a strong crust that can bear the weight of a moose or horse. Communication in

Sápmi, and the earlier central significance of SameNet, have resulted in networks and in a level of digital literacy that enables heterogeneous Sámi groups to make use of digital media for specific purposes.

Particularly illustrative of the impact of vernacular and institutional efforts facilitated by the web, is the case of Ume Sámi—one of the most endangered surviving Sámi languages. Up until April 2016, the language had no official orthography. Efforts for the recognition of the written language had been undertaken over several years, with strong dedication from two collaborating organizations, the Ubmeje (Umeå) Sámi association, *Såhkie*, and the association of Ume Sámi people, Álgguogåhtie, also Ubmeje-based. Interestingly, online projects to support the language had already begun taking place before the orthography was officially recognized and adopted. In 2014, the application Memrise Umesami phrases was developed under the initiative of Såhkie and Álgguogåhtie. Our point of departure is therefore Ubmeje, as an illustration and a symbol of the intertwining efforts for promoting and strengthening Sámi languages, efforts advanced by both official and less official actors in both online and offline contexts.

New Ways to Create a Narrative

Recent changes in the media landscape, not least with the increasing ubiquity of social media and digital channels for communication, mean that the diversity of voices has intensified and become woven together into an intricate web that can shape new conditions for Sámi languages and cultural expressions.

The situation for the Sámi languages is critical, especially regarding the use of the languages among younger generations—a key indicator for revitalization and survival. For a language to develop, it is crucial to ensure that it is passed on and actively used in as many domains as possible, at home and in public spaces. Within institutional frameworks, such as the educational system, the lack of teaching materials and teachers is in need of improvement, as pointed out repeatedly by various observers, including the European Council and the three Nordic Sámi parliaments. In this context, social media offers a platform outside of institutional frames, where various actors and initiatives can develop materials and share resources, sometimes as private initiatives and sometimes in more organized fashion. These platforms and efforts become channels for the negotiation of authority, where control over teaching, use of imagery, and ideological stands make active and productive use of these novel ways to create a narrative.

Reaching Out

Indigenous communication online can operate both as inreach and outreach communication (Landzelius 2006). Inreach communication practices contribute to community building, knowledge sharing, and identity construction. As Laurel Evelyn Dyson (2011) points out, online inreach communication also facilitates identity construction, contributes to developing or strengthening a sense of belonging, and thereby brings people closer together. Outreach communication practices address those outside the community, in order to increase visibility or to spread knowledge about the group among other segments of the population.

Both forms of communication, that within the community and that directed toward an outsider audience, have important roles to play. There is a need for channels of communication within the community, as illustrated previously by the SameNet discussion. The need for communicating and disseminating knowledge outside the community is also obvious, underscored by how the lack of knowledge about the Sámi in the broader society has consequences. These two forms of communication address different needs, although they are not distinct from each other.

We can find several examples of outreach uses of digital media, such as the @duodji_365 rotating account on Instagram, run by the

Foundation for Sámi Handicraft, which invites artists to post text and pictures and about their craft in order to teach and promote contemporary Sámi handicraft. Judging from the comments and replies to the posts and pictures, the account has a mixed audience: crafters, locals, tourists, and people interested in art in general. The posts do not only focus on pieces of art and handicraft, but also with some frequency on the significance of an artifact (for instance, a drum), or clothes (a gákti), or even political statements. The account thus becomes a way to provide information about Sámi handicraft, and to share knowledge about Sámi culture, cultural heritage, cultural politics, and the conditions for artists in Sápmi.

One major project that illustrates outreach communication through social media—by sharing snapshots of everyday life in Sápmi—is #MittSápmi. It was part of an initiative by the information center of the Swedish Sámi Parliament in partnership with the Sámi youth organization Sáminuorra. The campaign, #MittSápmi (My Sápmi), was initiated in 2014.

It responded to an increasing number of requests from school children and youngsters interested in learning more about Sámi life (Saami Parliament 2015b). It aims at increasing knowledge and awareness about what it is like to live as a Sámi youth in contemporary society. #MittSápmi was therefore created as a means for disseminating knowledge in a more efficient way than by answering individual emails and phone calls. Thus, the campaign is also an attempt to use social media as an educational resource and to complement other learning materials.

The intended audience is young people from age fifteen to twenty five. The campaign started as a six-month project, but after evaluation the information center decided to implement it among its other regular activities. #MittSápmi is conducted mainly through social media; a Facebook page for updates and promoting the campaign, and the account @mittsapmi on Instagram. The campaign is part of the work of the Sámi parliament for creating and sharing resources that can be used in schools, as support materials for teachers or as a source of information for children. For instance, the Sámi Information Center has published on its website interviews with fictional Sámi persons living in different places in Sweden, both inside and outside Sápmi. The aim is to convey information about the everyday life of Sámi people in a rather personal way, inspired by a variety of people but with no reference to any specific person. The eight fictional characters are between the ages of seven and eighty-one. They answer questions about favorite food, occupation, what it means to be Sámi, Sámi identity and history, and also about reindeer. The questions are based on the most common queries that the Sámi Information Center receives. Other parts of the campaign include a quiz and a booklet (available online) about prejudices against Sámi.

In the #MittSápmi campaign and through the rotating Instagram account @MittSápmi, every week someone shares pictures and short texts about his or her everyday life. The introduction of the account, in Swedish, reads "Ett samiskt stafettkonto. Vi delar med oss här för att ni behöver veta att vi finns. Ett urfolk mitt ibland er. Lika men ändå olika. Välkomna!" (A Sámi rotating account. We share [our knowledge] because you need to know that we exist. An Indigenous people among you. Same but still different. Welcome!). With these words, the text addresses directly the lack of knowledge of a non-Sámi audience.

In the case of #MittSápmi, Instagram was selected as the primary social media service. The project leader explains that one reason for this choice is that information in social media has value when a post is published, and rapidly disappears in the feed. A rotating account was a means for ensuring continuity in the flow of information, thanks to new account holder every week given the task and responsibility of posting updates on a regular basis during the seven-day period. Instagram is a social media service for photo sharing that allows registered users to upload pictures and videos. Similarly to other social media platforms, users can interact using comments, emojis, "likes," and "shares." Rotating accounts on social media have become popular in conducting campaigns and raising awareness, as for instance the

7.1. The rotating account Mitt-Sápmi (@mittsapmi) on Instagram is part of a campaign for sharing knowledge about how it is to live as a Sámi today.

@IndigenousX account on Twitter, an Australian-based account for raising awareness about Indigenous issues. The @sweden account on Twitter, administered by the Swedish Institute, is a project called "Curators of Sweden," which declares that "Sweden was the first country in the world to hand over its official Twitter account to its citizens." Since 2011, a new "curator" shares her or his life in Sweden every week.

Rotating accounts on social media platforms allow institutions or authorities to invite citizens and contributors to share perspectives, illustrate diversity, and shape an image (for instance, of a country). This choice of channel and mode of communication enables the institution (in this case, the Information Center of the Sámi parliament) to let people tell others about their everyday life and share ideas, illustrating the diversity and the variations that exist in Sámi culture (Saami Parliament 2015b: 6). Project leader Anamaria Fjällgren also explains that the choice of Instagram as the main channel was based on the fact that "this is where young people are." "Att finnas på sociala medier är bra av den anledningen att där kan också samiska ungdomar interagera, och skildra sin vardag, med egna ord, och egna bilder" (It is good to be on social media because that's also where young Sámi discuss and describe their everyday life in their own words and photos; Saami Parliament 2015b: 14). Social media is identified as a place where young people spend time. As a matter of fact, Instagram has become very popular during the last several years, especially among youngsters (Davidsson and Thoresson 2017). Other advantages of this Social Networking Service are that it allows publishing different kind of media (photos, films, and text), supports some degree of interaction and that, according to interviewed participants, there are fewer trolls than on Twitter, where users are protected by anonymity to a greater extent than on other SNS.

The participants—called *bievnijeh* (the South Sámi word for "participants")—are new each week and given the only one instruction, that they should introduce themselves in the first post they publish. Each of the bievnijeh begins with a brief introduction and a photo. The introduction contains information about name, age, place of origin, place of residence, and interests and occupation—such as, "I'm a student" or "I am a reindeer herder," Sometimes, the guest shares a few lines about his or her Sámi identity or heritage in the introductory post. Themes presented and discussed by the bievnijeh vary from food, herding, hunting, handicraft, to mental health, and other topics related to identity, for instance, in relation to being vegan or to a specific place.

One of the consultants, a young Sámi woman, tells how she chose the theme in her week as a guest on the account. "It shouldn't be something too sensitive that has to be explained," she says, "but it should be something important that is not discussed much in other contexts" [such as offline] (Interview 9).[1] She chose to write about what it is like to be a young woman and reindeer herder.

> Att vara ung och dessutom kvinna i renskötseln är inte alltid det lättaste. Det är många gånger jag har fått höra "-vad gör du här?

> Du borde göra något vettigare med ditt liv, börja plugga och skaffa ett riktigt jobb! Inte kommer du kunna leva på renskötsel" samtidigt som dom till jämnåriga killar säger att dom är så duktiga som satsar på det deras hjärta brinner för. Detta gör mig ledsen men jag tror det stärker mig ännu mer, för den tävlingsmänniska som jag är så brukar jag tänka att jag ska allt visa er! (Instagram, Mittsapmi, February 15, 2017)

> Being young and above this a woman in reindeer husbandry is not always the easiest thing. I have been told many times "What are you doing here? You should do something cleverer with your life, study and get a real job! You will not be able to live on reindeer herding," while at the same time, to the guys of the same age, they tell them that they are so talented and that it is great that they invest in what their heart is passionate for.
>
> This makes me sad, but I think it also gives me strength, because when it is a competition, then I think, "Well, I'll show you!"

After her Instagram posts that week, several acquaintances commented on the topic she had brought up, and she recounts that it opened an opportunity to discuss the topic offline with people with whom she otherwise would not have expected to exchange ideas about this issue.

This example illustrates how inreach and outreach communications are interwoven. For the consultant, the campaign has significance for a Swedish audience, who gets to see how different the lives of young Sámi people can be. But also and not least, it is of significance for a Sámi audience, because "people share their thoughts, and then one can feel 'I am not alone living with this, thinking about this,'" as the same observes.

The Sámi Information Center has no editing responsibility and does not correct or modify the posts, but acts as a moderator and offers support to the participants when needed. However, the task of moderating has been a minor part of the work, as we can read in the evaluation report:

> Det har aldrig varit några problem med de inlägg som lagts upp via våra sociala medier, allt har flutit på bra. Både våra bievnijeh och den åskådande allmänheten har hållit god ton, vilket har gjort att projektgruppen, som bara har ett övervakande uppdrag över Instagram, inte har behövt rycka in och svara på rasistiska och kränkande kommentarer. (Saami Parliament 2015b: 15)
>
> There have never been any issues with the posts published through our social media, everything has moved on well. Both our bievnijeh and the public in general have kept a good tone, which has meant that the project group, that only had a supervisory role over Instagram, has not had to intervene or respond to any racist and offensive comments.

This is confirmed by the project leader: "I keep an eye on the comments. I barely need to remove comments or block other users. I had expected more of that kind of reactions [i.e., racist comments]. As one participant comments, '[t]he account has been around for so long, I don't think people dare make inappropriate comments there'" (Interview 8).[2] Here, the account—with almost thirteen thousand followers as of July 2018—does not create a safe space, but a form of self-regulation by the users to an established audience, minimizing the risk and the occurrence of unpleasant or inappropriate comments.

Strengthening Communities and Languages

Global digital media are intrinsically well-suited for outreach communication. They enable the dissemination of information, reaching an audience independent of geographical location, and penetrating and overlapping with other networks. But global communication technologies can be successful for inreach communication for the purpose of strengthening communities.

The Twitter platform provides another example of inreach communication for strengthening languages. Through the use of hashtags such as #gollegiella ("golden language" in North Sámi, enhancing the value given to the language; #sámegiella ["Sámi language"]; or #åarjel "South" for South Sámi), communities of speakers create networks to support and encourage language use and learning (Cocq 2015). For Indigenous groups having limited access to information in their Indigenous languages, and rarely on their own terms, this form of knowledge production can play a significant role in a context of revitalization. But also—and not to be neglected—the sense of belonging, for instance to a linguistic group, becomes a motivation for specific media use (Cocq 2015; Vincze and Moring 2013).

Digital tools for distance learning and for sharing teaching resources are yet other examples of the application of global technological solutions to specific linguistic contexts. The e-school (E-skuvla ABC Company, a publishing house that also offers e-learning resources for the Sámi languages) illustrates this potential through a variety of applications for children and youngsters to practice languages. In addition to resources adapted to schools, the company also produces applications for smartphones and tablets, for example, games, dictionaries, and a lexicon with key words and phrases for flirting in Sámi. The initiators of E-skuvla, educators Kirsi Paltto and Jan Skoglund Paltto, were awarded the Gollegiella (Golden language) award in 2016 for their work for the Sámi languages with E-skuvla. Gollegiella, instituted in 2004 by the Sámi parliaments and the Sámi ministers in Sweden, Norway, and Finland, is awarded every second year to community members who contribute to the promotion, development, and preservation of the Sámi languages.

Memrise, mentioned in the introduction, is yet an example of how a global tool (the Memrise app, where users can create a "language course") was adapted and applied in order to fill the needs for a language resource in Ume Sámi. The Ume Sámi course was created within the frame of Memrise in 2014 by Såhkie, the Sámi association of Ubmeje, in collaboration with Álgguogåhtie, "the association of Ume Sámi people." It was developed in a first step as a lexicon. The user learns a vocabulary about, for instance, the weather, food, or family—starting with simple basic words, continuing with glossaries that follow different themes, and then simpler sentences, questions, and expressions. One also practices spelling and can train pronunciation. In a second step (2017), video recordings were added to the course, so that the user can see (and hear) different persons pronouncing words and phrases, thereby illustrating the variations within the language. The course had four hundred twenty-five registered users (individual accounts) as of August 2018.

Ume Sámi, as mentioned earlier, is one of the smallest and most endangered of the Sámi languages. There are a few teachers, almost no teaching materials, and courses and teaching resources are scarce. When the course was created and launched in 2014, the Ume Sámi language had no official orthography: it was only two years later that the Ume Sámi orthography was officially approved.

Instagram and rotating accounts are also applied for inreach communication, evidence of how groups of users appropriate, adapt, and apply tools and technologies based on their specific needs and interests. One example is the *aktavuohta* campaign on Instagram, spurred by an educational program for young reindeer herders preparing them for administrative tasks that working for a reindeer-herding unit often entails. The participants were encouraged to post pictures and short texts of their everyday life as reindeer herders, mostly to share knowledge, thoughts, and ideas.

One particularly interesting campaign of significance was *Sámás muinna* (Speak Sámi to me) organized by *Gïelejarnge*, the language center of the Sámi parliament of Sweden, which aimed to increase the visibility and the use of the Sámi languages. During the campaign conducted between May 2016 and January 2017, nineteen young language ambassadors from different areas of Sápmi made active use of their languages on social media in order to stimulate others to use the languages. Instagram was the main platform used, but also to a much lesser extent SnapChat and YouTube. Photos and short posts were shared on Instagram accounts @samasmuinna2, @samastamujna2, @samasthmujna2, and @saemesthmunnjien2 ("talk Sámi to me" in the North, Lule, South, and Ume Sámi languages). The hashtags #samasmuinna2, #samastamujna2, #samasthmujna2, and #saemesthmunnjien2 were also used.[3] The main target group was young Sámi. As Ingegerd Vannar from Gïelejarnge, owner of the project, explains:

> Sámás muinna-kampanjen, den har gett besked: att sociala medier, Instagram, har varit populär, och det är tack vare genom våra språkambassadörers försörj.
>
> Den statistiken vi har fått ta del av, den visar också att unga vuxna, ungdomar behöver riktade insatser och mötesplatser för de representeras inte heller utav våra andra aktiviteter. De behöver språkprojekt, språkprocesser, utifrån sitt vardagliga verktyg, och det är ofta telefonen, som initierar, stärker, utvecklar deras samiska språk. (Ingegerd Vannar, Digigiella17)

> The Sámás muinna campaign has given us clear indications: that social media, Instagram is popular among young people, and it is thanks to the work of our ambassadors. The figures we had showed that we needed to make specific efforts in order to reach young adults and youngsters, who are otherwise not sufficiently represented in the other activities we organize. They need language projects and processes based on a tool they use every day, and it is often their phone in order to develop their languages.

One of the ambassadors tells of the significance the campaign had for her personally:

> När man bor på sydsamiskt område, man har inte så många att prata med [. . .]. De som kan språket, det var de äldre [. . .] men det var ingen garanti för att de skulle använda språket [. . .]. Det var ett stort steg för dem att börja prata med oss, och då blir steget ännu större för oss barn att börja prata med de vuxna. Men med kampanjen plötsligt hade jag en anledning. Nu är det jag som ta steget; jag kan börja prata med barnen och ungdomarna hemma. Nu är det våran generations tur. Nu ska vi ta tillbaka språket. (Julia Rensberg, Digigiella17)

> When you live in the South Sámi area, you don't have many people to talk with [in the language]. The speakers are the older generation [. . .] but it is not obvious for them to speak Sámi with us [. . .]. It is a big step for them to start talking [South Sámi] with us, and then it is an even bigger step for us kids to speak Sámi with the adults. But with this campaign, all of a sudden, I had a reason. I had to take the step and start talking [Sámi] with children and youngsters at home. Now, it is our generation's turn. We are going to take our language back.

The posts during the campaign give snapshots of everyday life. They are composed of images, for instance a detail in a landscape, an animal, a photo representing an activity. They include a short bilingual text or terms, sometimes some conjugation or grammar. Recurring topics in text and images are handicraft, reindeer, food, snow. However, the content varies between the different accounts, those associated with each of the four languages. Variation is naturally based on the personality and interest of the account-holder (the language ambassador), but also on geographical location. For instance, ambassadors living in an urban environment more often share, not surprisingly, terms related to activities in the city, whereas pictures and words about the mountain environment occur more often on other accounts.

The posts in the Sámás muinna Instagram accounts form a composite narrative about active, strong, and community-grounded young people. The overall message in the accounts is supportive and encouraging, addressing young language speakers with the motto "Dare to speak Sámi."

When the campaign ended in January 2017, the group also released a song on the music platform Spotify. As one of the North Sámi ambassadors describes it, it is "a pep song," about being happy and proud of being a Sámi speaker. A phrase book was also published as part of the campaign, titled *A Funnier Way to Learn Sámi*. An earlier version of the book was produced by the earlier Norwegian Sámas muinna campaign. One of the most noteworthy additional changes in the version from 2017 is the use of Ume Sámi. The phrase book is thereby the first publication applying the new, officially acknowledged Ume Sámi orthography. It compiles words and phrases about such topics as school (*Edtjebe leaksoeh ektesne darjodh?* [Shall we do our homework together?]), relations at home and with friends (*Tjengkerem tjïektjedibie* [We go and play football]), or useful sentences when flirting (*Datne dan joekoen tjaebpies* [You are incredibly beautiful] or, with lots of humor (*Gosse datnem vuajnam dellie eevre goh dam voestes miesiem vuejnedh akten aareh gïjreaereden* [To see you again is like seeing the first reindeer calf on a spring morning]).

The statistics compiled at the end of the campaign indicate that the greatest number of followers were in the age group eighteen to thirty-four, that is, the very group that the project had hoped to reach. Following on the success of Sámas muinna, Gïelejarnge rapidly initiated another language project on Instagram with language ambassadors, *Instagiella* (2018). In other words, online initiatives for promoting and strengthening the Sámi languages have become recurring efforts, for instance in the work of the Gïelejarnge, the language center of the Sámi parliament. These examples of inreach initiatives strive for increasing the use and visibility of minority, locally and geographically based languages. They illustrate how the use of global media can be reframed

7.2. Phrase book, *A Funnier Way to Learn Sámi!*, produced during the *Sámas muinna* project. Photograph by Peter Steggo.

and adjusted to specific conditions and for specific purposes. They also illustrate how digital modes of communication provide new ways of engaging with the goals of language revitalization. For instance, language practices online show that, although an official orthography is important for the revitalization of a language, the lack or underdevelopment of it is not an obstacle for dedicated language speakers to make use of their languages in online settings, as it has been the case with Ume Sámi. A similar observation can be made in the case of Pite Sámi, which at present still lacks an officially agreed-upon orthography, but that is discussed and developed by dedicated speakers and cultural workers on social media platforms like Facebook groups.

Digital Activism and Political Action

Examples such as #Sámásmuinna2 and #MittSápmi illustrate how campaigns driven or curated by institutions are shaped by a multitude of voices and perspectives. Rotating accounts on social media platforms are means for bringing to the fore this variety within institutional frameworks. However, voices and perspectives also find expression outside of such frames. Social media, as mentioned earlier, is characterized by affordances and potentials for expressing alternative views and opinions. These forms of media are often approached as alternative media, in the sense that they can be used for expressing and claiming marginal views or for gaining visibility or contesting dominant media messages (Lievrouw 2011). They also facilitate individualized forms of mobilization (Segerberg and Bennett 2011). The ability for activist networks to expand and reach audiences across borders in Indigenous contexts has been proven, for instance, by the Idle No More movement (see chapter 5).

In Sápmi, as in many other settings, social media is used to a great extent by activist groups and/or for the purpose of challenging and countering perceptions and discourses emanating from the majority society. This form of media use is also highly connected to global movements, and diverse activist initiatives on the internet can become like rings on water that, through the ripple effect, spread outward and intersect with others.

The web 2.0 has enabled increased commitment and coordination, and social media has therefore become a natural channel for activism. Rather than being truly new forms of communication, however, these so-called "activist media" (Lievrouw 2011) differ from traditional communication only by being novel channels and by bypassing gatekeepers such as publishers or editors. Digital activism, also called "cyberactivism," "net activism," or "online activism," is a "form of activism that uses the internet and digital media as key platforms for mass mobilization and political action" (Fuentes 2018). More-or-less organized structures and networks can make use of internet communication in various ways and through various and intersecting platforms, such as Facebook (Harlow 2012; Mercea 2013), Twitter (Lindgren and Lundström 2011; Maireder and Schwarzenegger 2012; Penney and Dadas 2014; Theocharis 2013), YouTube (Cocq 2016; Hill

2013), and digital takes on offline tools such as e-petitions or virtual sit-ins (Ketcham Weber 2013).

Of great significance, visual media increasingly plays a central role in the uses of social media for activism. In the case of Gállok for instance (see chapter 5), Twitter and Facebook were mainly used to link to YouTube, blogs, and websites where the environmental movement documented, shaped, and illustrated the ongoing struggle through photos and videos.

As an example of activism through assessing image sovereignty, the artist group Suohpanterror (Lasso terror) brings the matter to a head. This collective of anonymous artists and activists create what they present as "propaganda posters from Sápmi," appropriating pictures, themes, and other items from popular culture or famous visual media, with text in Sámi (often) and political connotations and direct references. By reframing, remixing, and re-appropriating images, aesthetics, and slogans, Suohpanterror creates protest posters about Indigenous rights. The group brings together anonymous artists, but it is not art or a specific artistic form that defines Suohpanterror. As the group's homepage states, "it's about the necessity of our collective liberation and survival. We either fight or we die. There is no ultimate victory, just perpetual struggle. Everything old shall be new again, and again: this is the eternal return of a sacred struggle."[4] The Suohpanterror group started in 2012 and their art is disseminated to a great extent via social media, but has also been displayed in several offline exhibitions mostly in the Nordic Countries but also in Hungary, the Netherlands, and Germany.

Suohpanterror creates a form of imagery from an explicitly Sámi standpoint, but is accessible and appealing to an international audience by its references to artistic expressions, visual patterns, characters, and symbols from popular culture. The artist group makes use of, for instance, Andy Warhol's Pop Art iconography, re-engaging with the political standpoint of Pop Art pioneers. As an illustrative example, one of the protest posters displays five persons wearing gákti (from different areas of Sápmi) and the Guy Fawkes mask. They are standing against a black background, looking into the camera. In a corner at the bottom, we can read these few lines:

> We are anonymous.
> We are legion.
> We do not forgive.
> We do not forget.
> Expect us!

Suohpanterror makes here explicit reference to the activist group Anonymous—a hacktivist cluster that has become internationally known for its cyberattacks against governmental institutions and authorities. The lines on the Suohpanterror poster are the watchwords of this group. The Guy Fawkes mask from the film *V for Vendetta* is used by Anonymous and is internationally known as a protest symbol. Suohpanterror thereby affiliates itself with the group and its efforts to reveal injustice. Here, the Sámi standpoint is presented by the Sámi clothes—a strong marker of identity—and the message is explicit for a broad, international audience. Suohpanterror thus does not only reuse themes and aesthetics from popular culture, but also from other activist networks and movements.

Yet another example of this form of linkage is a poster displaying four persons in gákti with their faces covered by colorful balaclavas and reading the words "pussy Sápmi." The aesthetics and the text explicitly reference the Russian feminist protest group Pussy Riot. Founded in 2011, the Russian collective became known globally for its provocative performances in public spaces filmed and distributed on the internet—as, for instance, at the World Cup Final 2018, when four protesters entered the field and interrupted the game. The collective took credit for the interruption on social media, calling for the release of political prisoners and the end of illegal detentions. They were arrested and jailed for fifteen days.

Another example of a protest poster by Suohpanterror creates a direct link between the Sámi storytelling tradition and contemporary mining exploitations. The poster represents one of the čuđit, cruel enemies that plundered and killed Sámi in the past according to many legends and the chief villains in Nils Gaup's seminal film *Ofelaš*, discussed in chapter 3. The poster is inspired by the one produced to advertise the 1987 film. Stories about the čuđit can be found in most collections of Sámi folklore (e.g., Gaski et al. 2004; Cocq 2008). These narratives could be reflections of conflicts experienced by the Sámi in contact with other ethnic groups in the past (Laestadius and Pentikäinen 2002: 253–54). The stories typically recount how a band of čuđit comes to a siida looking for the inhabitants and their resources. But all they can find is one unlikely foe (a young boy, woman, or old woman, depending on the version of the legend). They force the Sámi character to lead them to where the other members of the siida are. The character does so, guiding them at night, in the darkness, and in the end tricks them to fall down a high and steep cliff (or become drowned in a lake, or freeze to death, depending on the version). Thus, the pathfinder rescues the rest of the villagers by preventing their enemies from finding them.

In the poster by Suohpanterror, the traditional legend is reframed in a contemporary context. The picture represents a menacing man looking right into the camera and pointing a crossbow at us. The picture is blurred in the foreground, but sharp at the level of the face and the eyes of the man. In every corner and at the bottom, logos from mining companies involved in exploitations in Sápmi in Sweden, Norway, and Finland are displayed. In the middle of the poster, a text reads: "SÁPMELAŠ! Čuđit leat fas dappe. Dál son háliidit min minerálaid" (Sámi people! The čuđit are back. And they want our minerals). This reference to the traditional legend—with visual links and close rewording of actual lines from Gaup's 1987 film (see chapter 3)—gives us a reading of the situation in Sápmi today. What is happening in Sápmi is nothing new, although today's plunderers are not interested in money or food so much as land and its mineral wealth. Protests against the mining industry give a new frame for old stories to emerge and be shaped through activist media: the posters and the protests are disseminated and circulated through social media. The poster informs and characterizes through making an allusion: rather than storytelling, it is rather an instance of story contextualizing. In the context of protests in Sápmi—against the mining industry and the mining boom that threatens reindeer herding areas—the poster or illustration circulated widely on Facebook and other social media in 2013 in connection with the Gállok protests and their aftermath.

Suohpanterror is mostly known for its posters, but the group also engages in political statements occasionally through videos on YouTube, for instance with the video "America first, Saami second." It was uploaded in February 2017, as part of the unofficial video contest "Who wants to be second?/Every Second Counts," initiated by the Netherlands in response to the newly elected US president who, in his inauguration speech, declared that his vision will be "America first." Several satirical videos were uploaded on YouTube, presenting with self-irony what the US president might like about the Netherlands, and why it should be second after America.

The video by Suohpanterror follows the same genre. The short film of three minutes, in English, is introduced as a "message from the Saami" and an "introduction video to the Saami." It uses rhetoric from the US president, describing the Sámi as "the best and only" Indigenous people of Europe. This introduction to Sápmi mentions the four countries, Sámi artists (making fun of their names), politicians ("we have more presidents than the 4 countries together," referring to the Sámi parliaments), and the different Sámi languages. The Sámi are described as "so cool that others want to be like us," referring to cultural appropriation. Other insinuations to contemporary contexts are made, for instance with "we are kind of like you [. . .] every time someone writes about us in the media, the comment section is filled with angry people," referring to racism and how it is expressed online.

As often in the art of Suohpanterror, we find references to popular culture, for instance, here an allusion to the American TV series *Game of Thrones*: "we know how to survive when winter is coming" thanks to Indigenous knowledge, "the best knowledge." In a few instances, messages appear on the slides, passing by, with no reference in the speech. One example is the hashtag #DoNotAlterNativeFacts—as an exhortation and a play of words. Also, a short note appears on a slide: "BTW, what happened in Sweden?" referring to the president's statement in February 2017, "[l]ook at what's happening in Sweden last night," citing a nonexistent incident.

The slide show makes use of several of Suohpanterror's posters along with pictures of reindeer, snowy landscapes, a goahti, that is, elements that are associated with representations of Sámi. Such representations are often questioned as stereotypical, giving an ironic tone to the video. While the other countries "competing" for being second end their videos with the slogan "America first. The Netherlands/Finland/ etc. second," Suohpanterror ends declaring that Sápmi does not want to be in the competition: "We just want you and the other countries to put the mother nature first." At this point, there is an interruption in the video. The music stops, the tone in the voice changes and a new slide appears with the text "you think it is a motherfucking game?" The voice declares, "or otherwise we as humans are totally fucked." The voice and the wording indicate that it is serious, as the video shifts genre and tone.

The Suohpanterror video is not as satirical as most of the videos produced within the "Who wants to be second" genre. There is some degree of self-irony, for instance when mentioning Sámi names, joking about having many presidents, and referring to participation in cultural appropriation with "[s]ometimes we let Finns and Swedes use us to promote their countries for tourists." But the video is to a great extent about claiming and putting forward a message—and not only a criticism about contemporary US politics. The video is both about denouncing injustices in historical and contemporary times and about conveying a defiantly Sámi message and agenda, one ultimately focused on the environment and Mother Earth.

The work of Suohpanterror is a clear illustration of the assessment of visual sovereignty. The collective re-engages with artistic expressions in a way that reframes global and international motifs through the lens of Sámi aesthetics: the visual language of Andy Warhol or The Anonymous, for example, is in the protest posters made explicitly Sámi, referring to Sámi issues and conveying a message that matters in a Sámi context. Suohpanterror also recycles stereotypical representations of Sámi people that have circulated in majority society, jokes about cultural appropriation, and thereby takes control of the imagery and assessment and underscores the collective's primacy of interpretation.

The activist group also illustrates the increasing entwinement between the digital and the offline. The use of social media for spreading messages, raising awareness, and urging people to take a stand for human rights and for the environment disseminates and shares knowledge as well as increases Sámi visibility through a visually powerful online presence. However, Suohpanterror is not about establishing an international global network, even though solidarity and collaboration with other Indigenous groups is important. It is first and foremost about Sámi rights, that is, highly localized and anchored in geographical communities rather than in more diffuse or nebulous "virtual" ones.

As observed in other contexts, the internet contributes to a network or a group's strategies by facilitating online communication and offering technical competences (Dahlberg-Grundberg 2016: 535). Language revitalization and political activism are not internet phenomena. However, the work, strategies, and agendas of Sámi groups are supported, enhanced, strengthened, and disseminated through digital media. One cannot underestimate the key role of actors with digital skills and understandings of social media dynamics in this process. Network building, web presence, and modes of digital publication are central for both inreach and outreach efforts.

In the case of Sámás muinna, we see how young adults (the language ambassadors) create and shape their own spaces—expressing not only that using the Sámi languages is possible, but also portraying it as cool and as a source of pride. It also changes the status of the language by writing it in a public space—which is what Instagram offers. The image of the Sámi languages is not defined by Sámi officials and authorities but, rather, by the speakers and those who affiliate with their heritage language. While early language resources were produced and decided upon by Lappologists (e.g., Nielsen 1932; Wiklund 1917, 1935; Bergsland 1957)—established academic scholars but not native speakers, and with little interest in language variation—the speakers themselves, together with other dedicated community members, have today taken on the role of experts.

Initiatives for strengthening languages, supporting language speakers, and increasing visibility and awareness about Indigenous issues give us insight into how authority becomes negotiated. The online presence of Sámi groups (cultural workers, activists, etc.) who traditionally have been marginalized to a great extent in mainstream media, means that voices and perspectives come to the fore and can no longer be disregarded. But not least, the networks that are organized, concretized, and strengthened online contribute to an increased empowerment in terms of control of (re-)presentation and imagery.

The examples provided here illustrate the linking of vernacular and institutional authority observed by other folklorists working on digital culture. Being Sámi today is increasingly defined by Sámi themselves, and discourse and representations about the Sámi (discourses of exoticism, victimization, paternalism) are now not the only ones available in the repertoire when someone—a tourist, a student, an educator—looks for information. The participants or curators on the Instagram accounts, along with the activists, in fact add new narratives to the repertoire about contemporary Sápmi. In terms of empowerment, what is achieved here is the possibility of speaking out for oneself instead of being talked about–the power of defining who you are and who your community is.

The conditions and prerequisites for this empowerment have been established by the works and initiatives done in the past. Artists and cultural workers from the Tjïekere and the Sijvo eras, early digital initiatives such as SameNet, and others have built the ruövddietjarvva that carries contemporary generations faster and further.

Fiehta

Conclusion

THE OPENING PLACE FOR THIS CHAPTER, AND THEREBY THE place where this book ends, is Gállok. As we have described, narrated, and referred to at several instances in the previous chapters, Gállok has become a symbol for Sámi mobilization and activism in the 2010s. As described in chapter 5, the events of summer 2013 were not only reactions to mining prospecting in this reindeer-grazing area—it was also a milestone in history when Sámi groups, politicians, and artists took a stand against the increasing exploitation of Sápmi, and for Indigenous rights. Gállok also links back to Álttá, the place at focus in chapter 2. The events of Gállok—similarly in manner to Álttá, as an awakening for majority society and a means for Sámi groups to present images of their presence, situation and intentions—and how they were covered contributed to an awareness of contemporary Sámi life and culture, to a great extent in contrast with the stereotypes and misrepresentations that exist in the Nordic majority societies. Gállok was not only about protests and activism. It was also a milestone in Sámi politics. The unanimous statement—"The Sámi parliament cannot accept the exploitations of Sápmi"—from the Sámi parliament of Sweden was read in public on site at Gállok, August 28, 2013, and sent to the Ministry of Enterprise and Innovation.[1]

C.1. Camp Gállok, summer 2013. The sign says, "Change the Mineral Law." Photograph by Peter Steggo.

We have described the vivid, active, and conscious work of artists, cultural workers, and other dedicated community members for communicating, taking control of, and revitalizing Sámi representations and imagery. Even though the examples illustrate the vitality, power of resilience, and force of change in Sámi communities, it is, however, important to bear in mind the resistance that they meet and the setbacks they face. Misrepresentations, discrimination, and racism have proven to be part of life for many Sámi, with consequences for identities, physical and mental health, and a high risk for psychosocial illness (Axelsson et al. 2016; Omma et al. 2012; Hallett et al. 2007). These experiences, and Sámi defenses and resistance to them, take place on the internet and in social media, but also in other public and private spaces, in Sápmi and away from Sápmi.

Despite the fact that the Sámi languages are official national minority languages in Norway, Sweden, and Finland, and that national and

European legislation aims at guaranteeing access to learning Sámi at school, the implementation of the law and the conditions for ensuring such education have proven inadequate repeatedly (Council of Europe 2016, 2017). The lack of culturally sensitive education that prevents young Indigenous people from pursuing a course of studies that embraces and develops Indigenous identity or agendas (Keskitalo et al. 2012; Linkola 2014), is also discussed as a problem and an issue of priority for maintaining and developing Sámi culture and languages.

Representations of Sámi in popular culture, for instance in film and television series, often lead to discussions and debates. The warm reception, wide appreciation, and amazing success of the film *Sameblod* was not without controversy. In the national Swedish newspaper *Dagens Nyheter*, a June 2017 critique of the film proved an example of "conservative nationalism" rather than a story about how Sámi have been discriminated against in Sweden (Andersson 2017). The Swedish-French television series *Midnight Sun* (2016) is yet another example that provoked chronicles and essays in the press, questioning among other things the existence of racism against Sámi as presented in several episodes (Brodrej 2016).

In sum, if the climate and the conditions have improved in Sápmi through stronger minority legislation, increased awareness in majority population, and a greater degree of self-representation, much remains to be done in order to guarantee the implementation and effectiveness of Sámi rights, to strengthen the power of decision-making in issues that directly concern and affect Sámi groups, and to counteract discrimination and racism.

The multitude of initiatives, efforts, and examples of the work of artists, cultural workers, and others has challenged us to select, choose, and inevitably leave out many remarkable examples and individual artists as well as other uses of multimedia, such as for business development, education and training, community economic development, and so on. But this also shows that Sápmi is teaming with devoted, skilled, and knowledgeable community members building on and proudly maintaining a strong heritage, finding new paths and innovative ways to enhance identity and culture in contemporary contexts. The title of this chapter, *Fiehta*, illustrates this: like the first occasion for grazing when there is no more snow on the ground, the vitality of Sápmi gives optimism and marks at the same time a beginning and renewal, and a cycle of continuity.

The ways in which Sámi artists, activists, cultural workers, and other community members make use of media–from produced to social media–to advocate for a Sámi agenda can be traced back to the 1970s and even earlier. The Álttá protests were an occasion of powerful and pervasive use of image-making strategies, building on a form of aesthetics, communication, and expression with strong roots in Sápmi. In a similar manner, communication, as observed today on social media, builds on cultural patterns, prerequisites, and needs that were characteristic for Sápmi and Sámi groups long before digital communication made its entry in the media landscape.

We have presented a number of image makers and strategies for self-representations through different media: literature, film, music, social media, activism, and artivism. These are some of the media through which Sámi activist "spears," borrowing Jörgen Stenberg's word (see introductory chapter, *Arvi*), can reach their targets. Our examples however only represent part of the Sámi agenda: not all artistic expressions can be defined as activist spears or as ideological statements. And some Sámi artists simply want to make art, without addressing the political situations or injustices that are continuing parts of their experience. To be simply an "artist who is Indigenous," rather than an "Indigenous artist" is a wished for status for many Sámi, as for many artists of other minority groups the world over.

This study, however, illustrates Noam Chomsky's statement quoted in the introductory chapter, that "the indigenous populations are [. . .] taking the lead in trying to protect the Earth." This leadership can be seen not only through contemporary examples related to protests, like those associated with the 2015 Paris climate negotiations or resistance to mining exploitations. As we have shown, the central role given to nature and the Earth, and our responsibility toward her, was already evident during the Tjïekere and the Sijvo eras, powerfully symbolized by Nils Aslak Valkeapää's *Eanni, eannážan* (2001; The Earth, my mother) and discussed by Sámi scholars such as Rauna Kuokkanen (2009).

However, the involvement, activism, and power of action that can be witnessed in Sápmi today is not only about environmental awareness. What we see happening is part of a process of decolonization, where Sámi and other Indigenous groups take control of representing themselves and create a distinct agenda that is proactive rather than reactive. In Sápmi, these efforts include: striving for decolonizing education (e.g., Nutti 2013; Balto 2005), research (Porsanger 2004; Sehlin McNeil 2015), epistemology (Kuokkanen 2000; Keskitalo et al. 2012), politics (Kuokkanen 2011), and many other areas.

Giela Gielain

Strongly entwined with cultural and artistic expressions is language, as a means for communication, as a vehicle for culture and identities or, as for Paulus Utsi, something to be captured (see Utsi 1980 *Giela gielain* [Capturing the language]). While Sámi literature has been disseminated and exported for obvious reasons through translations, music and film have brought Sámi languages (in most cases, North Sámi, but increasingly other Sámi languages) abroad. That moviegoers could watch a film in North or South Sámi, or listen to music in Lule or Inari Sámi, creates a level of excitement and acknowledgement that remains all to novel and therefore exhilarating in a Nordic context in which most majority-culture members would not be able to count to three in a Sámi language. The fact that part of this language work has today moved to the internet—as, for instance, the campaigns led by the language centers of the Sámi parliaments—has many implications. The internet is not only a means to reach young people; it also implies that the Sámi languages can expand into new domains, increasing their visibility and contributing to creating positive attitudes toward Sámi culture. The process of increasing the physical presence of minority and Indigenous languages in public domains, such as through signs or city names, progresses slowly forward. The fact that languages—even those that lack official orthography, such as Ume Sámi until 2016 or Pite Sámi—become visible and browsable in digital environments, is a positive step, even if it is only with great caution that we can look for indicators of positive impact on strengthening and learning the languages. Another positive effect is that these online initiatives contribute to increasing awareness about multilingualism and bear witness to the vitality of the Sámi languages, counteracting the stereotype of Sámi as "dying languages."

The internet cannot revitalize languages by itself, but it can facilitate the promotion and development of minority and Indigenous languages absent from majority media, and support communities of speakers. Revitalization in itself is a process that has to involve all generations, cross long distances, overtake domains, and be implemented in everyday practices. Media and digital environments can only provide tools to use among others in that endeavor. It is also noteworthy that the internet has helped extend and advance strategies for successful language revitalization, such as the Maori "language nest" system of immersion in preschools, that has been successfully replicated in Sámi contexts for revitalizing threatened Sámi languages (Outakoski 2015), including Inari Sámi (Pasanen 2015). The internet provides revitalizers with a further tool and channel for sharing expertise and advice in the ongoing struggle to maintain and strengthen Indigenous languages in specific local contexts.

#Indigenous

In a similar way, it would be misleading to say that the Sámi population is empowered by the media. Rather, the Sámi population takes power, through media, based on the circumstances they have to some extent created and negotiated. From that perspective, the global networks and the collaborations coordinated at an international level through social media are key factors for bringing to the forefront Indigenous issues, bringing together Indigenous groups struggling for the same goals and against similar injustices, and "taking the lead." The examples of #IdleNoMore (see chapter 5), and, more recently, #NoDAPL, illustrate the powerful and influential effects of bringing together Indigenous groups from around the world to take a united stand.

Illustrative of this globalization of Indigenous activism in the era of the internet was the visit by three Sámi women to the Standing Rock reservation during the Dakota Access Pipeline (#NoDAPL) protests of the summer and fall of 2016. The protests drew tens of thousands of Indigenous people and non-Indigenous allies from across North America and abroad, in what became the largest Indigenous protest in the United States in generations. The three Sámi women–Inger Biret Kvernmo Gaup, Sara Marielle Gaup Beaska, and Sofia Jannok, committed Sámi activists and accomplished joikers–joined the protests in late September, gifting the Lakota Standing Rock Tribal Chairman David Archambault II (Tokala Ohitika) with water from Sápmi. They also raised a Sámi flag in solidarity and led the protesters in singing Gaup Beaska's joik *Gulahallat eatnamiin* (discussed in chapter 5). The moving gestures were captured expertly in photographs taken by Jeff Schad and in participant video, which were then uploaded on YouTube (e.g., Utiseta 2016; Mantila 2016) and shared widely via social media. Images and their messages soon made their way into press accounts of the events.

In a *NRK Sápmi* account of the visit on September 20, 2016, Sara Marielle Gaup Beaska notes that Sámi participation would help fulfill a prophecy of racial cooperation in defense of the Earth (Pulk and Rasmus 2016), while in an October 7, 2016, account in the *ETC Umeå* newspaper, Sofia Jannok is quoted stating: "Jag känner igen kampen, det är samma kamp som vi samer för hemma i Sverige. Utvinningen

C.2. Sámi women at Standing Rock. Image from a YouTube video documenting the visit of the Sámi artists at the site for protests against the Dakota pipeline (www.youtube.com/watch?v=VTL87q606Kw).

av naturresurser har blivit mycket värre de senaste åren och det enda sättet för oss att kunna påverka, det är att gå ihop" (Holm 2016; I recognize the battle: it is the same fight we Sámi have here at home in Sweden. The extraction of natural resources has become much worse in recent years and the only way for us to be able to influence the situation is to unite in action). Their acts, and the widely disseminated images of them provided by social media channels, helped lead to the decision of the Norwegian government to divest from the energy company responsible for the Dakota Access pipeline, and prompted the Swedish parliament to pass a resolution in support of the people of Standing Rock. The latter gesture afforded Sámi activists in turn the opportunity to call attention to the fact that Swedish lawmakers were prompt at criticizing foreign abuses of Indigenous rights but less willing to recognize and honor Indigenous rights within Sweden. While the technological mechanisms of these international protest acts were novel, the pattern and strategy remain the same that underlay the Álttá protests: harness international attention and sympathy in ways that call attention to Sámi Indigenous rights and shame Nordic governments into action. It is striking that in this new globalized internet arena for Sámi protests, Sámi artists like Sofia Jannok and Mari Boine have begun more and more to resort to English as a language of communication with the wider world, a strategy that has developed alongside their longstanding commitment to performance in, and celebration of, Sámi language.[2] Where Nordic groups like ABBA and A-ha, discussed in chapter 3, used English to disguise their Nordic identities, Sámi today may choose to use English to articulate their Sámi identities to a broader international audience.

Multiartists

This book covers a variety of different media: literature, music, film, and digital and social media. In our contemporary highly mediated social context, it is important to remember how different media are getting more and more integrated. Actions at Camp Gállok were coordinated through verbal communication, SMS, disseminated through Facebook pages and blogs, covered by video recordings uploaded on YouTube, and distributed through various social media. Later they were covered in international press and interpreted through visual arts, music, and spoken words on-site and in exhibition halls—and in turn distributed through digital media. With the increasing ubiquity of digital technologies in the world we live in, different media are not only becoming more and more integrated, they are also becoming more and more part of our lives. This has meant that the digital and the nondigital—digital and physical places—are also becoming more and more entwined. The collective Suohpanterror, for instance, works with highly localized, specific issues through globalized media, online and offline, where the offline is facilitated and made visible thanks to digital media, and where the online is anchored in a material, geographic, and earthly ground.

As we have taken pains to point out, the use and combination of various forms of expression is nothing new in Sápmi. Nils-Aslak

Valkeapää's written and artistic production illustrates how multiple forms of expression become intertwined when words and images are woven together. His Poem 54 of *Beaivi, áhčážan* (1989) seems to predict the internet activism of the future, while signaling the importance of cross-cultural, and cross-species communication:

54. gii livččii jáhkkán
váilevuođa rabasteaddjin
headjuvuođa áhpin
oidnosii iežá máilmmit
ođđa
beljii'e eará jienat
gii livččii jáhkkán
ádjaga jávohis mánás
lottiiguin hupmá, bovccuiguin
geđggiid guođaha
biekkain sepmoha
gii livččii jáhkkán
njealgái jámášii
ii bovccos heagga
muhto nu lea amas
ii'an dieđe
mii'al dahkes

(Valkeapää 1989)

54. who would have thought
weakness a way out
frailty at sea
other worlds appeared
new
other sounds to my ears
who would have thought
the spring's silent child

speaking with birds, reindeer
herding stones
delirious with the wind
who would have thought
would have died from starvation
without life in the reindeer
but so strange
one doesn't know
what it is

(Valkeapää 1997)

This poem illustrates how multiple forms of expression become intertwined into a new composite artwork. The graphic design echoes the words and creates a flow that takes shape along the page. "Gii livččii jáhkkán?" (Who would have thought?).

The entwinement of artistic forms such as words, songs, duodji, and storytelling explains why many Sámi artists have been called "multiartists." A contemporary multiartist worth particular mention is Britta Marakatt-Labba (see chapter 4), whose work attracted much interest on the international art scene with her participation in the 2017 exhibition Documenta 14 in Kassel. Marakatt-Labba, however, has had a long career as textile artist and painter, and her embroidered stories are not only exhibition pieces: they also decorate public buildings, as for example the twenty-four-meter long *Historja* (Historia/History), an embroidered history of the Sámi people, at the University of Tromsø, or Garjját (Kråkorna/The crows) depicting the Álttá protests and confrontation with the police (see chapter 2), there represented as crows. Some of Marakatt-Labba's works have been published in book format in *Sággon muitalusat* (2010; Embroidered stories)—a collection of stories based on historical events, older sayings, and experiences of reindeer husbandry and fishing or from specific items like the Sámi drum. The book's title refers to the materialization of stories through embroidery and to an aesthetic tradition, namely of narrating with pictures and remembering with stories, for example, through the narrative genre *muitalus*, or with the yoik as a form of remembering.

Mu Ruoktu Lea Mu Váimmus

Sápmi as a geographical area and point of reference is the core and foundation for many authors, artists, activists, and other community members—as powerfully symbolized by Valkeapää's famous wording and poem *Mu ruoktu lea mu váimmus* (1985; My home is in my heart). Beginning each chapter with our choice of place, we have tried to highlight and acknowledge the central role of the land. A recurring theme in political debates and in art when narrating and depicting the land is the colonization of the cultural landscape, and its consequences for land rights and use of natural resources.

The author Paulus Utsi, for instance, expressed this theme in poems about nature and reindeer herding (chapter 2). Today, when Sápmi witnesses a mining boom, Sámi artists and writers take a stand by putting words to what is happening in their areas—just as Utsi did earlier—such as Suohpanterror (chapter 7) and Timimie Märak (1992) from Jåhkåmåhkke, with the powerful spoken word performance "What local people" (2013) in Gállok as a response to and a comment on plans for exploitation of the area:

> Och snart växer inget mer
> Inga fler barn kommer att stå där
> Vare sig i en skog eller i hagen
> För den dagen närmar sig med stora steg
> Och alla som teg
> Kommer att gråta sina kinder våta
> Och då ska vi inte förlåta.
> De ska skämmas, stämmas
> För varje damm som skulle dämmas
> Varje träd du vill fälla

Varje plats du vill spränga
Kommer att tränga fram 1000 röster
Från oss, som är, "what local people?"!

And soon nothing more will grow
No place left for children to go
Be it in forest or in pasture
For that day approaches ever faster
And all who didn't shout out loud
Will cry their eyes out
And we will not forgive.
They will be ashamed, be blamed,
For every dam that was dammed up
For every tree that was cut down
For every place that was blown up
A thousand voices will resound
From us, who are "What local people?"[3]

This bitingly critical poem, which Märak performed on site at Gállok during the protests of the summer of 2013, belongs to the rap-inspired international spoken-word genre, and the aesthetics, intonation, and voice inflection regrettably and inevitably are lost when the lines are transcribed in writing. On YouTube, in contrast, more of the poem's resonance and power can come through, when the performance is filmed and uploaded and shared through social media, as Märak's poem was. The immediacy and urgency of Märak's message comes through on YouTube in a manner very different from what is possible in a printed poem alone.

Märak depicts a dystopian future where nothing grows anymore and children are nowhere to be found. The poem describes the regret, guilt, and shame of those who kept silent. But it ends by reminding listeners of the strength and presence of the locals—the thousand voices of "us, who are 'what local people?'" Referring to the revealingly oblivious words of the mining executive Saintclair-Poulton—when asked by investors whether local people in and around Gállok would be in favor of the proposed mine—Märak "owns the label" by identifying and including the performance's listeners as the supposedly nonexistent local people affected and concerned about the proposed mine (see chapter 5). "What local people?" articulates a struggle against the colonization of Sápmi. This is what Paulus Utsi experienced and wrote about; it is what Nils-Aslak Valkeapää narrated; and it is now what Timimie Märak embodies in this poem today.

In the globalizing context of the internet, specific cultural interventions take place within the affordances and parameters of an international technology and evolving digital media and products operating online. International trends emerge and converge, diverge and transfer, all through seemingly mysterious strings of zeros and ones. And yet, each Indigenous context and experience remains in part unique and specific, as members of Indigenous communities engage with technology in ways that respond to their own situations, experiences, and opportunities. It is our hope that by documenting the history of Sámi engagement with multimedia image making, as it has unfolded over decades in ways that predicted and then profited from the affordances of the internet, we will remind our readers of *gulahallan* (communication), of the importance and indeed necessity of culturally specific examinations and expertise. For if the Sámi case bears resemblances with that of Indigenous people elsewhere in the world, it also stands as a uniquely Sámi experience, one which we hope to have chronicled here for the present and future.

Glossary

Aanaar/Anár Inari, Finland
Åanghkerenjeeruve Ankarede, Sweden
Aerviesjaevrie Arvidsjaur, Sweden
Álttá Alta, Norway
åppås (Lule Sámi) fresh, unprinted snow
arvi rain
Čohkkeras Jukkasjärvi, Sweden
doalli (North Sámi) fresh snow fallen over an established trail
duodji (North Sámi) handicraft
eatnu river
Faepmie Fatmomakke, Sweden
fiehta (Lule Sámi) first grazing after the melting of all snow
gákti (North Sámi) the traditional Sámi costume
Gállok Kallak Sweden
Gárasavvon Karesuando, Sweden
Giema Kemi, Finland
Giron Kiruna, Sweden
goahti (North Sámi) traditional Sámi tent
Guovdageaidnu Kautokeino, Norway
Jåhkåmåhkke Jokkmokk, Sweden
Jiellevárri Gällivare, Sweden
joik (North Sámi) traditional Sámi musical genre encapsulating the essence of a being
Kárášjohka Karasjok, Norway
lávvu (North Sámi) traditional teepee-like Sámi tent
luohti (North Sámi) traditional vocal genre, see joik
Njauddâm Neiden, Norway
noaidevuohta (North Sámi) traditional activities and practices of a noaidi
noaidi (North Sámi) ritual specialist in traditional Sámi healing and religion
Ohcejohka Utsjoki, Finland
rahte a path in the snow that results from where people have walked, hiked, and transported goods

ruövddietjarvva (Ume Sámi) snow with hard crust capable of withstanding weight of a large animal like a moose or horse

sállat putting down new tracks in snow where no one has traveled yet

Sámediggi (North Sámi) Sámi parliament

Sámiid Riikkasearvi The National Union of the Sami People in Sweden

Samij Åhpadusguovdásj the Sámi education center

sieidi (North Sámi) sacred site or object that was/is the recipient of offerings and entreaties in traditional Sámi ritual life and religion

siida (North Sámi) a collective of one or more extended families that share(d) responsibility and labor related to a reindeer herd or other traditional source of livelihood in Sámi culture

sijvo (Inari Sámi) smooth ski conditions

tjïekere (South Sámi) loose snow pawed up by reindeer

vuolle (South Sámi) term for joik

Notes

Arvi: Introduction

1 WeChat (Weixin in Chinese) is an instant-messaging service for text and voice messaging.

Chapter 5. *Rahte*: Contextualizing Sámi Uses of Digital Media

1 Sveriges Radio, Sameradion & SVT Sápmi, www.sr.se/sameradion.
2 Interview, April 6, 2017.
3 Interview, April 11, 2017.
4 The preparation for confirmation (or affirmation of Baptism) in the Lutheran Church often takes place through participation in a youth camp. Such a confirmation camp, especially for young Sámi, is organized by the Church of Sweden every year.
5 *Allhelgonacup*, an annual indoor soccer tournament in Sápmi.
6 Interview, April 19, 2017.
7 What Local People?, www.whatlocalpeople.se.
8 "Gulahallat Eatnamiin: We Speak Earth," www.youtube.com/watch?v=H2LhBAi-Q8I.

Chapter 6. *Sállat*: New Tracks

1 Interview, April 19, 2017.
2 In the case of the south and central Sámi languages. The east Sámi languages use a Cyrillic script.
3 Efforts toward computerization of households took place in Sweden at that time, for instance, through the so-called "home PC reform" in 1998 that gave employees in Sweden an opportunity to borrow tax-free, or to rent, a personal computer against gross salary deductions.

4 Bridge-It Thematic Network, www.lmi.ub.es/bridge-it/samenetsami-network-connectivity.html.
5 Interview, November 29, 2016.
6 Samiska Posten, www.facebook.com/groups/214215213713.
7 Campaign on social media (Facebook, Twitter, Instagram) organized by the Sameradion & SVT Sápmi (the Sámi radio and the Swedish television) in the spring of 2017, encouraging people to share their experiences of racism under the hashtag #vardagsrasismmotmigsomsame ("everyday racism against me as a Sámi").
8 Interview, September 27, 2017.
9 Interview, September 29, 2017.

Chapter 7. *Ruövddietjarvva*: Beyond the World Wide Web

1 Interview, September 25, 2017.
2 Interview, October 10, 2017.
3 A similar campaign with the same name took place in Norway in 2014; therefore the campaign on the Swedish side of Sápmi received the number 2.
4 Suohpanterror, www.suohpanterror.com.

Fiehta: Conclusion

1 Sámi parliament of Sweden, www.sametinget.se/61174.
2 We are grateful for the insights and assistance of Tim Frandy in recounting this episode in Sámi activism.
3 Translated by Thomas DuBois and approved by Timimie Märak.

Bibliography

Ahvenniemi, Ulla. 2015. "Angelin tyttö Ursula Länsman palasi kotiin ja teki isänsä onnelliseksi." *Kodin kuvalehti*, November 3, 2015. www.kodinku valehti.fi/artikkeli/lue/ihmiset/angelin_tytto_ursula_lansman_palasi _kotiin_ja_teki_isansa_onnelliseksi.

Aikio, Ande. 2004. "An Essay on Substrate Studies and the Origin of Saami." In *Etymologie, Entlehnungen und Entwicklungen: Festschrift för Jorma Koivulehto zum 70. Gerburtsdag*, edited by I. Hyvärinen, P. Kallio, and J. Korhonen, 5–34. Helsinki: Société Néophilologique.

Akana, Collette Leimomi, and Kiele Gonzalez. 2015. *Hānau ka ua: Hawaiian Rain Names.* Honolulu: Kamehameha Publishing.

Alia, Valerie. 2010. *The New Media Nation: Indigenous Peoples and Global Communication.* New York: Berghahn Books.

Álgu database. 2019. Kotimaisten kielten keskus. http://kaino.kotus.fi/algu /index.php?t=etusivu.

Alonso, Francisco. 2014. "Zapatistas: Twenty Years of Reinventing Revolution." *Roar*, Ja nuary 4, 2014. https://roarmag.org/essays/zapatista -autonomy-reinventing-revolution.

Amft, Andrea. 2000. *Sápmi i förändringens tid: En studie av svenska samers levnadsvillkor under 1900–talet ur ett genus–och etnicitetsperspektiv.* Umeå: Samiska Studier.

Amft, Andrea, and Mikael Svonni, eds. 2006. *Sápmi Y1K: Livet i samernas bosättningsområde för ett tusen år sedan.* Umeå: Sámi Dutkan.

Anderson, Benedict. 2006. *Imagined Communities.* London: Verso.

Andersson, Lena. 2017. "Även samer kan längta bort ibland." *Dagens Nyheter*, June 9, 2017.

Andersson, Nils Mattias. 2005. "Åvlavuelien råantjoeh." In Åvtese jåhta, edited by Harald Gaski and Lena Kappfjell, 85–95. Guovdageaidnu: DAT.

Andrews, Marilyn. 2012. "Mapuche Communication and Self-Representation: Indigenous Expressions of Identity in New Media." PhD dissertation, University of Wisconsin, Madison.

Angelin tytöt. [Aŋŋel Nieiddat/Angelin Tytöt/Angelit]. 1992. *Dolla*. Mipu Music. MIPUCD 102. Compact disc.

——. 1993. *Giitu*. Mipu Music. MIPUCD 204. Compact disc. Re-released Finlandia Records 1999: 3984-268542.

——. 1995. *Skeaikit*. Mipu Music. MIPUCD 402. Compact disc. Re-released Finlandia Records 1999: 3984-26855-2.

——. 1997. *Girls of Angeli: The New Voice of the Earth*. Mipu Music. Compact disc.

——. 1999. *Mánnu*. Finlandia Records. Innovator Series 3984-25790-2. Compact disc.

——. 2003. *Reasons*. Finlandia Records. 0927-49873-2. Compact disc.

Antill, Peter, and Peter Dennis. 2005. *Berlin 1945: End of the Thousand Year Reich*. Oxford: Osprey Publishing.

Appadurai, Arjun. 1990. "Disjuncture and Difference in the Global Cultural Economy." *Public Culture* 2 (2): 1–24.

——. 1996. *Modernity at Large: Cultural Dimensions of Globalization*. Minneapolis: University of Minnesota Press.

Arnberg, Matts, Israel Ruong, and Håkon Unsgaard. 1997. *Jojk*. Kristianstad: Sveriges Radios Förlag.

Arnberg, Matts, Pål-Nils Nilsson, and Thomas Öhrström. n.d. "Då, när jag var mannen på Oulavuolie." Part 1. www.youtube.com/watch?v=hWHjJposcSQ.

——. n.d. "Då, när jag var mannen på Oulavuolie." Part 2. www.youtube.com/watch?v=BWy_B9jS5e8.

Ashcroft, Bill, Gareth Griffins, and Helen Tiffin. 2000. *Post-colonial Studies: The Key Concepts*. 2nd ed. New York: Routledge.

Associated Press. 1989. "CDs Overtake LPs for the First Time, Industry Says." January 26, 1989. www.apnews.com/9d2d59fd4bece253fe0ba00959e4a023.

Axelsson, Per, Tahu Kukutai, and Rebecca Kippen. 2016. "The Field of Indigenous Health and the Role of Colonization and History." *Journal of Population Research* 33:1, 1–7.

Bäckman, Louise, and Åke Hultkrantz. 1977. *Studies in Lapp Shamanism*. Stockholm Studies in Comparative Religion 16. Stockholm: Almqvist & Wiksell.

Balto, Asta. 2005. "Traditional Sámi Child Rearing in Transition: Shaping a New Pedagogical Platform." *AlterNative: An International Journal of Indigenous Peoples* 1 (1): 85–105.

Barberá, Pablo, John T. Jost, Jonathan Nagler, Joshua A. Tucker, and Richard Bonneau. 2015. "Tweeting from Left to Right." *Psychological Science* 26 (10): 1531–42.

Barthes, Roland. 1978. "The Photographic Message." In *Image, Music, Text*, 15–31. New York: Macmillan.

Beaton, Brian, Terence Burnard, Adi Linden, and Susan O'Donnell. 2016. "Keewaytinook Mobile: An Indigenous Community-Owned Mobile Phone Service in Northern Canada." In *Indigenous People and Mobile Technologies*, edited by Laurel Evelyn Dyson, Stephen Grant, and Max Hendriks, 109–25. New York: Routledge.

Belausteguigoitia, Marisa. 2006. "On Line, Off Line and In Line: The Zapatista Rebellion and the Uses of Technology by Indian Women." In *Native on the Net: Indigenous and Diasporic Peoples in the Virtual Age*, edited by Kyra Landzelius, 97–111. London: Routledge.

Bergman, Ingmar, dir. 1967. *Persona*. Film. Svensk Filmindustri, Stockholm.

Bergmo, Tonje. 2017. "Reindeer Herding with NRK 'Slow TV'" Press release. www.nrk.no/presse/reindeer-herding-with-norwegian-broadcasting-_slow-tv_-1.13462443.

Bergsland, Knut. 1957. *Sámien Lukkeme-Gärjá: Sydlapsk Läsebok: Med Grammatik Och Ordlista*. Svensk uppl. Gardvik: P. J. Fjellström.

Bernal, Victoria. 2005. "Eritrea On-Line: Diaspora, Cyberspace, and the Public Sphere." *American Ethnologist* 32 (4): 660–75.

Berners-Lee, Tim, and Mark Fischetti. 1999. *Weaving the Web: The Original Design and Ultimate Destiny of the World Wide Web by Its Inventor*. London: Orion Business.

Bijker, Wiebe, and John Law, eds. 1992. *Shaping Technology/Building Society*. Studies in Sociotechnical Change. Cambridge, MA: MIT Press.

Bjørklund, Ivar. 2000. *Sápmi: Becoming a Nation: The Emergence of a Sami National Community*. Tromsø: Tromsø University Museum.

Blank, Trevor, and Robert Howard. 2013. *Tradition in the Twenty-First Century: Locating the Role of the Past in the Present*. Boulder: University Press of Colorado.

Blind, Marica. 2015. "Hálgu lär sig en miljöjojk." Sámeradion & SVT Sápmi, November 13, 2015. https://sverigesradio.se/sida/artikel.aspx?programid=2327&artikel=6299517.

Blommaert, Jan, and Gosia Szabla. 2017. "Does Context Really Collapse in Social Media Interaction?" Paper presented at the conference Moving Texts: Mediations and Transculturations, Aveiro, Portugal.

Bock, Sheila. 2017. "Ku Klux Kasserole and Strange Fruit Pies: A Shouting Match at the Border in Cyberspace." *Journal of American Folklore* 130 (516): 142–65.

Boine, Mari. 1985. *Jaskatvuođa maŋŋá/Etter stillheten/After the Silence.* Hot Club Records. HCR 1001. Compact disc.

——. 1989. *Gula gula!* EmArcy 0044001778124; Universal 0044001778124. Compact disc.

——. 1993. Goaskinviellja. Lean MBCD 62. Also released on Verve World 521388-2. Compact disc.

——. 1998. Bálvvoslatnja. Lean 5590232. Also released on Antilles 5590232. Compact disc.

——. 2009. "Mari Boine synger Mitt lille land." Uploaded to YouTube by Mittlillelandnorge, November 23, 2009. www.youtube.com/watch?v=QQ8hpam-F3M.

Bourdieu, Pierre.1965. *Un art moyen. Essai sur les usages sociaux de la photographie.* Paris: Les Éditions de Minuit.

——. 1979. *La distinction: Critique sociale du jugement.* Paris: Les Éditions de Minuit.

——. 1996. *Sur la télévision.* Paris: Raisons d'Agir.

Brand, Peter, Tracey Herbert, and Shaylene Boechler. 2016. "Language Vitalization through Mobile and Online Technologies in British Columbia." In *Indigenous People and Mobile Technologies*, edited by Laurel Evelyn Dyson, Stephen Grant, and Max Hendriks, 265–73. New York: Routledge.

Brantenberg, Terje. 2014. "Politics of Belonging–The Sámi Movement." In *Sámi Stories: Art and Identity of an Arctic People*, edited by Marit Anne Hauan, 37–56. Tromsø, Norway: Tromsø University Museum and Orkana Akademisk.

Bridge-It Thematic Network. n.d. "SAMENET/Sámi Network Connectivity." www.lmi.ub.es/bridge-it/samenetsami-network-connectivity.html.

Brodrej, Gunilla. 2016. Samisk exotism i SVT:s thrillerserie. *Expressen*, November 13, 2016. www.expressen.se/kultur/gunilla-brodrej/samisk-exotism-i-svts-thrillerserie.

Brown, Dee. 1970. *Bury My Heart at Wounded Knee: An Indian History of the American West*. New York: Holt, Rinehart & Winston.

——. 1973. *Haudatkaa sydämeni Wounded Kneehen: Lännen valloitus intiaanien näkökulmasta*. Helsinki: Otava.

——. 1974a. *Begrav mitt hjerte ved Wounded Knee*. Oslo: Gyldendal.

——. 1974b. *Begrav mitt hjärta vid Wounded Knee: Erövringen av vilda västern ur indianernas perspektiv*. Stockholm: P. A. Norstedt & Söners.

Browne, Donald R. 1996. *Electronic Media and Indigenous Peoples: A Voice of Our Own?* Ames: Iowa State University Press.

Bruns, Axel. 2008. *Blogs, Wikipedia, Second Life, and Beyond: From Production to Produsage*. New York: Peter Lang.

Buddle, Kathleen. 2008. "Transistor Resistors: Native Women's Radio in Canada and the Social Organization of Political Space from Below." In *Global Indigenous Media: Cultures, Poetics, and Politics*, edited by Pamela Wilson and Michelle Stewart, 128–44. Durham, NC: Duke University Press.

Buder, Emily. 2017. "'Sami Blood': Why Amanda Kernell Broke All 3 Rules for Making a Feature Debut." No Film School, June 12, 2017. https://nofilmschool.com/2017/06/sami-blood-amanda-kernell.

Burns, Alex, and Ben Eltham. 2009. "Twitter Free Iran: An Evaluation of Twitter's Role in Public Diplomacy and Information Operations in Iran's 2009 Election Crisis." Communications Policy and Research Forum 2009, November 19–20, 2009, University of Technology, Sydney.

Bydler, Charlotte. 2010. "Forlandlinger om det samtidlige—Anders Sunnas kunstnerskap." *Ottar* 4 (2010): 9–14.

Cache Collective. 2008. "Cache: Provisions and Productions in Contemporary Igloolik Video." In *Global Indigenous Media: Cultures, Poetics, and Politics*, edited by Pamela Wilson and Michelle Stewart, 74–88. Durham, NC: Duke University Press.

ČálliidLágádus. 2016. "Samisk aktivisme—et fjernt minne! Ny bok om Alta-demonstrasjonene. Lørdag var det lansering på GG/Samisk Litteratur senter." www.calliidlagadus.org/web/index.php?odas=330&giella1=nor.

Campbell, Heidi. 2007. "Who's Got the Power? Religious Authority and the Internet." *Journal of Computer-Mediated Communication* 12 (3): 1043–62.

Castells, Manuel. 2001. *The Rise of the Network Society: The Information Age. Economy, Society, and Culture*. Malden, MA: Wiley-Blackwell.

Ceruzzi, Paul E. 2005. "Moore's Law and Technological Determinism: Reflections on the History of Technology." *Technology and Culture* 46 (3): 584–93.

Cespooch, Ataya. 2013. "Virtual Reservation: NDNs in the Digital Age." In *Writing American Cultures: Studies of Identity, Community and Place*, edited by Sam Schrager, 3–31. Olympia, WA: Evergreen State College Press.

Chevalier, Jacques, and Daniel J. Buckles. 2013. *Participatory Action Research: Theory and Methods for Engaged Inquiry*. New York: Routledge.

Chilisa, Bagele. 2012. *Indigenous Research Methodologies*. London: Sage.

Christensen, Cato. 2012. "Reclaiming the Past: On the History-Making Significance of the Sámi Film *The Kautokeino Rebellion*." *Acta Borealia* 29 (1): 56–76.

——. 2015. "Sami Shamanism and Indigenous Film: The Case of Pathfinder." In *Nordic Neoshamanisms*, edited by S. E. Kraft, T. Fonneland, and J. R. Lewis, 175–90. Palgrave Studies in New Religions and Alternative Spiritualities. New York: Palgrave Macmillan.

Christie, Michael. 2008. "Digital Tools and the Management of Australian Desert Aboriginal Knowledge." In *Global Indigenous Media: Cultures, Practices and Politics*, edited by P. Wilson and M. Stewart, 270–86. Durham, NC: Duke University Press.

Cobo, José R. Martinez. 1986. *Study of the Problem of Discrimination against Indigenous Populations*. United Nations Economic and Social Council Commission on Human Rights, Sub-commission on Prevention of Discrimination and Protection of Minorities. UN doc. E/CN.4/Sub.2/1986/7 and Add. 1–4.

Cocq, Coppélie. 2008. *Revoicing Sámi Narratives: North Sámi Storytelling at the Turn of the 20th Century*. Umeå: Institutionen för Språkstudier.

——. 2014. "Traditionalisation for Revitalisation: Tradition as a Concept and Practice in Contemporary Sámi Contexts." *Folklore: Electronic Journal of Folklore* 57:79–100.

——. 2015. "Indigenous Voices on the Web: Folksonomies and Endangered Languages." *Journal of American Folklore* 128 (509): 273–85.

———. 2016. “Exploitation or Preservation? Your Choice! Digital Modes of Expressing Perceptions on Nature and the Land.” In *The Environment in the Age of the Internet: Activists, Communication, and the Digital Landscape*, 53–74, edited by Heike Graf. Cambridge: Open Book Publishers.

Cocq, Coppélie, and Kirk Sullivan, eds. 2019. *Perspectives on Indigenous Writing and Literacies*. Studies in Writing Series 37. Leiden: Brill.

Cormack, Mike. 2013. “Towards an Understanding of Media Impact on Minority Language Use.” In *Social Media and Minority Languages: Convergence and the Creative Industries*, edited by Elin Haf Gruffydd Jones and Enrique Uribe-Jongbloed, 255–65. Bristol: Multilingual Matters.

Cosgrove, Ben. 2014. “Unforgettable Eisenstaedt: 22 Amazing Photos by a Master.” *Time*, November 3, 2014. http://time.com/3491299/unforgettable-eisenstaedt-22-amazing-photos-by-a-master.

Council of Europe, Advisory Committee on the Framework Convention for the Protection of National Minorities. 2016. Fourth Opinion on Finland. ACFC/OP/IV(2016)00.

———. 2017. Fourth Opinion on Sweden. ACFC/OP/IV(2017)004.

Croker, Richard. 2007. *The Boomer Century, 1946–2046: How America’s Most Influential Generation Changed Everything*. New York: Springboard Press.

Crottet, Robert. 1949a. *The Enchanted Forest and Other Tales*. London: Richards Press.

———1949b. *Forêts de la lune: Légendes lapones-scoltes*. Neuchâtel: A la Baconnière.

Cultural Survival. 1998. “Aboriginal Media, Aboriginal Control.” June 1998. www.culturalsurvival.org/publications/cultural-survival-quarterly/22-2-aboriginal-media-aboriginal-control.

Cunliffe, Daniel, and Rhodri ap Dyfri. 2013. “The Welsh Language on YouTube: Initial Observations.” In *Social Media and Minority Languages: Convergence and the Creative Industries*, edited by Elin Haf Gruffydd Jones and Enrique Uribe-Jongbloed, 130–45. Bristol: Multilingual Matters.

Cunliffe, Daniel, Delyth Morris, and Cynog Prys. 2013. “Investigating the Differential Use of Welsh in Young Speakers’ Social Networks: A Comparison of Communication in Face-to-Face Settings, in Electronic Texts and on Social Networking Sites.” In *Social Media and Minority Languages: Convergence and the Creative Industries*, 75-86, edited by Elin Haf Gruffydd Jones and Enrique Uribe-Jongbloed. Bristol: Multilingual Matters.

Dahlberg-Grundberg, Michael. 2016. "Technology as Movement." *Convergence: The International Journal of Research into New Media Technologies* 22 (5): 524–42.

Dana, Kathleen Osgood. 2003. Áillohaš the Shaman-Poet and *His Govadas-Image Drum: A Literary Ecology of Nils-Aslak Valkeapää*. Oulu: Giellegas Instituhtta, University of Oulu.

Davidsson Pamela, and Anders Thoresson. 2017. *Svenskarna och internet 2017* (The Swedes and the internet 2017). Internetstiftelsen i Sverige. https://2017.svenskarnaochinternet.se.

Dean, Jodi. 2003. "Why the Net Is Not a Public Sphere." *Constellations* 10 (1) (March): 95–112.

Deatnogátte Nuorat. 1974. *Tanabreddens Ungdom/Deatnogátte Nuorat.* LP album. Oslo: MAI no. 7402.

Dégh, Linda. 1994. *American Folklore and the Mass Media*. Bloomington: Indiana University Press.

Deloria, Vine, Jr. 1969. *Custer Died for Your Sins: An Indian Manifesto.* Norman: University of Oklahoma Press.

Denning, Dorothy E. 2000. "Activism, Hacktivism, and Cyberterrorism: The Internet as a Tool for Influencing Foreign Policy." *Computer Security Journal* 3 (16): 15–35.

Digigiella. 2017. http://stream.humlab.umu.se/?streamName=digigiella17.

Dijck, Jose van. 2013. *The Culture of Connectivity: A Critical History of Social Media*. New York: Oxford University Press.

DiNucci, Darcy. 1999. "Fragmented Future." *Print Magazine* 4 (32): 32, 221–22.

Dokka, Ingrid. 2015. "From Conceptions of Sami Culture in Norwegian Film to an Independent Sami Film Expression." In *Visions of Sápmi*, edited by Anna Lydia Svalastog and Gunlög Fur, 107–28. Røros, Norway: Arthub Publisher.

Douglas, Susan J. 1987. *Inventing American Broadcasting, 1899–1922*. Baltimore: Johns Hopkins University Press.

DuBois, Thomas A. 1996. "Native Hermeneutics: Traditional Means of Interpreting Lyric Songs in Northern Europe" *Journal of American Folklore* 109 (403): 235–66.

——. 1999. *Nordic Religions in the Viking Age*. Philadelphia: University of Pennsylvania Press.

——. 2000. "Folklore, Boundaries and Audience in *The Pathfinder*." In *Sami Folkloristics*, edited by Juha Pentikäinen, 255–74. Turku: NIF.

——. 2006. *Lyric, Meaning, and Audience in the Oral Tradition of Northern Europe*. Notre Dame, IN: University of Notre Dame Press.

——. 2008. "Un chanteur devenu poète: Sirma Ovllá et le début de la littérature samie." In *L'image du Sápmi*, edited by Kajsa Andersson, 307–19. Humanistica Oerbroensia. Artes et linguae 15. Göteborg: Humanistic Studies at Örebro University.

——. 2013. "Ethnomemory: Ethnographic and Culture-Centered Approaches to the Study of Memory." *Scandinavian Studies* 85 (3) (2013): 306–31.

——. 2014. "Borg Mesch: The Role of a Culture Broker in Picturing the North." *Journal of Northern Studies* 8 (2) (2014): 45–70.

——. 2016. "Performances, Texts, and Contexts: Olaus Sirma, Johan Turi, and the Dilemma of Reifying a Context-Dependent Oral Tradition." *Classics@* 14. http://nrs.harvard.edu/urn-3:hlnc.essay:DuBoisT.Performances_Texts_and_Contexts.2016.

——. 2017. "Sacralizing." In *Nordic Literature: A Comparative History*, vol. 1, *Spatial Nodes*, edited by Thomas A. DuBois and Dan Ringgaard, 519–29. Amsterdam: John Benjamins Publishing Company.

——. 2018. *Sacred to the Touch: Nordic and Baltic Religious Wood Carving.* Seattle: University of Washington Press.

Dyson, Laurel Evelyn. 2011. "Indigenous Peoples on the Internet." In *The Handbook of Internet Studies*, edited by C. Ess and M. Consalvo, 251–69. Oxford: Wiley-Blackwell.

Dyson, Laurel Evelyn, Max A. N. Hendriks, and Stephen Grant, eds. 2007. *Information Technology and Indigenous People.* Hershey, PA: Idea Group Inc.

Dyson, Laurel Evelyn, Stephen Grant, and Max Hendriks, eds. 2016. *Indigenous People and Mobile Technologies.* New York: Routledge.

Eikjok, Jorunn, and Ola Røa, eds. 2013. *Sámi Images in Modern Times.* Kárášjohka-Karasjok: ČálliidLágádus.

Eira, Inger Marie Gaup. 2012. "Muohttaga jávohis giella. Sámi árbevirolaš máhttu muohttaga birra dálkkádatrievdanáiggis" (The silent language of snow. Sámi traditional knowledge of snow in times of climate change). Čálus grádii (PhD dissertation), Institutt for språkvitenskap, Fakultet for humaniora, samfunnsvitenskap og lærerutdanning, Universitetet i Tromsø. https://munin.uit.no/handle/10037/9843.

Eira, Inger Marie Gaup, Ole Henrik Magga, and Nils Isak Eira. 2010. "Muohtatearpmaid sisdoallu ja geavahus." *Sámi dieđalaš áigečála* 2

(2010): 3–24. http://site.uit.no/aigecala/files/2014/06/SDA-2-2010-eira-ja-magga-ja-eira.pdf.

Eira, Nils Isak. 1984. *Boazobargi giella*. Dieđut 4-2008. Guovdageaidnu: Sámi Allaskuvla.

Elokuvasaatio. 2017. "Dokumentti kolttamummon ja sveitsiläiskirjalilijan ystävyydestä valloittaa maailmaa." *Sessio: Suomen elokuvasäätiön blogi*, February 9, 2017. https://sessessio.wordpress.com/tag/native.

Eriksen, Thomas Hylland. 2007. *Globalization: The Key Concepts*. New York: Berg Publishers.

EscLIVEmusic1. 2012. "Sámiid Ædnan." Uploaded to YouTube by EscLIVE music1, March 29, 2012. www.youtube.com/watch?v=AyMdsQOT8vI.

Ess, Charles, Akira Kawabata, and Hiroyuki Kurosaki. 2007. "Cross-Cultural Perspectives on Religion and Computer-Mediated Communication." *Journal of Computer-Mediated Communication* 12 (3): 939–55.

Ess, Charles, and Fay Sudweeks. 2001. "On the Edge." *New Media and Society* 3(3): 259–69.

Essed, Philomena. 1991. *Understanding Everyday Racism: An Interdisciplinary Theory*. London: Sage.

——. 2004. "Naming the Unnameable: Sense and Sensibilities in Researching Racism." In *Researching Race and Racism*, edited by M. Bulmer J. Solomos, 119–33. London: Routledge.

Fitzgerald, Timothy. 2000. *The Ideology of Religious Studies*. New York: Oxford University Press.

Fjällgren, Jon Henrik. 2014. "Jon Henrik–Daniels Jojk. Talang Sverige 2014." Uploaded to YouTube by Talang Sverige, February 18, 2014. www.youtube.com/watch?v=woEcdqqbEVg.

——. 2015a. *Goeksegh*. Cupol. 88843083952. Compact disc.

——. 2015b. "Melodifestivalen 2015. Jon Henrik Fjällgren–Jag är fri (Manne leam frijje)." Uploaded to YouTube by wiwibloggs, March 7, 2015. www.youtube.com/watch?v=BTiOfuMv1Lg.

Fuchs, Christian. 2010. "Alternative Media as Critical Media." *European Journal of Social Theory* 13 (2): 173–92.

Fuentes, Marcela A. 2018. "Digital Activism." *Encyclopaedia Britannica*. https://www.britannica.com/topic/digital-activism.

Gaski, Harald, ed. 1996. *In the Shadow of the Midnight Sun: Contemporary Sami Prose and Poetry*. Kárášjohka: Davvi Girji.

——. 2000a. "The Reindeer on the Mountain, the Reindeer in the Mind: On Sámi Yoik Lyrics." In *Rights to Language: Equity, Power, and Education*, edited by Robert Phillipson, 93–200. London: Routledge.
——. 2000b. "The Secretive Text: Yoiks Lyrics as Literature and Tradition." In *Sami Folkloristics*, edited by Juha Pentikäinen, 191–214. Åbo, Finland: Nordic Network of Folklore.
——. 2008a. "Nils-Aslak Valkeapää: Indigenous Voice and Multimedia Artist." *AlterNative* 4 (2): 156–78.
——, ed. 2008b. *Ivdnesuotna: Sámi čáppagirjjálašvuođa čoakkáldat*. Guovdageaidnu: DAT.
——. 2011a. "More than Meets the Eye: The Indigeneity of Johan Turi's Writing and Artwork." *Scandinavian Studies* 83 (4): 591–608.
——. 2011b. "Song, Poetry and Images in Writing: Sami Literature." *NordLit* 27:33–54.
——. 2015. "Looking Both Ways: Future and Tradition in Nils-Aslak Valkeapää's Poetry." In *Mapping Indigenous Presence: North Scandinavian and North American Perspectives*, edited by Kathryn W. Shanley and Bjørg Evjen, 250–78. Tucson: University of Arizona Press.
Gaski, Harald, and Lena Kappfjell, eds. 2005. Åvtese jåhta. Guovdageaidnu: DAT.
Gaski, Harald, John T. Solbakk, and Aage Solbakk, eds. 2004. *Min njálmmálaš árbevierru: Máidnasat, myhtat ja muitalusat*. Kárášjohka: Davvi Girji.
Gaup, Elisabeth Utsi. 2009. "Duovdagiid giella–Bálggesčuovga lunddolaš oahppanarenaid ozadettiin sámegiela oahpahusa olis." *Sámi dieđalaš áigečála* 1 (2) (2009): 46–61. http://site.uit.no/aigecala/sda-1-2-2009_gaup.
Gaup, Nils, dir. 1987. *Ofelaš* (Pathfinder). Prod. John M. Jacobsen. Film. Filmkameratene A/A, Mayco, Norsk Film, Norway.
——. 2008. *Guovdageainnu stuimmit/Kautokeino opprøret* (Kautokeino uprising). Film. Borealis Production, Filmlance International, Metronome Productions, Rubicon TV.
Gauriloff, Katja, dir. 2007. *Huuto tuuleen* (Shout into the wind). Film. Oktober, Finland.
——. 2012. *Säilöttyjä unelmia* (Canned dreams; 2012). Film. Final Cut for Real, Aljazeera English, Arte France.
——. 2016. *Kuun metsän Kaisa* (Kaisa's enchanted forest). Film. Oktober, Finland.

Gauriloff, Katja, and Jonas Berghäll, dir. 2013. *Voimanlähde* (Source of strength). Film. Oktober, Finland.

Gergely, Tamás. n.d. "Det gränslösa Sápmi: Intervju med Henrik Micael Kuhmunen" (Interview with Henrik Micael Kuhmunen, principal for the Sámi education center of Jokkmokk, operator for SameNet). www.oocities.org/istjan/intercsi/henkhu_sv.htm.

Giddens, Anthony. 1991. *Modernity and Self-Identity: Self and Society in Late Modern Age.* Stanford, CA: Stanford University Press.

Gideon, Valerie. 2006. "Canadian Aboriginal Peoples Tackle E-health: Seeking Ownership versus Integration." In *Native on the Net: Indigenous and Diasporic Peoples in the Virtual Age*, edited by Kyra Landzelius, 61–79. London: Routledge.

Ginsburg, Faye. 1991. "Indigenous Media: Faustian Contract or Global Village?" *Cultural Anthropology.* 6 (1): 92–112.

——. 1994. "Embedded Aesthetics: Creating a Discursive Space for Indigenous Media." *Cultural Anthropology* 9 (3): 365–82.

——. 2002. "Screen Memories: Resignifying the Traditional in Indigenous Media." In *Media Worlds: Anthropology on New Terrain*, edited by Faye D. Ginsburg, Lila Abu-Lughod, and Brian Larkin, 39–57. Berkeley: University of California Press.

Godard, Jean-Luc, and Jean-Pierre Gorin, writers, dir. 1972. *Letter to Jane.* Film. Janus Films/Criterion Collection, Paris.

Grenoble, Lenore A., and Linsay J. Whaley. 2006. *Saving Languages: An Introduction to Language Revitalization.* Cambridge: Cambridge University Press.

Greve, Bredo, dir. 1980. *La elva leve!* Film. Fotfilm Filmgruppe 1.

Gripenstad Georg. 1990. *Kautokeino 1852: Några tidsdokument.* Luleå: Tornedalica.

Guttorm, Eino. 1985. *Varahuvvan Bálgát.* [Tana]: Jår'galæd'dji.

Haf Gruffydd Jones, Elin, and Enrique Uribe-Jongbloed, eds. 2013. *Social Media and Minority Language: Convergence and the Creative Industries.* Bristol: Multilingual Matters.

Hafstein, Valdimar Tr. 2018. *Making Intangible Heritage: El Condor Pasa and Other Stories from UNESCO.* Bloomington: Indiana University Press.

Hagerman, Maja. 2015. *Käraste Herman: Rasbiologen Herman Lundborgs gåta.* Stockholm: Norstedts.

———. 2016. “Svenska kyrkan och rasbiologin.” In *De historiska relationerna mellan Svenska kyrkan och samerna*, edited by Daniel Lundmark and Olle Sundström, 961–92. Skellefteå: Artos & Norma Bokförlag.

Hallett, D., M. J. Chandler, and C. E. Lalonde. 2007. “Aboriginal Language Knowledge and Youth Suicide.” *Cognitive Development* 22 (3): 392–99.

Hällgren, Katarina, ed. 2017. #vardadsrasismmotmigsomsame. Sveriges Radio, Sameradion & SVT Sápmi.

Hansen, Hanna Horsberg. 2007. *Fortellinger om samisk samtidskunst*. Kárášjohka: Davvi Girji.

———. 2014. “Sámi Artist Group 1978–1984—A Story about Sámi Traditions in Transition.” In *Sámi Stories: Art and Identity of an Arctic People*, edited by Charis Gullickson and Sandra Lorentzen, 89–105. Stamnsund, Norway: Northern Norway Art Museum and Orkana Akademisk.

Harlow, Summer. 2012. “Social Media and Social Movements: Facebook and an Online Guatemalan Justice Movement That Moved Offline.” *New Media and Society* 14 (2): 225–43.

Harner, Michael. 1980. *The Way of the Shaman*. San Francisco: Harper SanFrancisco.

Harvey, Dennis. 2016. “Film Review: ‘Kaisa’s Enchanted Forest.’” *Variety*, May 6, 2016. https://variety.com/2016/film/reviews/kaisa-enchanted-forest-review-1201767852.

Heiska, Susanna. 2011. “Joikuja revontulten ääreltä” Loviisan sanomat, February 4, 2011. www.loviisansanomat.net/lue.php?id=4717.

Heith, Anne. 2014. “Valkeapää’s Use of Photographs in Beaivi, áhčážan: Indigenous Counter-history versus Documentation in the Age of Photography.” *Acta Borealia* 31 (1): 41–58.

Henriksen, John B. 1999. *Saami Parliamentary Co-operation: An Analysis*. Guovdageaidnu and Copenhagen: International Work Group for Indigenous Affairs.

Henrysson, Sten. 1992. “Saami Education in Sweden in the 1990’s.” In *Readings in Saami History, Culture and Language III*, edited by Roger Kvist, 103–12. Umeå: Center for Arctic Cultural Research, Umeå University.

Hilder, Thomas R. 2015. *Sámi Musical Performance and the Politics of Indigeneity in Northern Europe*. London: Rowman & Littlefield.

Hill, Symon. 2013. *Digital Revolutions: Activism in the Internet Age*. Oxford: New Internationalist.

Hillier, Lynne, and Lyn Harrison. 2007. "Building Realities Less Limited Than Their Own: Young People Practising Same-Sex Attraction on the Internet." *Sexualities* 10 (1): 82–100.

Ho, David Y. F. 1995. "Selfhood and Identity in Confucianism, Taoism, Buddhism, and Hinduism: Contrasts with the West." *Journal for the Theory of Social Behaviour* 25 (2): 115–39.

Hochman, Brian. 2014. *Savage Preservation: The Ethnographic Origins of Modern Media Technology*. Minneapolis: University of Minnesota Press.

Holck, Per. 1991. "The Occurrence of Hip Joint Dislocation in Early Lappic Populations of Norway." *International Journal of Osteoarchaeology* 1 (1991): 199–202.

Holm, Liselott. 2016. "Sofia Jannoks kamp för Standing Rock." ETC, October 7, 2016. http://umea.etc.se/kultur-noje/sofia-jannoks-kamp-standing-rock.

Holmberg, Niillas, and Jenni Laiti. 2015. "Saami Manifesto 15: Reconnecting through Resistance." Idle No More, March 15, 2013. www.idlenomore.ca/the_saami_manifesto_15_reconnecting_through_resistance_the_saami_manifesto_15_reconnecting_through_resistance.

Hooper-Greenhill, E. 2000. "Preface." In *Museums and the Interpretation of Visual Culture*, ix–xiv. London: Routledge.

Howard, Robert G., and Coppélie Cocq. 2017 "Introduction: The Inheritance of the Digital: Ethnographic Approaches to Everyday Realities in, of, and through Digital Technologies." *Cultural Analysis* 16.

Ijäs, Arne Johansen. 2011. *Sámi preassahistorjá–Samisk pressehistorie: Fra Muitalægje til Ávvir.* Kárášjohka: ČállidLágádus.

Iseke-Barnes, Judy, and Deborah Danard. 2007. "Indigenous Knowledges and Worldview: Representations and the Internet." In *Information Technology and Indigenous People*, edited by Laurel Evelyn Dyson, Max Hendriks, and Stephen Grant, 27–37. Hershey, PA: Information Science Publishing.

Jacobs, Seth. 2006. *Cold War Mandarin: Ngo Dinh Diem and the Origins of America's War in Vietnam, 1950–1963*. Lanham, MD: Rowman & Littlefield.

Jannok, Sofia. 2007. Čeaskat (White). DAT. DATCD-41. Compact disc.

———. 2008. Áššogáttis (By the embers). Caprice Records. CAP 21801. Compact disc.

———. 2013a. Áhpi (Wide as oceans). Songs to Arvas. STACD001. Compact disc.

——. 2013b. "Sofia Jannok–Áhpi (Wide as Oceans) Official Video." Dir. Oskar Njajta Östergren. Bautafilm. Uploaded to YouTube by Sofia Jannok, October 15, 2013. www.youtube.com/watch?v=hr13WV7UkgA.

——. 2016. *ORDA* (This is my land). Gamlestands Grammofonbolag. GG04. Compact disc.

Jansen, Fieke. 2010. "Digital Activism in the Middle East: Mapping Issue Networks in Egypt, Iran, Syria and Tunisia," *Knowledge Management for Development Journal* 6 (1): 37–52.

Jårgalæđđji. 2016. "Jårgalæđđji Å/S." www.wikiwand.com/no/J%C3%A5rgal%C3%A6%C4%91%C4%91ji.

Jenkins, Henry. 2006. *Fans, Bloggers, and Gamers: Exploring Participatory Culture*. New York: NYU Press.

Jernsletten, Nils. 1994. "Tradisjonell samisk fagterminologi." In *Festkrift til Ørnulf Vorren*. Tromsø Museums skrifter XXV. Tromsø: Tromsø Museum/Universitetet i Tromsø.

——. 1997. "Sami Traditional Terminology." In *Sami Culture in a New Era*, edited by Harald Gaski, 86–108. Kárášjohka: Davvi Girji.

Johansson Lönn, Eva. 2014. "Varför ska dom få? Vardagsrasism mot samer i läsarkommentarer på tre svenska nyhetssajter." *Kulturella perspektiv–Svensk etnologisk tidskrift* (1): 41–49.

Johnson, Ian. 2013. "Audience Design and Communication Accomodation Theory: Use of Twitter by Welsh-English Biliterates." In *Social Media and Minority Languages: Convergence and the Creative Industries*, edited by Elin Haf Gruffydd Jones and Enrique Uribe-Jongbloed, 99–118. Bristol: Multilingual Matters.

Jones-Bamman, Richard. 1993. "As Long as We Continue to Joik, We'll Remember Who We Are." In *Negotiating Identity and the Performance of Culture: The Saami Joik*. PhD dissertation, University of Washington, Seattle.

Keefer, Michael. 2013a. "Noam Chomsky: Indigenous People Are the Ones Taking the Lead in Trying to Protect All of Us." *Two Row Times*, November 3, 2013. https://tworowtimes.com/news/national/noam-chomsky-indigenous-people-are-in-the-lead.

——. 2013b. "Noam Chomsky: Harper Energy Policies Are Destroying the Environment 'as Fast as Possible.'" *Canadian Charger*, November 5, 2013. www.thecanadiancharger.com/page.php?id=5&a=1630.

Kernell, Amanda. 2015. *Stoerre Vaerie* (Northern Great Mountain). Film. Nordisk Film Production Sverige AB, Bautafilm, Sveriges Television (SVT).

——. 2017. *Sameblod* (Sami blood). Film. Bautafilm et al., Umeå.

Keskitalo, Jan Henry. 1997. "Sami Post-secondary Education–Ideals and Realities." In *Sami Culture in a New Era: The Norwegian Sami Experience*, edited by Harald Gaski, 155–71. Kárášjohka: Davvi Girji.

Keskitalo, Pigga, Kaarina Määttä, and Satu Uusiautti. 2012. "Re-thinking Sámi Education." *Linguistics, Culture and Education* 1 (1):12–41.

——. 2014. "'Language Immersion Tepee' as a Facilitator of Sámi Language Learning." *Journal of Language, Identity and Education* 13 (1): 70–79.

Ketcham Weber, Jessica. 2013. "Virtual Sit-In." *Encyclopaedia Britannica*. https://www.britannica.com/topic/virtual-sit-in.

Kilpatrick, Jacquelyn. 1999. *Celluloid Indians: Native Americans and Film*. Lincoln: University of Nebraska Press.

Kirshenblatt-Gimblett, Barbara. 1996. "The Electronic Vernacular." In *Connected: Engagements with Media*, edited by George E. Marcus, 21–66. Chicago: University of Chicago Press.

Kitchin, Robert M. 1998. "Towards Geographies of Cyberspace." *Progress in Human Geography* 22 (3): 385–406.

Kjellström, Rolf, Gunnar Ternhag, and Håkan Rydving. 1988. *Om jojk*. Hedemora: Gidlunds Bokförlag.

Kovach, Margaret. 2009. *Indigenous Methodologies: Characteristics, Conversations, and Contexts*. Toronto: University of Toronto Press.

Kraft, Siv Ellen. 2007. "Natur, spiritualitet og tradisjon: Om akademisk romantisering og feilslåtte primitivismeoppgjør." *Din: Tidsskrift for religion og kultur* (1–2): 53–62.

Kral, Inge. 2009. *The Literacy Question in Remote Indigenous Australia*. CAEPR Topical Issue no. 6. Canberra: Centre for Aboriginal Economic Policy Research.

——. 2010. *Plugged In: Remote Australian Indigenous Youth and Digital Culture*. CAEPR Working Paper no. 69. Canberra: Centre for Aboriginal Economic Policy Research.

Kral, Inge, and Robert J. Schwab. 2012. *Learning Spaces: Youth, Literacy and New Media in Remote Indigenous Australia*. Canberra: Australian National University Press.

Kulonen, Ulla-Maija, Irja Seurujärvi-Kari, and Risto Pulkkinen, eds. 2005. *The Saami: A Cultural Encyclopaedia*. Helsinki: Suomalaisen Kirjallisuuden Seura.

Kuokkanen, Rauna. 2000. "Towards an Indigenous Paradigm: From a Sami Perspective." *Canadian Journal of Native Studies* 20 (2): 411–36.

———. 2003. "'Survivance' in Sami and First Nations Boarding School Narratives: Reading Novels by Kerttu Vuolab and Shirley Sterling." *American Indian Quarterly* 27 (3- 4): 697–726.

———. 2009. *Boaris dego eana: Eamiálbmogiid diehtu, filosofiijat ja dutkan* (As old as the Earth: Indigenous knowledge, philosophies, and research). Čálliidlágádus: Sámi Academica Series. Kárášjohka: ČálliidLágádus.

———. 2011. "Self-Determination and Indigenous Women–'Whose Voice Is It We Hear in the Sámi Parliament?'" *International Journal on Minority and Group Rights* 18:39–62.

Kuutma, Kristin. 2006. *Collaborative Representations: Interpreting the Creation of a Sámi Ethnography and a Seto Epic*. FF Communications no. 289. Helsinki: Suomalainen Tiedeakatemia.

———. 2011. "Encounters to Negotiate a Sámi Ethnography: The Process of Collaborative Representations." *Scandinavian Studies* 83 (4): 491–518.

Kvernmo, Siv, Kirsi Strøm Bull, Ann Ragnhild Broderstad, May Britt Rossvoll, Bent Martin Eliassen, and Jon Petter Stoor. 2018. *Proposal for Ethical Guidelines for Sámi Health Research and Research on Sámi Human Biological Material*. Sámediggi, Karasjok, Norway.

Kvist, Roger. 1992. "Swedish Saami Policy, 1550-1990." In *Readings in Saami History, Culture and Language III*, edited by Roger Kvist, 63–78. Umeå: Center for Arctic Cultural Research, Umeå University.

Laestadius, Lars Levi, and Juha Pentikäinen. 2002. *Fragments of Lappish Mythology*. Beaverton, ON: Aspasia Books.

Landzelius, Kyria, ed. 2006. *Native on the Net: Indigenous and Diasporic Peoples in the Virtual Age*. London: Routledge.

Lantto, Patrik. 2012. *Lappväsendet: Tillämpningen av svensk samepolitik 1885–1971*. Umeå: Centrum för Samisk Forskning, Umeå Universitet.

Laula Renberg, Elsa.1904. *Inför lif eller död? Sanningsord i de Lappska förhållandena*. Stockholm: Wilhelmsson Boktryckeri.

Leary, Kevin. 2006. "Joe Rosenthal: 1911-2006; Photo Was His Fame–His Pride 'My Marines.'" *San Francisco Chronicle*, August 21, 2006, A1.

Leavy, Brett. 2007. "Digital Songlines: Digitising the Arts, Culture and Heritage Landscape of Aboriginal Australia." In *Information Technology and Indigenous People*, edited by Laurel Evelyn Dyson, Max Hendriks, and Stephen Grant, 159–69. Hershey, PA: Information Science Publishing.

Ledman, Anna-Lill. 2012. "Att representera och representeras: Samiska kvinnor i svensk och samisk press, 1966–2006" (To represent and be represented: Sami women in Swedish and Sami press, 1966–2006). PhD dissertation, Skrifter från Centrum för Samisk Forskning, Umeå Universitet, Umeå.

Lehtola, Veli-Pekka. 2004. *The Sámi People: Traditions in Transition*. Aanaar-Inari: Kustannus -Puntsi.

———. 2008. *Muitaleddjiid maŋisboahttit: Beaivvaš sámi teáhtera historjá*. Oulu: Giellagas-Instituhtta.

Lehtola, Veli-Pekka, and Jovnna-Ánde Vest. 2001. *Sámi jietna: Sámi radio 1947–1997*. Helsinki: Yleisradio.

Leijonhufvud, Margareta, ed. 1980. *Avannaamiut erinarsuutit, Davvilávlagat, Nordsange, Nordsanger, Nordsånger, Norðurlendskir sangir, Norðursöngvar, Pohjolan lauluja*. Stockholm: Utbildningsradion.

Lievrouw, Leah. 2011. *Alternative and Activist New Media*. Cambridge: Polity Press.

Liliequist, Marianne, and Coppélie Cocq, eds. 2017. *Samisk kamp: Kulturförmedling och rättviserörelse*. Umeå: Bokförlaget H:ström–Text & Kultur.

Lindgren, Simon, and Coppélie Cocq. 2017. "Turning the Inside Out: Social Media and the Broadcasting of Indigenous Discourse." *European Journal of Communication* 32 (2).

Lindgren, Simon, and Ragnar Lundström. 2011. "Pirate Culture and Hacktivist Mobilization: The Cultural and Social Protocols of #WikiLeaks on Twitter." *New Media and Society* 13 (6): 999–1018.

Linkola, Inker-Anni. 2014. "Saamelaisen koulun kielimaisema: Etnografinen tutkimus saamen kielestä toisen asteen oppilaitoksessa." PhD dissertation, Sámi Allaskuvla, Kautokeino, Norway.

Lõhmus, Jaak. 2010. *Dances for the Milky Way: Lennart Meri's Film Journeys*. Film.Estinfilm. Uploaded to YouTube May 14, 2014. www.youtube.com/watch?v=xq_x_qpPXxs.

Londoño, Ernesto. 2018. "Tribe's Lone Survivor Glimpsed in Amazon Jungle, Healthy and at Work." *New York Times*, July 20, 2018.

Louis, Renee Pualani. 2007. "Can You Hear Us Now? Voices from the Margin: Using Indigenous Methodologies in Geographic Research." *Geographical Research* 45 (2): 130–39.

Lovink, Geert. 2005. *The Principle of Networking: Concepts in Critical Internet Culture*. Amsterdam: Amsterdam University Press.

Lundmark, Bo. 1982. *Bæi'vi mánno nástit: Sol- och månkult samt astrala och celesta föreställingar bland samerna*. Acta Bothniensia Occidentalis/ Skrifter i västerbottniska kulturhistoria 5. Umeå: UTAB.

Lundmark, Lennart. 1998. *Så länge vi har marker: Samerna och staten under sexhundra år*. Stockholm: P. A. Norstedt & Söner.

Lundström, Jan-Erik. 2015. "Reassemble, Remap, Recode: Some Strategies among Three Contemporary (Sami) Artists." In *Visions of Sápmi*, edited by Anne-Lydia Svalastog and Gunlög Fur, 89–106. Røros: Arthub Publisher.

Magga, Ole Henrik. 2006. "Diversity in Saami Terminology for Reindeer and Snow." *International Social Science Journal* 58 (187): 25–34. www.arcticlanguages.com/papers/Magga_Reindeer_and_Snow.pdf.

——. 2014. "Lullisámegiela muohtasánit" / "Lullisámegiela muotasánit." *Sámi dieđalaš áigečála* 1 (2014): 27–49. http://site.uit.no/aigecala/files/2015/03/SDA-1-2014-magga.pdf.

Maireder, Axel, and Christian Schwarzenegger. 2012. "A Movement of Connected Individuals." *Information, Communication and Society* 15 (2): 171–95.

Mantila, Mavis. 2016. "Raising the Sami Flag at Standing Rock." Uploaded to YouTube September 30, 2016. www.youtube.com/watch?v=khqAPDFZR5M.

Marakatt-Labba, Britta. 2010. *Broderade Berättelser: Embroidered Stories = Sággon Muitalusat*. Kiruna: Koncentrat.

Markham, Annette, and Elizabeth Buchanan. 2012. "Ethical Decision-Making and Internet Research Recommendations from the AoIR Ethics Working Committee (Version 2.0)." Association of Internet Researchers (AoIR). https://aoir.org/reports/ethics2.pdf.

Marwick, Alice E., and Danah Boyd. 2011. "I Tweet Honestly, I Tweet Passionately: Twitter Users, Context Collapse, and the Imagined Audience." *New Media and Society* 13 (1): 114–33.

——. 2018. "Understanding Privacy at the Margins—Introduction." *International Journal of Communication* 12:1157–65.

Mathisen, Hans Ragnar Keviselie. 2019. "Art and the Sámi Revitalization." www.keviselie-hansragnarmathisen.net/141466668.

Mathisen, Stein R. 1993. "Folklore and Cultural Identity." In *Nordic Frontiers: Recent Issues in the Study of Modern Traditional Culture in the*

Nordic Countries, edited by Pertti J. Anttonen and Reimund Kvideland, 35–47. Turku: Nordic Institute of Folklore.

Mayhall, Laura E. Nym. 2003. *The Militant Suffrage Movement: Citizenship and Resistance in Britain*. New York: Oxford University Press.

McLuhan, Marshall. 1962. *The Gutenberg Galaxy: The Making of Typographic Man*. New York: New American Library.

———. 1964. *Understanding Media: The Extensions of Man*. New York: McGraw-Hill.

Meadows, Michael. 1994. "The Way People Want to Talk: Indigenous Media Production in Australia and Canada." *Media Information Australia* 73:64–73.

Media Smarts. n.d. "The Development of Aboriginal Broadcasting in Canada." http://mediasmarts.ca/digital-media-literacy/media-issues/diversity-media/aboriginal-people/development-aboriginal-broadcasting-canada.

Meehan, Mairtin Óg. 2006. *Finely Tempered Steel: Sean McCaughey and the IRA*. Dublin: Republican Publications.

Meier, Don. 1977. "The World of the Lapps Parts I and II." *Mutual of Omaha's Wild Kingdom*. Don Meier Productions. 24 + 24 min. Uploaded to YouTube by *Mutual of Omaha's Wild Kingdom*, April 20, 2011. www.youtube.com/watch?v=jta8IoXdJ-M&list=PL3NTgAkSxGbUKFTiRJVh4t47-tWYpr152&index=2; www.youtube.com/watch?v=M5ZNWUoNwg8&list=PL3NTgAkSxGbUKFTiRJVh4t47-tWYpr152&index=3.

Mennel, Barbara, and Amy Ongiri. 2000. "In a Desert Somewhere between Disney and Las Vegas: The Fanasy of Interracial Harmony and American Multiculturalism in Percy Adlon's Bagdad Cafe." *Camera Obscura* 44 (15): 50–175.

Mercea, Dan. 2013. "Probing the Implications of Facebook Use for the Organizational Form of Social Movement Organizations." *Information, Communication and Society* 16 (8): 1306–27.

Meri, Lennart. 1977. *Linnutee tuuled, Tallinnfilm and MTV.* 53 min. Uploaded to YouTube by FennoDoc, July 6, 2012. www.youtube.com/watch?v=i_dYIfsS9Cc.

Michael, Ib. 1981. *Snedronningen: Beretningen om Alta–et nulpunkt i Sameland*. København: Tiderne Skrifter.

Moore, Rebekah. 2004. "Rewriting the Soundscape: Towards a New Understanding of Sámi Popular Music and Identity in the New Millennium." PhD dissertation, University of Maryland, College Park.

Morozov, Evgeny. 2011. *The Net Delusion: The Dark Side of Internet Freedom*. New York: Public Affairs.

Morset, Kari-Synnøve. 2009. "Stemmene fra nord: Samisk revitalisering; Den kunstneriske kampen som levendegjorde en truet samisk kultur" (Voices of the North: Sami revitalization; The artistic struggle that revived a threatened Sami culture). PhD dissertation. University of Wisconsin, Madison.

Mungiu-Pippidi, Alina, and Igor Munteanu. 2009. "Moldova's 'Twitter Revolution.'" *Journal of Democracy* 20 (3): 136–42.

Nathan, David. 2000. "Plugging in Indigenous Knowledge: Connections and Innovations." *Australian Aboriginal Studies* 1 (12): 39–47.

Ní Bhroin, Niamh. 2015. "Social Media-Innovation: The Case of Indigenous Tweets." *Journal of Media Innovations* 2 (1): 89–106.

Nickul, Karl. 1948. *The Skolt Lapp Community Suenjelsijd during the Year 1938*. Acta Lapponica 5. Stockholm: Hugo Gerbers Förlag.

Nielsen, Konrad. 1932. *Lappisk Ordbok–Lapp Dictionary*. Oslo: Instituttet for Sammenlignende Kulturforskning.

Nordic Council. 2016. "The Nordic Council. The Official Inter-parliamentary Body." www.norden.org/en/nordic-council.

Nordström, Marika. 2017. "Om drömmar, motstånd och identitet: Samiska musiker berättar om sitt musikskapande." In *Samisk kamp: Kulturförmedling och rättviserörelse*, edited by Marianne Liliequist and Coppélie Cocq, 16–61. Umeå: Bokförlaget H:ström–Text & Kultur.

NRK. 2010. *Farlige fronter*. Television series. Brennpunkt. Dir. Lars Kristiansen. https://tv.nrk.no/serie/brennpunkt/MDUP11001810/02-11-2010.

Nutti, Ylva Jannok. 2012. "Förändringsarbete för en kulturellt baserad samisk matematikundervisning." *Tangenten* (2): 48–52.

——. 2013. "Indigenous Teachers' Experiences of the Implementation of Culture-Based Mathematics Activities in Sámi School." *Mathematics Education Research Journal* 25 (1): 57–72.

Nystad, Kristine. 2016. "Ole Heandarat–giellaprofessor ja eamiálbmotpolitihkar." http://site.uit.no/aigecala/files/2011/08/SDA-1-2-2007-giellaprofes sor-nystad.pdf.

Ođđašat. 2018. News broadcast, July 20, 2018. https://tv.nrk.no/serie/odd asat-tv/SANY70072018/20-07-2018.

O'Hara, Kieron. 2014. "In Worship of an Echo." *IEEE Internet Computing* 18 (4): 79–83.

Ó Laoire, Muiris. 2008. "Indigenous Language Revitalisation and Globalization." *Te Kaharoa*, vol. 1: 203–16.

Oliver, Kendrick. 2006. *My Lai Massacre in American History and Memory*. Manchester: Manchester University Press.

O'Neil, Mathieu. 2014. "Hacking Weber: Legitimacy, Critique, and Trust in Peer Production." *Information, Communication and Society* 17 (7): 872–88.

Omma, Lotta. 2013. "Ung same i Sverige: Livsvillkor, självvärdering och hälsa." PhD dissertation, Umeå Universitet, Umeå.

Omma, Lotta, Lars Jacobsson, and Solveig Petersen. 2012. "The Health of Young Swedish Sami with Special Reference to Mental Health." *International Journal of Circumpolar Health* (71).

Oscarsson, Erik-Oscar. 2016. "Rastänkande och särskiljande av samer." In *De historiska relationerna mellan Svenska kyrkan och samerna*, edited by Daniel Lundmark and Olle Sundström, 943–60. Skellefteå: Artos & Norma Bokförlag.

Outakoski, Hanna. 2015. "Multilingual Literacy among Young Learners of North Sámi: Contexts, Complexity and Writing in Sápmi." PhD dissertation, Umeå Universitet, Umeå.

Outakoski, Hanna, Coppélie Cocq, and Peter Steggo. 2018. "Strengthening Sámi Languages in the Digital Age: Social Media–Supported Learning in Sápmi." In "Indigenous Innovation in Social Media," edited by Tanja Dreher and Bronwyn Carlson, special issue, *Media International Australia* 169 (1): 21–31.

Owens, Kay, Pat Doolan, Maria Bennet, Patricia Paraides, Patricia Logan, and Ylva Jannok Nutti. 2012. "Continuities in Education: Pedagogical Perspectives and the Role of Elders in Education for Indigenous Students." *Journal of Australian Indigenous Issues* 15 (1): 20–39.

Paine, Robert. 1982. *Damn a River, Damn a People?* Copenhagen: International Working Group for Indigenous Affairs.

Papacharissi, Zizi. 2010. *A Private Sphere: Democracy in a Digital Age*. Digital Media and Society Series. Cambridge: Polity.

Pariser, Eli. 2011. *The Filter Bubble: What the Internet Is Hiding from You*. London: Viking.

Pasanen, Annika. 2015. *Kuávsui já peeivičuovâ 'Satastus ja päivänvalo'—Inarinsaamen kielen revitalisaatio*. Uralica Helsingiensia 9. Helsinki: Tiedekirja.

Peck, Danielle, and Alex Seaborne, dir. 1995. *Bones of Contention.* Television program. London: BBC-TV Horizon.

Penney, Joel, and Caroline Dadas. 2014. "(Re)Tweeting in the Service of Protest: Digital Composition and Circulation in the Occupy Wall Street Movement." *New Media and Society* 16 (1): 74–90.

Pentina, Iryna, and Monideepa Tarafdar. 2014. "From 'Information' to 'Knowing': Exploring the Role of Social Media in Contemporary News Consumption." *Computers in Human Behavior* 35 (June): 211–23.

People's Knowledge Editorial Collective. 2016. *People's Knowledge and Participatory Action Research: Escaping the White Walled Labyrinth.* Rugby, UK: Practical Action Publishing.

Peters, John Durham. 2000. *Speaking into the Air: A History of the Idea of Communication.* Chicago: University of Chicago Press.

Pietikäinen, Sari. 2008. "'To Breathe Two Airs' Empowering Indigenous Sámi Media." In *Global Indigenous Media: Cultures, Poetics, and Politics,* edited by Pamela Wilson and Michelle Stewart, 197–213. Durham, NC: Duke University Press.

Porsanger, Jelena. 2004. "An Essay about Indigenous Methodology." *Nordlit* 15: 105–20.

——. 2017. "Kaisa máinnasmáilmi." *Sámis* 25 (2017): 27–33. www.samifaga.org/samis/samis25/26.

Porsanger, Sverre, Samuli Aikio, and Jill Anne Aslaksen. 2009. *Spildis Bivlii: Muohta- ja dálvesániid čoakkáldat; Snø og vinterord i utvalg.* Deatnu: Deanu Giellagáddi.

Pratt, Tim, and James Vernon. 2005. "'Appeal from this fiery bed . . .': The Colonial Politics of Gandhi's Fasts and Their Metropolitan Reception." *Journal of British Studies* 44 (1): 92–114.

Pulk, Åse, and Jenna Rasmus. 2016. "På tur til Nord-Amerika: Standing Rock-folket trenger all støtte de kan få." NRK Sápmi, September 20, 2016. www.nrk.no/sapmi/pa-tur-til-nord-dakota_-_-standing-rock-folket-trenger-all-stotte-de-kan-fa-1.13141906.

Pulk, Åse, and Sara Ellen Anna Eira. 2009. "Historisk comeback: Máze Nieiddat holdt tirsdag sin første konsert på 30 år." NRK Sápmi report, April 11, 2009. www.nrk.no/sapmi/maze-nieiddat-pa-scenen-igjen-1.6848939.

Rainie, Harrison, Lee Rainie, and Barry Wellman. 2012. *Networked: The New Social Operating System.* Cambridge, MA: MIT Press.

Ranttila, Marja Aletta. 2017. Exhibition page. Vernissage, December 9–13, 2017. https://derniersjourscom.wordpress.com/2017/11/04/mysteres-de-laponie-femmes-mystiques-par-merja-aletta-ranttila.

Rennie, Ellie, Tyson Yunkaporta, and Indigo Holcombe-James. 2018. "Privacy versus Relatedness: Managing Device Use in Australia's Remote Aboriginal Communities." *International Journal of Communication* 12:1292–309.

Rheingold, Howard. 1994. *The Virtual Community: Finding Connection in a Computerized World*. London: Secker & Warburg.

Ritter, Christian A. 2017. "The Moroccan Diaspora in Istanbul: Experiencing Togetherness through Participatory Media." *Cultural Analysis* 16.

Roche, Gerald. 2017. "Introduction: The Transformation of Tibet's Language Ecology in the Twenty-First Century." *International Journal of the Sociology of Language* 245:1–35.

Ronfeldt, David, John Arquilla, Graham E. Fuller, Melissa Fuller. 1998. *The Zapatista Social Netwar in Mexico*. Santa Monica, CA: Rand.

Rothe, E. Nina. 2017. "'Kaisa's Enchanted Forest': A Talk with Skolt Sámi Filmmaker Katja Gauriloff." *Huffington Post*, March 24, 2017. www.huffingtonpost.com/entry/kaisas-enchanted-forest-a-talk-with-skolt-s%C3%A1mi_us_58d3cd5be4b099c777b9df58.

Ruong, Israel. 1969. *Samerna i historien och nutiden*. Stockholm: Bonnier-Fakta Bokförlag AB.

——. 1976. *Min sámigiella:* Tæk›sta- ja hár›jehallangir›ji. Text-och övningsbok. Stockholm: Liber Läromedel.

Ryd, Yngve, and Johan Rassa. 2007. *Snö: Renskötaren Johan Rassa berättar*. Stockholm: Natur og Kultur.

Saami Parliament. 2015a. *Förstudie om kartläggning av de samiska språken i Sverige* (Pilot study for a mapping of the Sámi languages in Sweden). https://www.sametinget.se/88549.

——. 2015b. #MittSápmi 3.2.7-2015-1100. Report.

——. 2018. *Kartläggning av rasism mot samer i Sverige* (Mapping out racism against Sámi people in Sweden). https://www.sametinget.se/kartlaggning_rasism.

Said, Edward W. 1994. *Culture and Imperialism*. London: Vintage.

Samediggi.fi. n.d. http://www.samediggi.fi/index.php?lang=davvi.

Samediggi.no. n.d. https://www.samediggi.no.

Samediggi.se. n.d. https://www.sametinget.se/lang/same.

Sameradion & SVT Sápmi. 2011. "SameNet går i graven." June 14, 2011. https://sverigesradio.se/sida/artikel.aspx?programid=2327&artikel=4553945.
Sandström, Moa. 2017. "DeCo2onising Artivism." In *Samisk kamp: Kulturförmedling och rättviserörelse*, edited by Marianne Liliequist and Coppélie Cocq, 62–115. Umeå: Bokförlaget H:ström–Text & Kultur.
——. Forthcoming. *Dekoloniseringskonst*. PhD diss., Umeå University.
Sara, Máret Ánne. 2017a. Artist statement. Documenta 14. www.documenta14.de/en/artists/13491/maret-anne-sara.
——. 2017b. "Pile of Sápmi." www.pileosapmi.com.
Sassen, Saskia. 2004. "Local Actors in Global Politics." *Current Sociology* 52 (4): 649–70.
Scannell, Kevin. n.d. Indigenous Tweets.Com. www.indigenoustweets.com.
Schefferus, Johannes. 1673. *Lapponia*. Frankfurt: Typis J. Andreae, ex officina C. Wolffii.
Scott, James. 1990. *Domination and the Art of Resistance*. New Haven, CT: Yale University Press.
Segerberg, Alexandra, and W. Lance Bennett. 2011. "Social Media and the Organization of Collective Action: Using Twitter to Explore the Ecologies of Two Climate Change Protests." *The Communication Review* 14 (3): 197–215.
Sehlin MacNeil, Kristina. 2015. "Shafted: A Case of Cultural and Structural Violence in the Power Relations between a Sami Community and a Mining Company in Northern Sweden." *Ethnologia Scandinavica* 45:73–88.
Seurujärvi-Kari, Irja. 2005. "Saami Council." In *The Saami: A Cultural Encyclopedia*, 344–46. Helsinki: Suomalaisen Kirjallisuuden Seura.
Sharf, Barbara F. 1997. "Communicating Breast Cancer On-Line: Support and Empowerment on the Internet." *Women and Health* 26 (1): 65–84.
Sides, Hampton. 2007. Foreword to *Bury My Heart at Wounded Knee: An Indian History of the American West*, xv–xx. New York: Henry Holt and Company.
Siida. 2017. "Historia." www.siida.fi/sisalto/saamelaismuseo/historia.
Silvén, Eva. 2016. "Hemfört, bortfört, återfört: Museerna och det samiska kulturarvet." In *Historiens hemvise. III. Minne, medier, och materialitet*, edited by Johan Hegardt and Trond Lundemo, 189–217. Göteborg: Makadam Förlag.

Simma, Paul Anders, dir. 1992. *Let's Dance*. Film. PAS Film, Finland.

——. 1994a. *Duoddara árbi*. Film. Epidem, Sweden, Finland, Norway.

——. 1994b. *Guovza* (Bear). Finland.

——. 1997. *Sagojoga minister* (Minister of state). Film. Eurimages, Sweden, Finland, Norway.

——. 1999. *Oaivveskaldjut* (Give us our skeletons). Film. First Run/Icarus Films, Sweden, Norway, Denmark, Finland.

Singer, Beverly R. 2001. *Wiping the War Paint Off the Lens: Native American Film and Video*. Minneapolis: University of Minnesota Press.

Sjoholm, Barbara. 2010. "How *Muittalus Samid Birra* Was Created." *Scandinavian Studies* 82 (3): 313–36.

——. 2017. *Black Fox: A Life of Emilie Demant Hatt, Artist and Ethnographer.* Madison: University of Wisconsin Press.

Skåden, Sigbjørn Ihpil. Láhppon mánáid bestejeaddji. http://ihpil.blogspot.com/2007.

Skarðhamar, Anne-Kari. 2008. "Changes in Film Representations of Sami Culture and Identity." *Nordlit* 12 (1): 293–304.

Skielta, Anna, Marie Enoksson, and Anders Suneson. 2014. *Fördomar och förklaringar.* Östersund: Samiskt Informationscentrum.

Smith, Carsten, et al. 1987. "Self Determination and Indigenous Peoples: Sámi Rights and Northern Perspectives." Compiled and edited from the seminar "Self-Determination and Indigenous Peoples," November 2–3, 1984, by the Oslo and Copenhagen Local Groups of IWGIA (International Work Group for Indigenous Affairs), Copenhagen.

Smith, Claire, and Graeme K. Ward. *Indigenous Cultures in an Interconnected World*. Vancouver: UBC Press, 2000.

Solbakk, Aage. 2011. *Sámit áiggiid čađa I: Prográmmafága sámi historjá ja servodat; Joatkkaskuvla J2 ja J3 Sámi Historjá*. Kárášjohka: ČálliidLágádus.

Solbakk, Jon Trygve. 1997. "Sami Mass Media–Their Role in a Minority Society." In *Sami Culture in a New Era: The Norwegian Sami Experience*, edited by Harald Gaski, 172–98. Kárášjohka: Davvi Girji.

——. 2006. *The Sámi People: A Handbook*. Karasjok: Davvi Girji.

——. 2010. Álttá-Guovdageainnu stuimmi birra/Kampen om Alta-Kautokeino elva. Kárášjohka: ČálliidLágádus.

Somby, Lawra. 2005. "Siivu." Adjágas. Track 6. Trust Me Records/Bureau Storm TMR027. Compact disc.

Somby, Niillas. 2016. *Gumppe diimus*. Kárášjohka: ABC-Company E-skuvla.

Søum, Veronika. 2009. "Mitt lille land på samisk." Norway TV 2 website, August 29, 2009. https://www.tv2.no/a/2874859.

Srinivasan, Ramesh. 2006. "Indigenous, Ethnic and Cultural Articulations of New Media." *International Journal of Cultural Studies* 9 (4) (December 1): 497–518.

Stenberg, Jörgen. 2013. "Kråkan." Uploaded to YouTube by Jörgen Stenberg, August 8, 2013. www.youtube.com/watch?v=o2TUN7VhUsg.

——. 2015a. "Vuortjis–Kråkan!" Uploaded to YouTube by Tor Tuorda, August 28, 2015. www.youtube.com/watch?v=ckyvGV5jgAg.

——. 2015b. "Gállok och Alta" Facebook post, August 28, 2015. www.facebook.com/J%C3%B6rgen-Stenberg-jojkare-109327822563187.

Sterling, Bruce. 1994. *The Hacker Crackdown: Law and Disorder on the Electronic Frontier.* London: Penguin.

Sternlund, Hans. 2015. "Åsa Simma skriver ett nytt brev om Kungabron." SVT Nyheter, September 19, 2015. www.svt.se/nyheter/lokalt/norrbotten/asa-simma-skriver-ett-nytt-brev-om-kungabron.

Stoor, Krister. 2003a. *Att jojka är att leva.* Umeå Universitet. UMUFCD-001. Compact disc.

——. 2003b. *To Yoik Is to Live.* Umeå Universitet. UMUFCD-002. Compact disc.

——. 2015. "Skogssamisk kultur under press: Jojkarna berättar." In *Från kust til kyst: Áhpegáttest áhpegáddáj;* Møter, miljø og migrasjon in pitesamisk område, edited by Bjørg Evjen and Marit Myrvoll, 143–68. Stamsund, Norway: Orkana Akademisk.

Stordahl, Vigdis. 1997. "Sami Generations." In *Sami Culture in a New Era: The Norwegian Sami Experience*, edited by Harald Gaski, 143–54. Kárášjohka: Davvi Girji.

Storfjell, Troy. 2001. "Colonial Palimpsest: Tracing Inscriptions of Sápmi and the Sámi." PhD dissertation, University of Wisconsin, Madison.

——. 2011. "From the Mountaintops to Writing: Traditional Knowledge and Colonial Forms in Turi's Hybrid Text." *Scandinavian Studies* 83 (4): 573–90.

——. 2017. "Worlding." In *Nordic Literature: A Comparative History,* vol. 1, *Spatial Nodes*, edited by Thomas DuBois and Dan Ringgaard, 651–61. Amsterdam: John Benjamins Publishing Company.

Streese, Konstanze, and Kerry Shea. 1992. "Who's Looking? Who's Laughing? Of Multicultural Mothers and Men in Percy Adlon's Bagdad Cafe." *Women in German Yearbook* 8:179–97.

Sunstein, Cass R. 2009. *Republic.com 2.0*. Princeton, NJ: Princeton University Press.

Suohpanterror. n.d. https://suohpanterror.com.

Svalastog, Anne-Lydia, and Gunlög Fur, eds. 2015. *Visjoner av Sápmi* (Visions of Sápmi). Røros: Arthub Publisher.

Svonni, Mikael. 2011. "Johan Turi: First Author of the Sámi." *Scandinavian Studies* 83 (4): 483–90.

Theocharis, Yannis. 2013. "The Wealth of (Occupation) Networks? Communication Patterns and Information Distribution in a Twitter Protest Network." *Journal of Information Technology and Politics* 10 (1): 35–56.

350.org. 2015. "Gulahallat Eatnamiin: We Speak Earth." Uploaded to YouTube by 350.org, October 14, 2015. www.youtube.com/watch?v=H2LhBAi-Q8I.

Thuen, Trond. 1995. *Quest for Equity: Norway and the Saami Challenge*. St John's: Institute of Social and Economic Research, Memorial University of Newfoundland.

Tremlett, Annabel. 2017. "Visualising Everyday Ethnicity: Moving beyond Stereotypes of Roma Minorities." *Identities* 24 (6): 720–40.

Tuhiwai Smith, Linda. 1999. *Decolonizing Methodologies: Research and Indigenous Peoples*. London: Zed Books.

——. 2012. *Decolonizing Methodologies: Research and Indigenous Peoples*. Second edition. London: Zed Books.

Turi, Johan. 1910. *Muittalus Samid birra*. Stockholm: AB Nordiska Bokhandel.

——. 2011a. *An Account of the Sámi*. Trans. Thomas A. DuBois. Chicago: Nordic Studies Press.

——. 2011b. *Muitalus Sámiid birra*. Karasjok: ČálliidLágádus.

Turner, Fred. 2006. *From Counterculture to Cyberculture: Stewart Brand, the Whole Earth Network, and the Rise of Digital Utopianism*. Chicago: University of Chicago Press.

Turner, Terence. 1992. "Defiant Images: The Kayapo Appropriation of Video." *Anthropology Today* 8 (6).

UNESCO (United Nations Educational, Scientific, and Cultural Organization). 2012. "International Day of the World's Indigenous People 2012." www.unesco.org/new/en/unesco/events/prizes-and-celebrations/celebrations/international-days/international-day-of-the-worlds-indigenous-people.

United Nations Department of Economic and Social Affairs. 2004. "The Concept of Indigenous Peoples." Document no. PFII/2004/WS.1/3. Background paper prepared by the Secretariat of the Permanent Forum on Indigenous Issues for the Workshop on Data Collection and Disaggregation for Indigenous Peoples, January 19–21, 2004, New York.
United Nations Division for Social Policy and Development. 2016. "Division for Social Policy and Development: Indigenous Peoples." www.un.org/development/desa/indigenouspeoples/unpfii-sessions-2.html.
United Nations Economic and Social Council. 2019. "International Year of Indigenous Languages." https://en.iyil2019.org.
United Nations General Assembly. 1966. International Covenant on Civil and Political Rights. 2200A (XXI). https://www.ohchr.org/en/professionalinterest/pages/ccpr.aspx.
——. 2007. *United Nations Declaration of the Rights of Indigenous Peoples.* www.un.org/esa/socdev/unpfii/documents/DRIPS_en.pdf.
United Nations International Labour Organization. 1990. Indigenous and Tribal Peoples Convention 169. www.ilo.org/dyn/normlex/en/f?p=NORMLEXPUB:12100:0::NO::P12100_ILO_CODE:C169.
Utbildningsradion. 2010. Cugu. www.gulldalit.se/cugu.
Utiseta. 2016. "Sami Women at Standing Rock." Uploaded to YouTube by Utiseta, October 9, 2016. www.youtube.com/watch?v=VTL87q6O6Kw.
Utsi, Paulus, Inger Näkkäläjärvi Utsi, and Utsi, Per Mikael. 1980. *Giela Gielain: Divttat.* Porjus: Sameslöjd & Material.
Valkeapää, Nils-Aslak. 1971. *Terveisiä Lapista.* Helsinki: Otava.
——. 1979. *Helsing frå Sameland.* Oslo: Pax.
——. 1983. *Greetings from Lappland: The Sami—Europe's Forgotten People.* London: Zed Press.
——. 1985. *Trekways of the Wind.* Trans. Ralph Salisbury, Lars Nordström, Harald Gaski. Guovdageaidnu: DAT.
——. 1989. *Beaivi, áhčážan.* Guovdageaidnu: DAT.
——. 1994. *Boares nauti Johan Thuri.* Guovdageaidnu: DAT.
——. 1997. *The Sun, My Father.* Trans. Ralph Salisbury, Lars Nordström, Harald Gaski. Guovdageaidnu: DAT.
——. 2001. *Eanni, Eannážan.* Guovdageaidnu: DAT.
Vincze, Lásló, and Tom Moring. 2013. "Towards Ethnolinguistic Identity Gratifications." In *Social Media and Minority Languages: Convergence*

and the Creative Industries, edited by Elin Haf Gruffydd Jones and Enrique Uribe-Jongbloed, 47–57. Bristol: Multilingual Matters.

Vinterbo-Hohr, Aagot. 1987. *Palimpsest*. Kárášjohka: Davvi Media.

Vitak, Jessica. 2012. "The Impact of Context Collapse and Privacy on Social Network Site Disclosures." *Journal of Broadcasting & Electronic Media* 56 (4): 451–70.

Vivarelli, Nick. 2017. "Swedish-Sami Director Amanda Kernell on 'Sami Blood' and Past Racism against Sami People in the North of Sweden." *Variety*, December 14, 2016. https://variety.com/2016/film/festivals/swedish-sami-director-amanda-kernell-on-sami-blood-and-racism-against-sami-people-in-the-north-of-sweden-1201941707.

Vuolab, Kerttu. 1995. "Riggodagaid Botnihis Gáldu–Máidnasat Mearihis Mearkkašupmi." In *Cafe Boddu: Essayčoakkáldat* 2, 23–35. Kárášjohka: Davvi Girji.

Weinberger, David. 2008. "Echo Chambers = Democracy." In *Rebooting America: Ideas for Redesigning American Democracy for the Internet Age*, edited by M. Sifry, A. Rasiej, and J. Levy, 32–37. New York: Personal Democracy Press.

What Local People? n.d. www.whatlocalpeople.se.

Wiklund, Karl Bernhard. 1917. *Nomadskolans Läsebok*. Uppsala: Almqvist & Wiksell.

——. 1935. *Nomadskolans Läsebok Andra Boken*. Uppsala: Almqvist & Wiksell.

Wilson, Pamela, and Michelle Stewart, eds. 2008. *Global Indigenous Media: Cultures, Poetics, and Politics*. Durham, NC: Duke University Press.

Wood, Houston. 2008. *Native Features: Indigenous Films from Around the World*. New York: Continuum.

Yleisradio. 1977. "Joiku ei tarvitse sanoja." Suomen Yleisradio. http://yle.fi/aihe/artikkeli/2013/05/30/joiku-ei-tarvitse-sanoja.

——. 1978. "Ailluhas." Ajanvietetoimitus. Helsinki: Yleisradio TV. Uploaded to YouTube April 18, 2014. www.youtube.com/watch?v=DA9FwNAsmLg&list=PLwr-Ohu4iwex2MVEUUtVTzoBVZsUbbdjA&index=13.

Young, Stephanie. 2013. "Into the Jaws of Death: U.S. Coast Guard–Manned Landing Craft at Normandy." *Coast Guard Compass* blog. http://coastguard.dodlive.mil/2013/06/into-the-jaws-of-death-u-s-coast-guard-manned-landing-craft-at-normandy.

Zimmerman, Larry J., Karen P. Zimmerman, and Leonard R. Bruguier. 2000. "Cyberspace Smoke Signals: New Technologies and Native American Ethnicity." In *Indigenous Cultures in an Interconnected World*, edited by Claire Smith and Graeme K. Ward, 69–88. Vancouver: UBC Press.

Zorgdrager, Nellejet. 1989. "De strijd der rechtvaardigen, Kautokeino 1852: Religieus verzet van Samen tegen intern Noors kolonialisme." PhD dissertation, Universiteit Utrecht.

Zuckerberg, Mark. 2018. Facebook post, January 11, 2018. www.facebook.com/zuck/posts/10104413015393571.

Index

N

O